The Missouri Review

Volume XX Number 3   1997

University of Missouri – Columbia

The Missouri Review is published by the College of Arts & Science of the University of Missouri–Columbia, with private contributions and assistance from the Missouri Arts Council and the National Endowment for the Arts.

Web Page Site at http://www.missouri.edu/~moreview

Cartoons in this issue by Brad Veley.

"The Solitary Twin," from *I Know This Much Is True* by Wally Lamb. To be published by Regan Books, an imprint of HarperCollins. © 1998 by Wally Lamb.

Charlotte Brontë's *The Search After Happiness,* by permission of the British Library, Ashley, 156.

The editors invite submissions of poetry, fiction, and essays of a general literary interest with a distinctly contemporary orientation. Manuscripts will not be returned unless accompanied by a stamped, self-addressed envelope. Please address all correspondence to The Editors, *The Missouri Review,* 1507 Hillcrest Hall, University of Missouri, Columbia, Missouri, 65211.

SUBSCRIPTIONS
1 year (3 issues), $19.00
2 years (6 issues), $35.00
3 years (9 issues), $45.00

Copyright © 1997 by The Curators of the University of Missouri

ISSN 0191 1961   **ISBN** 1–879758–21–0

Typesetting by Stacia Schaefer   Printed by Thompson-Shore

Distributed by Ingram Periodicals, Small Changes

The Missouri Review

CONTENTS   1997

POETRY (continued)

ESSAYS

BOOK REVIEWS

"I must tell you, this is the most inspiring
and heart-warming revenge memoir I've ever
read!"

Foreword

In Lucy Ferriss' story "The Windmill," two American teenage boys walking in a field in Belgium are surrounded by a herd of cattle. Pressed on all sides, nuzzled and licked by the hot-breathed creatures, they don't quite know what to do. Afraid, embarrassed, these boys from the burbs aren't sure that they can even tell cows from bulls. Realizing the ridiculousness of the situation, however, they do figure out one thing: that they know very little about the world. "We're standing here like a pair of goofs," one of them says. Then their conversation slips from embarrassment to something larger, something that might become one of those curious lifetime memories.

Naïveté, youth, and the peculiar—often unexpected—nature of learning are themes that run through much of this issue. Franklin Fisher's splendidly realistic saga "Her New Last Name" chronicles the life of a girl growing to adulthood in the West of the early 1900s, weathering vicissitudes and undergoing the transformations of youth. Fisher's story calls into question the truism that life in the past was slower, suggesting that harsh material circumstances and the imminence of death can turn human experience into a roller coaster of change.

Ha Jin's story "Flame" is set in contemporary China, also a place of relative economic scarcity. A Chinese woman—a competent, married, relatively successful nurse—receives a note announcing that her old true love is about to come for a visit. While seemingly guileless, "Flame" is a sly critique of materialism in Chinese culture and expectations conditioned by selected memories of youth. "Flame" also suggests that the hard choices life throws up to the young often don't seem like choices at all. They are by definition "unfair" to the one who has to make them, an idea shared by Steve Yarbrough's unusually suspenseful story "The Rest of Her Life."

Wally Lamb's "The Solitary Twin" is from his upcoming novel *I Know This Much Is True*. In it, a thorny, lonely, not easily likable man is desperate to do something for his terminally ill mother, and he becomes caught up in an adventure of discovery almost despite himself. Lamb's first novel *She's Come Undone* was a blockbuster, and we expect great things for his new book, as well.

Walt McDonald is the poet of no excuses and no easy solutions. He often writes about pain and loss, in plain, no-nonsense, refreshingly unapologetic terms. Like McDonald's, Pamela Greenberg's poems are set in the open air; they describe a girl growing up who spends most of her memorable hours outdoors. At times, she walks in solitary bliss beneath the open sky with "whole cornfields swaying at my footsteps"; at others, "the field troubles [her] with longing." Sandra McPherson's poetry shares an interest in the young, particularly in the lessons learned through the odd details of education and experience. The constituents of knowledge and character, McPherson implies, come from unexpected places.

In her personal essay "A New Youth" Debora Freund describes growing up as a schoolgirl who moved to Israel in 1959. While she defiantly learns about the life around her, life in the streets, the naïveté and arrogance of youth blinds her to the life of her own mother.

This issue's found text is a story by Charlotte Brontë, written when she was still a child, over fifteen years before the appearance of *Jane Eyre* and her later adult novels. The story behind the story is part of the interest of this piece, and it has captivated readers of the Brontës beginning with Charlotte's first biographer.

The Brontës lived in the parsonage of a tiny village on the lonely Yorkshire moors. At quite young ages they began to create stories to entertain themselves. They made "plays," which were not just random creations but interconnected sagas that evolved like television serials. When Charlotte was eleven years old, she began to write down some of their stories, and eventually abandoned acting them out in favor of just writing them. At first, she constructed amazingly small "magazines," meant only for the eyes of children. How she wrote in such a tiny hand is part of the intrigue of these manuscript artifacts, but their real fascination lies in the fact that they are windows into the untutored mind of a great writer. "The Search After Happiness," one of the earliest of these surviving Brontë manuscripts, is a never-before-published story. It provides a glimpse into the effervescence of young genius, unmasked by the self-consciousness of adulthood.

SM

THE SOLITARY TWIN / *Wally Lamb*

ONE SATURDAY morning when my brother and I were ten, our family television set spontaneously combusted.

Thomas and I had spent most of that morning lolling around in our pajamas, watching cartoons and ignoring our mother's orders to go upstairs, take our baths, and put on our dungarees. We were supposed to help her outside with the window-washing. Whenever Ray gave an order, my brother and I snapped to attention, but our stepfather was duck hunting that weekend with his friend, Eddie Banas. Obeying Ma was optional.

She was outside looking in when it happened—standing in the geranium bed on a stool so she could reach the parlor windows. Her hair was in pin curls. Her coat pockets were stuffed with paper towels. As she Windexed and wiped the glass, her circular strokes gave the illusion that she was waving in at us. "We better get out there and help," Thomas said. "What if she tells Ray?"

"She won't tell," I said. "She never tells."

It was true. However angry we could make our mother, she would never have fed us to the five-foot-six-inch sleeping giant who snoozed upstairs weekdays in the spare room, rose to his alarm clock at 3:30 each afternoon, and built submarines at night. Electric Boat, third shift. At our house, you tiptoed and whispered during the day and became free each evening at 9:30, when Eddie Banas, Ray's fellow third-shifter, pulled into the driveway and honked. I would wait for the sound of that horn. Hunger for it. With it came a loosening of limbs, a relaxation in the chest and hands, the ability to breathe deeply again. Some nights, my brother and I celebrated the slamming of Eddie's truck door by jumping in the dark on our mattresses. Freedom from Ray turned our beds into trampolines.

"Hey, look," Thomas said, staring with puzzlement at the television. "What?"

Then I saw it, too: a thin curl of smoke rising from the back of the set. The *Howdy Doody Show* was on, I remember: Clarabel the Clown chasing someone with his seltzer bottle. The picture and sound went dead. Flames whooshed up the parlor wall.

I thought the Russians had done it—that Khrushchev had dropped the bomb at last. If the unthinkable ever happened, Ray had lectured us at the dinner table, the submarine base and Electric Boat were guaranteed targets. We'd feel the jolt nine miles up the road in Three Rivers. Fires would ignite everywhere. Then the worst of it: the meltdown. People's hands and legs and faces would melt like cheese.

"Duck and cover!" I yelled to my brother.

Thomas and I fell to the floor in the protective position the civil defense lady had made us practice at school. There was an explosion over by the television, a confusion of thick black smoke. The room rained glass.

The noise and smoke brought Ma, screaming, inside. Her shoes crunched glass as she ran toward us. She picked up Thomas in her arms and told me to climb onto her back.

"We can't go outside!" I shouted. "Fallout!"

"It's not the bomb!" she shouted back. "It's the TV!"

Outside, Ma ordered Thomas and me to run across the street and tell the Anthonys to call the fire department. While Mr. Anthony made the call, Mrs. Anthony brushed glass bits off the tops of our crewcuts with her whiskbroom. We spat soot-flecked phlegm. By the time we returned to the front sidewalk, Ma was missing.

"Where's your mother?" Mr. Anthony shouted. "She didn't go back in there, did she? Jesus, Mary, and Joseph!"

Thomas began to cry. Then Mrs. Anthony and I were crying, too. "Hurry *up!*" my brother shrieked to the distant sound of the fire siren. Through the parlor windows, I could see the flames shrivel our lace curtains.

A minute or so later, Ma emerged from the burning house, sobbing, clutching something against her chest. One of her pockets was ablaze from the paper towels; her coat was smoking.

Mr. Anthony yanked off Ma's coat and stomped the fire out of it. Fire trucks rounded the corner, sirens blaring. Neighbors hurried out of their houses to cluster and stare.

Ma stank. The fire had sizzled her eyebrows and given her a sooty face. When she reached out to pull Thomas and me to her, several loose photographs spilled to the ground. That's when I realized why she'd gone back into the house: to rescue her photo album from the bottom drawer of the china closet.

"It's all right now," she kept saying. "It's all right, it's all right." And, for Ma, it *was* all right. The house her father had built would be saved. Her twins were within arm's reach. Her picture album had been rescued. Just last week, I dreamt my mother—dead from breast cancer since 1987—was standing at the picture window at Joy's and my condominium, looking in at me and mouthing that long-ago promise. "It's all right, it's all right, it's all right."

Sometime during Ma's endless opening and closing of that over-stuffed photo album she loved so much, the two brass pins that attach the front and back covers first bent, then broke, causing most of the book's black construction paper pages to loosen and detach. The book had been broken for years when, in October of 1986, Ma herself was opened and closed on a surgical table at Yale–New Haven Hospital. After several months' worth of feeling tired and run down and contending with a cold that never quite went away, Ma had fingered a lump in her left breast. "It's no bigger than a pencil eraser," she told me over the phone, "But Lena Anthony thinks I should go to the doctor, so I'm going." At Yale–New Haven, Ma was tested and told she had breast cancer, and that it had already spread to the lymph system. With luck and aggressive treatment, the oncologist told her, she could probably live another six months to a year.

My brother and Ray and I struggled independently with our feelings about Ma's illness and pain—her death sentence. Each of us fumbled, in our own way, to make things up to her. Thomas set to work in the arts and crafts room down at the state hospital's Settle building. While Ma lay in the hospital being scanned and probed and plied with cancer-killing poisons, he spent hours assembling and gluing and shellacking something called a "hodgepodge collage"—a busy arrangement of nuts, washers, buttons, macaroni, and dried peas that declared: GOD = LOVE! Between hospital stays, Ma hung it on the kitchen wall, where its hundreds of glued doodads seemed to pulsate like something alive—an organism under a microscope, molecules bouncing around in a science movie. It unnerved me to look at that thing.

My stepfather decided he would fix, once and for all, Ma's broken scrapbook. He took the album from its keeping place in the china closet and brought it out to the garage. There he jerryrigged a solution, reinforcing the broken binding with strips of custom-cut aluminum sheeting and small metal bolts. "She's all set now," Ray told me when he showed me the re-bound book. He held it at arm's length and opened it face down to the floor, flapping the covers back and forth as if they were the wings of a captured duck.

My own project for my dying mother was the most costly and ambitious. I would remodel her pink 1950s-era kitchen, sheetrocking the cracked plaster walls, replacing the creaky cabinets with modern units, and installing a center island with built-in oven and cooktop. I conceived the idea, I think, to show Ma that I loved her best of all. Or that I was the most grateful of the three of us for all she'd endured on our behalf. Or that I was the sorriest that fate had given her first a volatile husband and then a schizophrenic son and then tapped her on the shoulder and handed her the "big C." What I proved, instead, was that I was the deepest in denial. If I was going to go to the trouble and expense of giving her a new kitchen, then she'd better live long enough to appreciate it.

I arrived with my toolbox at the old brick duplex early one Saturday morning, less than a week after her discharge from the hospital. Ray officially disapproved of the project and took off in a huff when I got there. Looking pale and walking cautiously, Ma forced a smile and began carrying her canisters and knickknacks out of the kitchen to temporary storage. She watched from the pantry doorway as I committed my first act of renovation, tamping my flatbar with a hammer and wedging it between the wainscoting and the wall. Ma's hand was a fist at her mouth, tapping, tapping against her lip.

With the crack and groan of nails letting go their hold, the four-foot-wide piece of wainscoting was pried loose from the wall, revealing plaster and lath and an exposed joist where someone had written notes and calculations. "Look," I said, wanting to show her what I guessed was her father's handwriting. Throughout our childhood, Thomas and I had been reminded that our grandfather, Domenico Onofrio Tempesta, had put the roof over our heads—had built our home "with his own two hands." But when I turned around, I realized I was addressing the empty pantry.

I was thirty-six at the time, unhappily divorced from my first wife, Dessa, for less than a year. Sometimes in the middle of the night, I'd still reach for Dessa, and her empty side of the bed would startle me awake. We'd been together for sixteen years.

I found my mother sitting in the front parlor, trying to hide her tears. The newly repaired photo album was in her lap.

"What's the matter?"

She shook her head, tapped her lip. "I don't know, Dominick. You go ahead. It's just that with everything that's happening right now . . . "

"You don't *want* a new kitchen?" I interrupted. The question came out like a threat.

"Honey, it's not that I don't appreciate it." She patted the sofa cushion next to her. "Come here. Sit down."

Still standing, I reminded her that she'd complained for decades about her lack of counter space. I described the new stoves I'd seen at Kitchen Depot—the ones where the burners are one continuous flat surface, a cinch for cleaning. I sounded just like the saleswoman who'd led me around from one showroom miracle to the next.

Ma said she agreed a new kitchen would be great, but that maybe what she really needed right now was for things to stay settled.

I sat.

"If you want to give me something," she said, "give me something small."

"Okay, fine," I huffed. "I'll just make you one of those collage things like Thomas's. Except mine will say LIFE SUCKS. Or JESUS CHRIST'S A SON OF A BITCH." My mother was a religious woman. I might as well have taken my flatbar and poked at her incision.

"Don't be bitter, honey," she said.

Suddenly, out of nowhere, I was crying—tears and strangled little barks that convulsed from the back of my throat. "I'm scared," I said.

"What are you scared of, Dominick? Tell me."

"I don't know," I said. "I'm scared for you." But it was myself I was scared for. Closing in on forty, I was wifeless, childless. Now I'd be motherless, too. Left with my crazy brother and Ray.

She reached over and rubbed my arm, "Well, honey," she said, "it's scary. But I accept it because it's what God wants for me."

"What God wants," I repeated, with a little snort of contempt. I dragged my sleeve across my eyes, cleared my throat.

"Give me something little," she repeated. "You remember that time last spring when you came over and said, 'Hey, Ma, get in the car and I'll buy you a hot fudge sundae'? *That's* the kind of thing I'd like. Just come over and visit. Look at my picture album with me."

Tucked inside the inside front cover pocket of my mother's scrapbook are two pictures of Thomas and me, scissored four decades earlier from the *Three Rivers Daily Record*. The folded newsprint, stained brown with age, feels as light and brittle as dead skin. In the first photo, we're wrinkled newborns, our diapered bodies curved toward each other like opening and closing parentheses. IDENTICAL TWINS RING OUT THE OLD, RING IN THE NEW, the caption claims and goes on to explain that Thomas and Dominick Tempesta were born at the Daniel P. Shanley Memorial Hospital on December 31, 1949, and January 1, 1950, respectively—six minutes apart and in two different years. (The article makes no mention of our father and says only that our unnamed mother is "doing fine." We were bastards, and our births would have been discreetly ignored by the newspaper, had we not been the New Year's babies.) "Little Thomas arrived first, at 11:57 p.m.," the article explains. "His brother Dominick followed at

12:06 a.m. Between them, they straddle the first and second halves of the twentieth century!"

In the second newspaper photo, taken on January 24, 1954, my brother and I have become Thomas and Dominick Birdsey. We wear matching sailor hats and woolen peajackets and salute the readers of the *Daily Record*. Mamie Eisenhower squats between us, one mink-coated arm wrapped around each of our waists. Mrs. Eisenhower, in her short bangs and flowered hat, beams directly at the camera. Thomas and I, age four, wear twin looks of bewildered obedience. This picture is captioned FIRST LADY GETS A TWO-GUN SALUTE.

The president's wife was in Groton, Connecticut, that winter day to break champagne against the *U.S.S. Nautilus*, America's first nuclear-powered submarine. Our family stood in the crowd below the dignitaries' platform, ticket-holding guests by virtue of our new step-father's job as a pipefitter for Electric Boat. E. B. and the Navy were partners in the building of the *Nautilus*, America's best hope for containing Communism.

According to my mother, it had been cold and foggy the morning of the launch, and then, just before the submarine's christening, the sun had burned through and lit up the celebration. Ma had prayed to Saint Anne for good weather and saw this sudden clearing as a small miracle, a further sign of what everybody knew already: that Heaven was on our side, was *against* the godless Communists who wanted to conquer the world and blow America to smithereens.

"That was the proudest day of my life, Dominick," she told me that morning when I started, then halted, the renovation of her kitchen and sat, instead, and looked. "Seeing you two boys with the President's wife. I remember it like it was yesterday. Mamie and some admiral's wife were up there on the VIP platform, waving down to the crowd, and I said to your father, 'Look, Ray. She's pointing right at the boys!' He said, 'Oh, go on. They're just putting on a show.' But I could tell she was looking at you two. It used to happen all the time. People get such a kick out of twins. You boys were always special."

Her happy remembrance of that long-ago day animated her gestures and strengthened her voice. The past, the old pictures, the sudden brilliance of the morning sun through the front windows: the mix made her joyful and took away, I think, a little of her pain.

"And then, next thing you know, the four of us were following some Secret Service men to the Officers' Club lounge. Ray took it in stride, of course, but I was scared to death. I thought we were in trouble for something. Come to find out, we were following Mrs. Eisenhower's orders. She wanted her picture taken with my two boys!

"They treated us like big shots, too. Your father had a cocktail with Admiral Rickover and some of the other big brass. They asked him all about his service record.

"Then a waiter brought you and your brother orange sodas in frosted glasses almost as tall as you two were. I was scared skinny one of you was going to spill soda all over Mamie."

"What did you and she have to drink?" I kidded her. "Couple of boilermakers?"

"Oh, honey, I didn't take a thing. I was a nervous wreck, standing that close to her. She ordered a Manhattan, I remember, and had some liver pâté on a cracker. She was nice—very down-to-earth. She asked me if I'd sewn the little sailor suits you and Thomas were wearing. She told me she still knitted some when she and the President traveled, but she'd never had a talent for sewing. When she stooped down to have her picture taken with you two boys, she told you she had a grandson just about your age. *David* Eisenhower is who she was talking about. Julie Nixon's husband. *Camp* David."

Ma shook her head and smiled, in disbelief still. "You know what I always used to wish about that day?" she said. She pulled a Kleenex from the sleeve of her bathrobe and wiped her eyes. "I always wished your grandfather could have lived to see it. First he comes to this country with holes in his pockets and the next thing you know, his two little grandsons are hobnobbing with the First Lady of the United States of America. Papa would have gotten a big kick out of that. He would have been proud as a peacock."

Papa.

Domenico Onofrio Tempesta—my maternal grandfather, my name-sake—is as prominent in my mother's photo album as he was in her life of service to him. He died during the summer of 1949, oblivious of the knowledge that the unmarried thirty-two-year-old daughter who kept his house—his only child—was pregnant with twins. Growing up, my brother and I knew Papa as a stern-faced paragon of accomplishment, the subject of a few dozen sepia-tinted photographs, the star of a hundred anecdotes. Each of the stories Ma told us about Papa reinforced the message that *he* was the boss, that *he* ruled the roost, that what *he* said went.

He had emigrated to America from Sicily in 1901 and gotten ahead because he was shrewd with his money and unafraid of hard work, lucky for us! He'd bought a half-acre lot from a farmer's widow—land that had once upon a time been part of the hunting grounds of the Occom Indians—and thus became the first Italian immigrant to own property in Three Rivers, Connecticut. Papa had put the roof over our heads—had built "with his own two hands" the brick Victorian duplex on Hollyhock Avenue where we'd lived as kids, where my mother had lived all her life. Papa had had a will of iron and a stubborn streak—just the traits he needed to raise a young daughter "all by his lonesome." If we thought *Ray* was strict, we should have seen Papa! Once when Ma was a girl, she was belly-aching about having to eat fried eggs for supper. Papa let her go on and on and then, without saying a word, reached over and pushed her face down in her plate. "I came up with egg yolk dripping off my hair and the tip of my nose and even my eyelashes. I was crying to beat the band. After that night, I just ate my eggs and shut up about it!"

Another time, when Ma was a teenager working at the Rexall store, Papa found her secret package of cigarettes and marched himself right down to the drugstore where he made her eat one of her own Pall Malls. Right in front of the customers and her boss, Mr. Chase. And Claude Sminkey, the soda jerk she had such an awful crush on. After he left, Ma ran outside and had to throw up at the curb with people walking by and watching. She had to quit her job, she was so ashamed of herself. But she never smoked again—never even liked the smell of cigarettes after that. Papa had fixed her wagon, all right. She had defied him and then lived to regret it. The last thing Papa wanted was a sneak living under his own roof.

Sometime during our visit with the photo album that morning, my mother told me to wait there. She had something she wanted to get. With a soft sigh of pain, she was on her feet and heading for the front stairs.

"Ma, whatever it is, let *me* get it for you," I called out.

"That's okay, honey," she called back down the stairs, "I know right where it is."

I flipped quickly through the pages as I waited—made my family a jerky, imperfect movie. It struck me that my mother had compiled mostly a book of her father, Thomas, and me. Other people made appearances: Ray, Dessa, the Anthonys from across the street, the Tusia sisters from next door. But my grandfather, my brother, and I were the stars of my mother's book. Ma herself—camera-shy and self-conscious about her cleft lip—appears only twice in the family album. In the first picture, she's one of a line of dour-faced schoolchildren posed on the front step of St. Mary of Jesus Christ Grammar School. (A couple of years ago, the parish sold that dilapidated old schoolhouse to a developer from Massachusetts who converted it into apartments. I bid on the inside painting, but Painters Plus came in under me.) In the second photograph, Ma looks about nine or ten. She stands beside her lanky father on the front porch of the house on Hollyhock Avenue, wearing a sacklike dress and a sober look that matches Papa's. In both of these photos, my mother holds a loose fist to her face to cover her defective mouth.

It was a gesture she had apparently learned early and practiced all her life: the hiding of her cleft lip with her right fist—her perpetual apology to the world for a birth defect over which she'd had no control. The lip, split just to the left of her front teeth, exposed a half-inch gash of gum and gave the illusion that she was sneering. But Ma never sneered. She apologized. She put her fist to her mouth for store clerks and Fuller Brush men, for mailmen and teachers on parents' visiting day, for neighbors, her husband, even, sometimes, for herself when she sat in the parlor watching TV, her image reflected on the screen.

She had made reference to her harelip only once, on a day in 1964 when she sat across from me in an optometrist's office. A month earlier, my ninth grade algebra teacher had caught me squinting at the blackboard and called to advise my mother to get my eyes tested. I'd protested angrily. Glasses were for brains, for losers and finky kids. I was furious because Thomas had developed no twin case of myopia— no identical need to wear stupid faggy glasses like me. *He* was the jerk, the brown-noser at school. *He* should be the nearsighted one. If she made me get glasses, I told her, I just wouldn't wear them.

But Ma had talked to Ray, and Ray had issued one of his supper-table ultimatums. So I'd gone to Dr. Wisdo's office, acted my surliest, and flunked the freaking wall chart. Now, two weeks later, my black plastic frames were being fitted to my face in a fluorescent-lit room with too many mirrors.

"Well, I think they make you look handsome, Dominick," Ma offered. "Distinguished. He looks like a young Ray Milland. Doesn't he, doctor?"

Dr. Wisdo didn't like me because of my bad attitude during the first visit. "Well," he said reluctantly, "now that you mention it."

This all occurred during the fever of puberty and Beatlemania. The summer before, at the basketball courts at Fitz Field, a kid named Billy Grillo had shown me and Marty Overturf a stack of rain-wrinkled paperbacks he'd found out in the woods in a plastic bag: *Sensuous Sisters, Lusty Days & Lusty Nights, The Technician of Ecstasy*. I'd swiped a couple of those mildewed books and taken them out past the picnic tables, where I read page after faded page, simultaneously drawn to and repelled by the things men did to women, the things women did to themselves and each other. It flabbergasted me, for instance, that a man might put his dick inside a woman's mouth and have her "hungrily gulp down his creamy nectar." That a woman might cram a glass bottle up between another woman's legs and that this would make both "scream and undulate with pleasure." I'd gone home from basketball that day, flopped onto my bed and fallen asleep, awakening in the middle of my first wet dream. Shortly after that, the Beatles appeared on *Ed Sullivan*. Behind the locked bathroom door, I began combing my bangs forward and beating off to my dirty fantasies about all those girls who screamed for the Beatles—what those same girls would do to me, what they'd let me do to them. So the last person I wanted to look like was Ray Milland, one of my mother's old-fart movie stars.

"Do you think you could just shut up, please?" I told Ma, right there in front of Dr. Wisdo.

"Hey, hey, hey, come on now. Enough is enough," Dr. Wisdo protested. "What kind of boy says 'shut up' to his own mother?"

Ma put her fist to her mouth and told the doctor it was all right. I was just upset. This wasn't the way I really was.

As if *she* knew the way I really was, I thought to myself, smiling inwardly.

Dr. Wisdo told me he had to leave the room for a few minutes, and by the time he got back, he hoped I would have apologized to my poor mother.

Neither of us said anything for a minute or more. I just sat there, smirking defiantly at her, triumphant and miserable. Then Ma took me by complete surprise. "You think *glasses* are bad," she said. "You should try having what I have. At least you can take your glasses off."

I knew immediately what she meant—her harelip. The unexpected reference to it pained me—hit me like a snowball in the eye. Of all the forbidden subjects in our house, the two *most* forbidden were the identification of Thomas' and my biological father and our mother's disfigurement. We had never asked about either—had somehow been raised not to ask and had honored the near sacredness of the silence. Now Ma herself was breaking one of the two cardinal rules. I looked away, shocked and embarrassed, but Ma wouldn't stop talking.

"One time," she said, "a boy in my class, a mean boy named Harold Kettlety, started calling me 'Rabbit Face.' I hadn't done anything to him. Not a thing. I never bothered anyone at all—I was scared of my own shadow. He just thought up that name one day and decided it was funny. 'Hello, there, Rabbit Face,' he used to whisper to me across the aisle. After a while, some of the other boys took it up, too. They used to chase me at recess and call me 'Rabbit Face.'"

I sat there, pumping my leg up and down, wanting her to stop, wanting Harold Kettlety to still be a kid so I could find him and rip his face off.

"And so I told the teacher and she sent me to the principal. Mother Agnes, her name was. She was a stern thing." Ma's fingers twisted her pocketbook strap as she spoke. "She told me to stop making a mountain out of a molehill. I was making things worse, she said, by calling it to everyone's attention. I should just ignore it. Then more boys got on the bandwagon, even boys from other grades. It got so bad, I used to get the dry heaves before school every morning. You didn't stay home sick in our house unless you had something like the measles or the chicken pox. That's the last thing Papa would have stood for— me home all day long just because some stinker was calling me a name."

I needed her to stop. Needed not to hear the pain and shaking in her voice. If she kept talking, she might tell me everything. "I don't see how any of this sob story stuff has anything to do with me," I said. "Are you planning to get to the point before I die of old age?"

She shut up after that, silenced, I guess, by the fact that her own son had joined forces with Harold Kettlety. On the drive home from the optometrist's, I chose to sit in the back seat and not speak to her. Somewhere en route, I drew my new glasses from their brown plastic clip-to-your-pocket case, rubbed the lenses with the silicone-impregnated cleaning cloth, and slipped them on. I looked out the window, privately dazzled by a world more sharp and clear than I remembered. I said nothing about this, spoke no apologies, offered no concessions.

"Ma's *crying* downstairs," Thomas informed me later, up in our bedroom. I was lifting weights, shirt off, glasses on.

"So what am I supposed to do about it?" I said. "Hold a snot rag to her nose?"

"Just try being decent to her," he said. "She's your *mother*, Dominick. Sometimes you treat her like s-h-i-t."

I stared at myself in our bedroom mirror as I lifted the weights, studying the muscle definition I'd begun to acquire and which I could now see clearly, thanks to my glasses. "Why don't you *say* the word instead of spelling it," I smirked. "Go ahead. Say 'shit.' Give yourself a thrill."

He'd been changing out of his school clothes as we spoke. Now he stood there, hands on his hips, wearing just his underpants, his socks, and one of those fake-turtleneck dickey things that were popular with all the brown-noser student council kids at our school. Thomas had them in four or five different colors. God, I hated those dickeys of his.

I looked at the two of us, side by side, in the mirror. Next to me, he was a scrawny beanpole. A joke. Mr. Pep Squad Captain. Mr. Goody-Goody.

"I *mean* it, Dominick," he said. "You better treat her right or I'll say something to Ray. I will. Don't think I won't."

Which was bullshit and we both knew it.

I grabbed my barbell wrench, banged extra weights onto the bar, lifted them. Mr. Fink. Mr. Pansy-Ass Dickey Boy. "Oh, gee, I'm nervous," I told him. "I'm so nervous I'll probably s-h-i-t my pants."

He stood there, just like Ma, his look of indignation melting into forgiveness.

"Just cool it is all I'm saying, Dominick," he said. "Oh, by the way I like your glasses."

When Ma came back down the stairs on that day of failed renovation, she was holding a gray metal strongbox. I put down the picture album. "Here, honey," she said. "This is for you."

"What's in it?" I asked.

"Open it up and see."

She had taped the key to the side of the box. "It's a good thing you don't work for Fort Knox," I said. Ma ignored my teasing. She was smiling down at the strongbox.

Inside was a large manila envelope curled around a small coverless dictionary and held in place with an elastic band that snapped as soon as I touched it. The envelope held a thick sheaf of paper—a manuscript of typed carbon pages. "It's Italian, right?" I said. "What is it?"

"It's my father's life story," she said. "He dictated it the summer he died."

"Dictated it?"

She nodded. "Remember the Mastronunzios from church? They had a cousin who came over here from Italy after the war. Angelo Nardi, his name was. He was a handsome fella—very dashing. He had been a courtroom stenographer in Palermo. Papa got it into his head that he wanted to tell the story of his life. He thought maybe boys and young men back in the Old Country would want to read about how one of their own had come to America and gotten ahead in life. So he hired Angelo to take it all down and then type it up on the typewriter. They used to work on it out back in the grape arbor every morning for a couple of hours. It went on all summer."

"Have you ever read it?" I asked.

"Oh, gosh, no. It was top secret. I wasn't even supposed to know what they were doing. It's funny, though. It wasn't at all like Papa to do something like that. He was always so private about everything. I'd ask him about the Old Country or about my mother and he'd tell me that was all water over the dam. But up there in the backyard with Angelo, he talked a blue streak. Some mornings I'd hear him crying. Papa had a lot of tragedy in his life. First he lost two brothers. Then his wife. I don't know. Maybe he knew the stroke was coming and he just wanted to get it all down."

The first page was hand-lettered in blue fountain pen ink, lots of flourishes and curliques. "I can read his name," I said, "What does the rest say?"

"Let's see. It says, 'The History of Domenico Onofrio Tempesta, a Great Man from . . . *Umile? Umile?* Humble! . . . 'The History of Domenico Onofrio Tempesta, a Great Man from Humble Beginnings.'"

I had to laugh. "He had a pretty good idea of himself, didn't he?"

Her eyes brimmed with tears. "He was a wonderful man," she said.

"Yeah, right. As long as you ate your eggs. And your cigarettes."

Ma stroked the small, coverless dictionary. "I've been meaning to give you this stuff for a long time, Dominick," she said. "Take it with you. It's for Thomas, too, if he wants to look at it, but I wanted to give it to you especially because you always used to ask about Papa."

"I did?"

She nodded. "When you were little. See this dictionary? This is the one he used right after he came over from the Old Country—the one he learned his English from."

I opened the tattered book. Its onion-skin pages were stained with grease from his fingers. On one page, I covered his thumbprint with my thumb and considered for the first time that Papa might have been more than just old pictures—old, repeated stories.

I took my mother into the kitchen and showed her the penciled notations on the joist. "Yup, that's his writing!" she said. "I'll be a son of a gun. Look at that! It almost brings him right back."

I reached out and rubbed her shoulder, the cloth of her bathrobe, the skin and bone. "You know what I think?" I said. "I think you should translate that story of his."

Ma shook her head. "Oh, honey, I can't. For one thing, my Italian is too rusty. And for another thing, I don't think he ever wanted me to read it. Whenever I went out into the yard to hang the clothes or bring them a cold drink, Papa would clam right up. Shoo me away. He was a regular J. Edgar Hoover with that project of his. Everything was top secret."

"But Ma, he's dead. He's been dead for almost forty years."

She stopped, was quiet. She seemed lost in thought.

"What?" I said. "What are you thinking about?"

"Oh, I was just remembering the day he died. He was out there in the backyard, all by himself. Angelo had just finished typing the last of his story—had just brought it over that morning—and Papa was up in the yard, reading it. And when I went out with his lunch, there he was, slumped over in his chair. These pages were all over the yard. Stuck in the hedges, stuck against the chicken coop. They'd blown all over the place. I ran inside and called the police. Then I went out there again and picked up pages. I knew he was dead, but I kept looking over, hoping I'd see him blink or yawn. Hoping and praying I was mistaken. That was the only thing I could think of to do until the police got there: pick up the pages of his story."

"Did he know about us?" I asked. "About Thomas and me?"

She looked away without answering me. "Well, anyway," she said. "I just don't think it was something he wanted me to read."

Before I left, I tapped the wainscoting back into place, covering once again Domenico's notes and calculations. I walked out the door and down the front porch steps, balancing my toolbox, the strongbox, and several foil-wrapped packages of frozen leftovers. ("I worry about you in that apartment all by yourself, Dominick. Your face looks too thin. I can tell you're not eating the way you should. Here, take these.") At the door of the truck, I heard her calling and ran back up the steps.

"You forgot this," she said, handing me the strongbox key. "*Il chiave.*"

"Come again?" I said.

"*Il chiave.* The key. The word for it just came back to me."

"*Il chiave,*" I repeated, and dropped the key into my pocket.

That night, I awoke from a sound sleep with the idea for the perfect gift for my dying mother. It was so simple and right that its obviousness had eluded me until 3:00 a.m. I'd have her father's life story translated, printed, and bound for her.

I drove up to the university and found the Department of Romance Languages office tucked into the top floor of a stone building dwarfed by two massive, leafless beech trees. The secretary drew up a list of possibilities for me to try. After an hour's worth of false leads and locked doors, I walked the narrow steps to a half-landing and knocked at the office door of Nedra Frank, the last person on my list.

She looked about forty, but it's hard to tell with those hair-yanked-back, glasses-on-a-chain types. As she thumbed through my grandfather's pages, I checked out her breasts (nice ones), the mole on her neck, her gnawed-down cuticles. She shared the office with another teacher; her sloppy desk and his neat one were a study in opposites. "I'm a scholar," she said when she looked up. She handed me back the manuscript. "What you're asking me to do is roughly the same as trying to commission a serious artist to paint you something that goes with the drapes and the sofa. How many pages is it?"

"Fifty-two," I said. Already, I'd begun backing out of her low-ceilinged office—a glorified closet, really, and not all that glorified.

She sighed. "Let me see it again." I handed back the envelope and she scanned several pages, frowning. "This is single-spaced," she said. "That's 104 pages, not 52."

"Yeah, well . . ."

"I could do it for eight dollars a page. More on the pages where explanatory footnotes are necessary."

"How much more?"

"Oh, let's say eleven fifty. I mean, fair is fair, right? If I'm actually *generating text* instead of just translating and interpreting, I should be paid more. Shouldn't I?"

I nodded, computing the math in my head: 832 big ones *without* the footnotes. Probably somewhere around a thousand bucks—more than I thought it would be, but a lot less than a kitchen renovation. "Are you saying you'll do it?" I said.

She sighed, kept me waiting for several seconds. "All right," she finally said. "To be perfectly honest, I have no interest in the project, but I need money for my car. Can you believe it? A year and a half old and the tranny's already got problems."

It struck me funny: this Marian the Librarian using gearhead lingo. "Why are you smiling?" she asked.

I shrugged. "No reason, really. What kind of car is it?"

"A Yugo," she said. "I suppose *that's* funny, too?"

Nedra Frank told me she wanted two hundred dollars up front and estimated the translation would take her a month or two to complete, given her schedule, which she described as oppressive. Her detachment annoyed me; she had looked twice at her wall clock as I spoke—of my grandfather's accomplishments, my mother's lymphoma. I wrote her a check, worrying that she might summarize or skip pages—shortchange me in spite of what she was charging. I left her office feeling vulnerable—subject to her abbreviations and interpretations, her sourpuss way of seeing the world. Still, the project was on its way.

I called her several times over the next few weeks, wanting to check her progress or to see if she had any questions. But all I ever got was an unanswered ring.

Whenever my mother underwent her chemotherapy and radiation treatments at Yale–New Haven, Ray drove her down there, kept her company, ate his meals in the cafeteria downstairs, and cat-napped in the chair beside her bed. By early evening, he'd get back on the road, driving north on I-95 in time for his shift at Electric Boat. When I suggested that maybe he was taking on too much, he shrugged and asked me what the hell else he was supposed to do.

Did he want to talk about it?

What was there to talk about?

Was there anything I could do for him?

I should worry about my mother, not him.

I tried to make it down to New Haven two or three times a week. I brought Thomas with me when I could, usually on Sundays. It was hard to gauge how well or poorly Thomas was handling Ma's dying. As was usually the case with him, the pendulum swung irregularly. Sometimes he seemed resigned and accepting. "It's God's will," he'd sigh, echoing Ma herself. "We have to be strong for each other." Sometimes, he'd sob and pound his fists on my dashboard. At other times, he was pumped up with hope. "I *know* she's going to beat this thing," he told me one afternoon over the phone. "I'm praying every day to Saint Agatha."

"Saint who?" I said, immediately sorry I'd asked.

"Saint Agatha," he repeated. "The patron saint invoked against fire, volcanoes, and cancer." He rambled on and on about his stupid saint: a virgin whose jilted suitor had had her breasts cut off, her body burned at the stake. Agatha had stopped the eruption of a volcano, had died a Bride of Christ, blah blah blah.

One morning, Thomas woke me at 6 a.m. with the theory that the Special K our mother ate for breakfast every day had been deliberately impregnated with carcinogens.

The Kellogg's Cereal company was secretly owned by the Soviets, he said. "They target the relatives of the people they're *really* after. I'm on their hit list because I do God's bidding." Now that he was on to them, he said, he was considering exposing Kellogg's, rubbing it right in their faces. He would probably end up as *Time* magazine's Man of the Year and have to go into hiding. Stalkers followed famous people. Look what had happened to poor John Lennon. Did I remember that song, "Instant Karma"? John had written it specifically for him, to encourage him to do good in the world after he'd gone. "Listen!" my brother said. "It's obvious!"

Instant karma's gonna get you—gonna look you right in the face.
You better recognize your brother and join the human race!

One Sunday afternoon when Thomas and I drove down to visit Ma, her bed was empty. We found her in the solarium, illuminated by a column of sun coming through the skylight, sitting by herself amongst clusters of visitors. By then, the chemo had stained her skin and turned her hair to duck fluff—had given her, once again, the singed look she'd had that day she emerged from the burning parlor on Hollyhock Avenue. Somehow, bald and shrunken in her quilted pink robe, she looked beautiful to me.

Thomas sat slumped and uncommunicative through that whole visit. He had wanted me to stop at McDonald's on the way down and I'd told him no—that maybe we could go there on the ride back. In the solarium, he pouted and stared trancelike at the TV and ignored Ma's questions and efforts at conversation. He refused to take off his coat. He wouldn't stop checking his watch.

I was angry by the time we left, angrier still when, during the drive home, he interrupted my speech about his selfishness to ask if we were still going to McDonald's. "Don't you get it, asshole?" I shouted at him. "Don't you even come up for air when your own mother's dying?" He undid his seatbelt and climbed over the front seat. Squatting on the back seat floor, he assumed a modified version of the old duck-and-cover.

I pulled over at the next rest stop and told him to get the fuck back in front—that I was sick and tired of his bullshit, fed up with *his* crap on top of everything else I was trying to juggle. When he refused to get up, I yanked him up. He pulled free and bolted, running across the interstate without even looking. Tires wailed, cars swerved wildly. Don't ask me how he made it across.

By the time I got across the highway myself, Thomas had disappeared. I ran, panic-stricken, through woods and yards, imagining the ugly thump of impact, Thomas ripped apart, his blood all over the road. He was lying in the tall grass at the side of the highway about a half mile up from where the car was. His eyes were closed, his mouth smiling up at the sun. When I helped him up, the grass was dented in the shape of his body. Like a visual aid at a crime scene. Like one of those angels he and I used to make in the new snow. Back in the car, I gripped the wheel to steady my hands and tried not to hear and see those cars that had swerved out of his way. In Madison, I pulled into a McDonald's and got him a large fries, a Quarter Pounder with cheese, a strawberry shake. If he was not exactly happy for the rest of the trip, he was at least quiet and full.

That evening, Nedra Frank picked up on the first ring.

"I know you're busy," I said. I told her what Ray had just called and told me: that my mother's condition had gotten worse.

"I'm working on it right now, as a matter of fact," she said. "I've decided to leave some of the Italian words and phrases intact to give you some sense of the music."

"The music?"

"Italian is a musical language. English isn't. I didn't want to translate the manuscript to death. But you'll recognize the words I've left untouched, contextually or phonetically. Or both. And some of the proverbs he uses are virtually untranslatable. I've left them in whole but provided parenthetical notations—approximations."

"So what's he like?" I asked.

There was a pause. "What's he like?" she repeated.

"Yeah. I mean, you know the guy better than I do at this point. I'm just curious. Do you like him?"

"A translator's position should be an objective one. An emotional reaction might get in the way of—"

The day had been brutal. I had no patience with her scholarly detachment. "Well, just this once, treat yourself to an emotional reaction," I said. "Do you like the guy?"

"Do I *like* him?"

"Yeah."

"Well, no, actually. He's pompous. And he's a misogynist."

"What?"

"A misogynist. A woman-hater."

"I know what a misogynist is. I just wasn't sure whether I heard you right."

"You *see*?" she said. "I knew I shouldn't have relinquished my objectivity. Now you're offended. I can hear it in your voice."

"I'm not offended," I told her. "I'm just impatient, I just want it to get done before she's too sick to enjoy it."

"Well, I'm doing the best I can. I told you about my schedule. And anyway, I think you'd better read it first before you decide to share it with her. If I were you, I wouldn't talk it up just yet."

Now her lack of objectivity was pissing me off. What right did she have to an opinion about what I did or didn't do? Screw you, I wanted to say to her. You're just the translator.

Ma's third round of chemo made her too sick to eat. In February, she landed back in the hospital weighing in at ninety-four pounds and looking like an ad for famine relief. By then, I'd stopped bringing Thomas to see her. The incident on the highway had scared me shitless, had kept me up more nights than one.

"This may jab a little going in, Sweetie Pie," the nurse said, her intravenous needle poised in front of my mother's pale face.

Ma managed a nod, a weak smile.

"I'm having a little trouble locating a good vein on you. Let's try it. You ready, Sweetheart?"

The insertion was a failure. The next one, too. "Let me see the other arm again," she said. "I'll try one more time and if that doesn't work, I'm going to have to call my supervisor."

"Jesus fucking Christ," I mumbled, walking to the window.

The nurse turned toward me, red-faced. "Would you rather step outside until we're finished?" she said.

"No. I'd rather you stopped treating her like she's a friggin' pin cushion. And as long as you're asking, I'd rather you stop calling her Honey and Sweetie Pie like we're all on fucking *Sesame Street* or something."

Ma began to cry—over my behavior, not her own pain. I've got this talent for making bad situations worse. "Later, Ma," I said, grabbing my jacket. "I'll call you."

Late that same afternoon, I was standing at the picture window in my apartment, watching unpredicted snow fall, when Nedra Frank pulled up unexpectedly in her orange Yugo, hopping the curb and coming to a sliding stop. She parked half on the sidewalk, half in the road.

"Come in, come in," I said. She was wearing a down vest, sweatshirt, denim skirt, sneakers—clothes I never would have predicted. She carried a bulging briefcase.

"So it's finished?"

"What?" Her eyes followed mine to the briefcase. "Oh, *no*," she said. "This is my doctoral thesis. The apartment house where I live was broken into last week, so I'm carrying this wherever I go. But I'm working on your project. It's coming along." She asked me nothing about my mother's condition.

"How did you know where I live?" I asked.

"Why? Is it a deep, dark secret or something?"

"No, I just—"

"From your check. I copied your address down before I cashed it. In case I had to get ahold of you. Then I was just out for a drive—I've been so stressed out lately—and I just happened to pass by your street sign and I remembered it. Hillyndale Drive. It's such an unusual spelling. Was someone trying to be quaint or something? Faux British?"

I shrugged, jingled the change in my pockets. "Couldn't tell you," I said.

"I'd been meaning to call you anyway. About the manuscript. Your grandfather used a lot of proverbs—country sayings—and they don't lend themselves to translation. I thought I'd just leave them as is and then paraphrase them in the endnotes. If that's okay? I mean, it's your money."

Hadn't we already had this conversation? She was just out for a drive, my ass. "That would be fine," I said.

I offered her a beer; she accepted.

"So why are you stressed out?" I said.

For one thing, she said, the two undergraduate classes they made her teach were certifiably "brain dead." They didn't want to learn anything; they just wanted A's. And for another thing, her department chair was threatened by her knowledge of Dante, which was superior to his. And for a third thing, her office mate had disgusting personal habits. He flossed his teeth right there at his desk. He manicured his fingernails with a nail clipper that sent everything flying over to her side. Just that day she had found two fingernails on her desk blotter, after she had *told* him . . . She was sick to death of academic men, she said—sucking, forever, on the breast of the university so that they wouldn't have to get on with real life. "What do you do for a living?"

"I paint houses," I said.

"A housepainter!" she said, flopping down on my couch. "Perfect!"

She finished her beer, said yes to another. She walked over to my bookcase and cocked her head diagonally to read the spines. "García Márquez, *Zen and the Art of Motorcycle Maintenance*, Solzhenitsyn," she said. "I must say, Mr. Housepainter, I'm impressed."

"Yeah," I said, "You'd think a dumb fuck like me would be reading—what?—Mickey Spillane? *Hustler*?"

"Or this," she said. She took my boxed Stephen King trilogy from the shelf, waving it like a damning piece of evidence. She walked over to the picture window. "Is this snow supposed to amount to anything? I never follow the forecast."

"It wasn't forecast," I said. "Let's see what they're saying." I clicked on the little weather radio I keep in the bookcase. The staticky announcer said three to five inches. Oh, great, I thought. Snowed in with this supercilious bitch. Just what I needed.

Nedra picked up the weather radio, looked at it front and back, clicked it on and off. "So you're a real fan of weather," she said.

"I'm not a *fan* of it," I said. "But you need to know what it's going to be doing out when you're in the painting business. In season, I mean. You need to keep on top of it."

"You need to keep on top," she repeated. "God, you men are all alike." She laughed—a fingernails-down-the-blackboard kind of shriek—and asked *me* if *I* wanted a beer. If I was planning to feed her or just get her drunk and then push her back out into the snowstorm.

I told her I didn't have much of anything, unless she liked chicken broth or stale croutons or Honey Nut Cheerios.

"We could order a pizza," she said.

"All right."

"I'm a vegetarian, though. If *that* changes anything."

The kid from Domino's arrived two beers later. I'd ordered a large mushroom and olive, but ours was the last stop before his shift ended, he said, and all he had left in his vinyl warmer bag were two medium pepperonis. "I'm sure it's my retarded manager's fault, not yours," he said. Snowflakes lit on the fur collar of his jacket, on the brim of his dorky Domino's hat. "Here," he said. "Free of charge. I'm quitting anyways."

When I closed the door and turned around again, I saw my quilt draped around Nedra Frank's shoulders. She had been in my bedroom.

At the kitchen table, she picked off all the pepperoni slices and stacked them like poker chips, then blotted the tops of the pizzas with paper towels. We opened a second six-pack.

It must have been a Thursday night because later *Cheers* was on—a show Nedra said offended her politically because all the women characters were either bimbos or bitches. She'd come late to feminism, she said, after having been daddy's little girl, then a majorette in high school, then a slave to a chauvinist husband and a Dutch colonial on Lornadale Road. "I had to go into therapy for three years just to give myself permission to get my Ph.D.," she said. "Take *this*!" She aimed the remote control at Ted Danson, deadening the TV.

"My wife was in *Ms.* magazine several years back," I said. "She and her friend, Jocelyn."

"You have a *wife*?"

"My ex-wife, I meant. She and this friend of hers organized day care for women welders down at Electric Boat. Plus they got the honchos down there to put into writing a policy about on-the-job harassment from the male workers. It was a year or two after E.B. started hiring women to work in the yard."

"You were married to a *welder*?" she asked, a smirk on her face.

"Her friend was a welder. Dessa ran the day care center. Runs it, I should say. Present tense. It's called *Kids, Unlimited!* Exclamation mark at the end."

"Fascinating," Nedra said. Except she didn't sound too fascinated. She was attacking that pizza like the shark in *Jaws* attacked those swimmers. "My ex-husband's a psychiatrist," she said. "He's an administrator down at the state hospital."

I almost told her about Thomas, but didn't want to encourage any wow-what-a-small-world connections between the two of us. I kept hoping she'd leave before those bald tires of hers ruled out leaving as one of her options. It frosted me a little that she'd just gone into my room and taken the quilt. Who knew what kind of liberties she was taking with my grandfather's story?

"Todd's crazier than the inmates, though," Nedra said. "Vicious, too. It was sort of like being married to the Marquis de Sade, except that it was all pain, no pleasure."

"Oh," I said. "Todd de Sade."

That screechy laugh again. I turned the TV back on. "God," I said. "*L.A. Law*'s on already. It must be after ten. I can drive you back in my truck if you don't want to chance it in this snow. It's four-wheel drive."

"You tell time by the television shows?" she said. "Amazing." I let her keep assuming what she assumed: that I was just some uneducated housepainter from Dogpatch, some goober she could use to get herself through a lonely evening. Back when I was teaching high school, I never would have called a class "brain-dead."

"So do you want me to? Drive you home?"

"Oh, I get it," she said. "You're the big four-wheel-drive hero and I'm the damsel in distress, right? Thanks but no thanks."

She lifted my quilt off her shoulders and tossed it on the sofa. "Let's listen to some music," she said. Before I could say yes or no, she hit the power switch on my tuner and went searching for a station. I'd have pegged her for a classical music type, but she settled on Tina Turner: *What's love got to do, got to do with it?*

She turned around and smiled. "Hello, there, Mister Housepainter," she said.

She walked over to me. Kissed me. Took my hands in hers and put them against her hips. Her tongue flicked around inside my mouth.

"Is this a turn-on, Mr. Housepainter?" she whispered. "Am I making you feel good?" I couldn't tell if she was being daddy's little girl or a majorette or what. I pretended I was kissing Dessa, but she was thicker than Dessa, damp to the touch no matter *where* I touched. I hadn't been with a woman since the divorce—had imagined it happening pretty differently. Had imagined being more a part of the decision, for one thing. I found Nedra a little scary, to tell the truth. The last thing I needed in my life was another nutcase. I wanted my wife.

"Um, this is very nice," I said, "but sort of unexpected. I'm not sure I'm really ready for—"

"I have one," she said. "Relax. Touch me."

She slid my hand down to her butt, slid my other hand up under her sweatshirt. Then suddenly, right in the middle of kissing her, I started laughing. A few little nervous burps of laughter at first that I tried to swallow back. Then worse: full-throttle, out-of-control stuff—the kind of laughing that turns into a coughing spell.

She stood there, smiling, humiliated. "What's so funny?" she kept asking. *"What?"*

I couldn't answer her. Couldn't stop laughing.

Nedra headed for the bathroom. She stayed in there for a good fifteen minutes, long enough for me to begin to wonder if a person could commit suicide by overdosing on Nyquil, cutting her wrists with a Bic plastic razor. She emerged, red-eyed. Without a word, she went for her coat, her briefcase. I told her I'd just been nervous—that I was really, really sorry.

"For what?" she said. "For getting your kicks by degrading women? Don't apologize. You're born to the breed."

"Hey, look," I said. "I didn't—"

"Oh, please! Not another word! I *beg* of you!"

At the door, she stopped. "Maybe I should call your ex-wife," she said. "We could commiserate about sexual harassment." She pronounced it in that alternative way—William Henry *Harass*ment.

"Hey, wait a minute. *You* put the moves on *me.* How did I harass *you?*"

"What's her number, anyway? Maybe I'll call her. Maybe she and I can have our picture in *Ms.* magazine."

"Hey, listen. All I ever contracted you for was an overpriced translation. The rest of this was your idea. Leave my wife out of it."

"Overpriced? *Overpriced?* That work is painstaking, you bastard! You unappreciative—!" Instead of finishing her sentence, she swung her briefcase at me, whacked me in the leg with her twenty-pound thesis.

She slammed the door behind her and I yanked it open again, scooped up some snow, packed it, and let it fly. It thunked against her Yugo.

She gave me the finger, then got into her car and revved up for take-off. Oblivious to the road conditions, she gunned it all the way down the street, slipping and sliding and nearly front-ending a honking city plow.

"Your lights!" I kept yelling at her. "Put on your lights!"

By March, the oncology team at Yale had begun to sound like snake oil salesmen. Ma was in near-constant pain; what little comfort she was getting was coming from an old Polish priest, the hospice volunteers. Painting season had begun, jump-started by an early spring that I couldn't afford not to take advantage of. It was mid-April before I got the time and the stomach to drive back to the university and walk the steps up to Nedra Frank's little cubicle. Finished or not, I wanted my grandfather's story back.

Nedra's office buddy told me she'd withdrawn from the degree program. "Personal reasons," he said, rolling his eyes. Her desk was a clean slate, the bulletin board behind her stripped to bare cork.

"But she's got something of mine," I protested. "Something important. How can I get ahold of her?"

He shrugged.

The head of the department shrugged, too.

The head of Humanities told me she would attempt to locate Ms. Frank and share my concerns, but that she couldn't promise I'd be contacted. The agreement we had made was between the two of us, she reminded me; it had nothing whatsoever to do with the university. Under no circumstances could she release Nedra Frank's forwarding address.

My mother slipped out of consciousness on May 1, 1987. Ray and I kept a vigil through the night, watching her labored, ragged breathing and thwarting, until the very end, her continual attempts to pull the oxygen mask from her mouth. "There's a strong possibility that someone in a coma can hear and understand," the hospice worker had told us the evening before. "If it feels right to you, you might want to give her permission to go." It *hadn't* felt right to Ray; he'd balked at such an idea. But ten minutes before she expired, while Ray was down the hall in the men's room, I leaned close to my mother's ear and whispered, "I love you, Ma. Don't worry. I'll take care of him. You can go now."

Her death was different from the melodramatic versions I'd imagined during those final months. She never got to read her father's history. She never sat up in her deathbed and revealed the name of the man with whom she'd conceived my brother and me. From early childhood, I had formed theories about who our "real" father was: Buffalo Bob; Vic Morrow from *Combat;* my seventh grade shop teacher, Mr. Nettleson; Mr. Anthony from across the street. By the time of Ma's death, my suspicions had fallen on Angelo Nardi, the dashing, displaced courtroom stenographer who had first written in shorthand, then typed my grandfather's life story. But that, too, was just a theory. I told myself it didn't really matter.

After the hospital paperwork had been gotten through, Ray and I drove to the funeral parlor to make final arrangements, then drove back to Hollyhock Avenue and drank Ray's good Scotch. The old photo album was out, sitting there on the dining room table. I couldn't open it up—couldn't look inside the thing—but on impulse, I took it with me when we went down to the hospital to tell my brother the news.

Tears welled up in Thomas's eyes when he heard, but there was no scene—no difficult overreaction, as I'd imagined. Dreaded. When Ray asked Thomas if he had any questions, he had two. Had she suffered at the end? Could Thomas have his GOD IS LOVE collage back now?

Ray left after half an hour or so, but I stayed behind. If Thomas was going to have a delayed bad reaction, I told myself, then I wanted to be there to help him through it. But that wasn't entirely true. I stayed there because I needed to—needed on the morning of our mother's death to be with my twin, my other half, no matter who he had become, no matter where all this was going.

"I'm sorry, Tommy," I said.

"It's not your fault," he said. "You didn't give her the cancer. God gave it to her." With grim relief, I noted that he was no longer blaming the Kellogg's Cereal company.

"I mean, I'm sorry for blowing up at you. That time we visited her? In the car on the way home? I shouldn't have lost my cool like that. I should have been more patient."

He shrugged, bit at a fingernail. "That's okay. You didn't mean it."

"Yeah, I *did*. I meant it at the time. That's *always* my problem. I let stuff eat away and eat away inside of me and then—bam!—it just explodes. I do it with you, I did it with Ma, with Dessa. Why do you think she left me? Because of my anger, that's why."

"You're like our old TV," Thomas sighed.

"What?"

"You're like our old TV. The one that exploded. One minute we were watching a show and the next minute—ka-boom!"

"Ka-boom," I repeated, softly. For a minute or more, neither of us spoke.

"Do you remember when she came running out of the house that day?" Thomas finally said. He reached over and grabbed the photo album, touched its leather cover. "She was holding this."

I nodded. "Her coat was smoking. The fire had burned off her eyebrows."

"She looked just like Agatha."

"Who?"

"Agatha. The saint I prayed to while Ma was sick." He got up and took his dog-eared book from the bottom drawer of his nightstand. *Lives of the Martyred Saints.* Flipped through the lurid color paintings of bizarre suffering: the faithful, besieged by hideous demons; afflicted martyrs gazing Heavenward, bleeding from gaping, Technicolor wounds. He found Agatha's full-page illustration and held it up. Dressed in a nun's habit, she stood serene amidst chaos, holding a tray that bore two women's breasts. Behind her, a volcano erupted. Snakes fell out of the sky. Her body was outlined in orange flame.

Thomas shuddered twice and began to cry.

"It's all right," I said. "It's all right. It's all right." I reached back for the scrapbook. Opened it. We looked in silence, together.

When Ray had repaired my mother's broken book, he'd made no effort first to restore the loose pages to their proper chronological order. The result was a book of anachronisms: Instamatic snapshots from the sixties opposite turn-of-the-century studio portraits; time shuffled up and bolted. Here were Thomas and I in front of the Unisphere at the 1964 World's Fair; Ray in his Navy uniform; Papa in a greased handlebar mustache, arm in arm with his young bride who, later, would drown at Rosemark's Pond. Though my grandfather had died several months before Thomas and I were born, in Ma's book, we met him face to face. Stupidly, carelessly, I had lost his dictated story, but my mother had entered the fire and rescued his image.

Thomas unfolded the old newspaper clipping of the two of us in our sailor suits, saluting the camera and flanking Mamie Eisenhower. Despite my sadness, I had to smile at those two bewildered faces.

Thomas told me he had no recollection whatsoever of that day when the *Nautilus*, America's first nuclear submarine, eased down the greased ways and into the Thames River to help save the world from Communism. As for me, my memories are fragments—sounds and sensations that may have more to do with my mother's retelling of the story than with any electrical firings in my own brain. What I seem to recall are these: the crack of the water as the flag-draped submarine hits the river, the prickle of orange soda bubbles against my lip, the tickle of Mamie's mink.

Wally Lamb is the author of *She's Come Undone*. His first story, "Astronauts," which originally appeared in *The Missouri Review*, won the William Peden Prize for fiction. This is an excerpt from his forthcoming novel *I Know This Much Is True*.

"Like most of my other novels, this one is virtually writing itself!"

THE WINDMILL/*Lucy Ferriss*

THE TROUGH in the landscape was what fooled you—made the windmill appear to lie just over a hill, when the real distance might be miles. Jess pushed for it still. You'd just dip down, he insisted, looking out the wide picture window from the refectory, and then climb back up again. An hour at the most.

"Hour at the least, you mean," said Neal, who balanced caution and adventure better than Jess.

"We'd still have time to hang, once we got there. Waste the afternoon."

Neal shrugged; he wasn't much of a waster. "Might be on someone's property."

"We can just tell the owners we got lost."

"Better to tell them we wanted a look at their windmill."

"They can't care much about it. It's never running." Jess turned back to the deserted table and, standing, knocked off his glass of warm beer, followed by a coffee biscuit. Everyone else had gone—the boarders to the front area where their parents picked them up for the weekend, Steve Mack to Bruges where his girlfriend directed the girls' program. Only the monks in the kitchen remained, waiting to clean up in time for afternoon prayers or whatever they did. Over the tables at the north end of the dining hall, the lights had already been turned off. "What's Russ the Bus doing?" asked Jess.

"Eating *tarte tatin* with the *préfecture*, probably, who knows," said Neal. Neal was the oldest exchange student, Jess the youngest. Russell, in the middle—they'd lost two others to homesickness early in the fall—was already buying his school uniform a size larger than when he started.

"We should probably leave the Mack a note."

"Uh-uh. Easier to ask forgiveness than permission."

"*Vous mettez les plats, non?*" came the lunch prefect's gravelly voice as they started out. Trotting back under his black stare, they slid their trays down the chute, then clattered down the iron steps to the broad soccer field. Hoisting his backpack, Jess shaded his eyes. Clearly there was a deep grassy descent, and a field of rye, and then the windmill rose, its great propeller exactly like the cut-out on those cookies Jess' mother used to buy, back home. The sun winked off the motionless blades. Upstairs in the chapel, the chants had begun; from the other side of the school, you could hear the occasional honk of a car leaving. Those who stayed for weekends—long-distance boarders, plus the Americans— would get a van trip into town later and probably a soccer match.

"Free at last," said Neal as they angled across the field.

"For five hours."

"Yeah, well hold up, okay? You don't have a train to catch."

With effort, Jess shortened his stride; already, at fifteen, he was taller than Neal, taller than most boys he knew. In his backpack he had a dozen coffee-iced biscuits, along with four green apples and two bottles of Pipps. Neal hadn't thought to grab anything—he was one of those guys who'd grown up with other people taking care of the snacks, the clothes, the arrangements. Neal played soccer well enough to have been taken on the school team here. That was apparently part of the motivation, giving Neal soccer abroad. Plus there was the appeal of new places, the language, the way Europeans went about everything. Neal's eyes shone as he explained this enthusiasm to Jess, who never quite caught it but thought his friend would probably ride the crest of girls, college, career, everything that threatened to drown the ordinary guy. Still, Jess was the one who'd remembered the snacks.

The day was warm for October; by the time they scrambled over the fence they'd both shucked their flannel jackets. The school had uniforms, blue twill trousers and white shirts with brown ties, so Jess had brought only these jeans and a few T-shirts for days off. His parents weren't rich, like Neal's. The week before he left, his dad had said the hospital was sucking them dry. Still, his dad had coughed up the fare, the program fee. Not that this abroad thing had been Jess' idea. If it weren't for Neal, he'd have gotten on the plane home with those other guys.

"Fuck," said Neal. "There's a fucking ravine."

"Maybe we can bushwhack it," said Jess. They were barely out of sight of the school, and here already was a glitch they hadn't foreseen—a knife-slice of brambles and rocks cutting through the field down to a dry streambed.

"No way, not here anyhow. Take a look at those thorns."

The barbs were a half-inch long, along vines that wrapped around the gnarly bushes and ran across the larger rocks. Farther down was no different. Jess didn't know much about ravines, and he figured Neal didn't either, both of them being products of manicured lawns and b-ball courts, of the rare summer hike up a graded trail. At one point Jess tried to slide underneath a thorn-choked bush to a log jutting across the ravine, but his jeans got yanked up and his calves raked by a branch he hadn't seen. "Shit," he said as he pulled himself back up by roots to level ground. "It stings."

"You want to forget about this?" Neal had opened Jess' backpack and was munching an apple. With his square shoulders, his close-cropped hair, he looked already like a piece of Wall Street.

"No." Jess stood up, dusting his hands against his lean hips, and shielded his eyes for a look down toward the right. "There's that wall there," he said.

"Yeah, I noticed that. It's the long way around."

"Muddy, too."

"But if we drop down into the field on the other side, and then make it up the rise, we ought to find a place to climb over once we're on that ridge, there." Coming up beside Jess, Neal marked a long arc with his finger. It looked a lot farther than it had from the dorm. Which made the windmill a lot bigger, Jess realized, and a surge of excitement gathered in his chest.

"Let's do it," he said, and set off at his natural pace, ahead of Neal. When they reached the brick wall at the lower end of the hill, he found a weedy tree to help hoist himself up, then sat at the top and waited for Neal to throw the pack up to him before they both leaped down. It was an eight-foot drop, at least; their sneakers sank into mud at the bottom. Neal took the pack and they slapped each other high fives.

They were in a greenish-yellow sweep of a pasture, with a small copse farther over at this low end and some haystacks farther up. "Cow pies," Neal said as they started walking along the brick wall. *"Tartes de vache."*

They did look just like pies, round and flat, crusted at the top. *"Vachement* gross," said Jess. But he didn't think where they came from until the group of cattle started out from the copse toward them.

The cows didn't trundle over, the way he'd seen them do on PBS. They ran. They headed straight for the two boys at a sort of canter—not charging, but definitely in a hurry.

"Hold still," Neal said, putting his hand on Jess' arm.

Jess remembered the old rule about not running from a dog who charges you. Not that there was anywhere to run—the cows were spreading out from the copse, coming at them from three sides, with the brick wall at their backs.

"Jesus," Jess breathed. Lumbering to within five feet, the big animals suddenly stopped and surrounded them, a half-circle of cattle cut by the wall. "Are they cows or bulls?" he asked.

"Both," said Neal. "Look at the horns."

"I read somewhere cows can have horns, too."

"Well, I'm not bending down to look. Best thing's just to stand still. Don't scare 'em." Neal said this with a touch of authority, but Jess had known him long enough now to tell that it was just a habit of speaking.

"What if we just walk slowly?"

"Okay. Okay, try it."

Flies had surrounded them, along with the cows; their hum rose in the warm air. The cows' heads were lowered, their foreheads and horns—short, thick, curved like quote marks—pointing vaguely at the boys, their wide eyes scanning them at knee level. Being farther uphill, Jess took the first step. The cows clustered in that direction moved closer together, shuffling toward him even as he tried to show determination. He got close enough to touch their huge heads, to smell their cud, and still they didn't move back. "This is stupid," he said. "They're not budging."

"No, not this way either," said Neal, who'd moved a couple of paces from the wall.

"They'll get bored with us," Jess said in what he thought was a reassuring tone. "Look, even if they're bulls, they don't eat meat, right? They're just curious. Let's hang here, and they'll move away. Right?"

"Right," said Neal. And at that, the cows shuffled closer.

There were sixteen of them. Jess had plenty of time to count. Six with horns, ten without. The one time he bent down, to check out genitals, they moved closer still—but he got a chance to see the udder before he straightened up. Girls with horns, he thought. Their coats were mottled, the hair worn off in patches, crusted with mud elsewhere—reddish-brown, mostly, some of them white on the faces, as if they were wearing clown masks. Flies gathered in the moist underbrow of their eyes. Their oversized noses were baby-pink, the nostrils like vacuum hoses. They did not move, except forward. This is really stupid, he and Neal kept saying. This is the dumbest thing we've ever done. Still, the boys didn't move either, neither of them willing to push against those broad implacable flanks, to risk those horns or the sheer weight of the beasts. "We don't know a fucking thing," Neal said at one point. "You realize that? Not a damn fucking thing." By which Jess knew he meant that a farmer's son would have been out of there in thirty seconds.

The sun broiled. This side of the wall, the sweet October breeze had died. They drank the Pipps, ate the apples. When Jess tossed the core, one of the cows shuffled forward and pulled it into her mouth with her big, dry lips, then started making those round chewing motions. *Gueule,* Jess remembered—that was what you called an animal's mouth; *engueuler,* to gorge, stick in your gullet. The other cows followed suit, not finding apples but moving their huge dumb bodies even closer, some of them swinging to the side as they did so, until they were presenting their shoulders rather than their lowered heads, making a wall. Their skin hung over their lifted spines as rugs would on a hanger, bloating below.

"They keep moving like this," Jess said, "They'll crush us against that wall."

"C'mon."

"No. I mean it. They're too stupid to know any better. They just follow each other."

"That one's the leader," said Neal, pointing at a horned one, totally brown. "She moves, the others follow. You noticed that?"

"Hey, Bossy," Jess said, but the brown cow just moved her head slowly, dipping and raising it the way she'd been doing for five minutes now.

Soon they all had names, at least the ones in the front line—Bossy and Sugar, Toast and Shitface. "I got to pee," said Neal at one point, and turned to aim at the wall, but Shitface moved in on that signal, so he turned and pointed the stream outward, holding her off. "Helluva way to die," he said when he'd zipped up. "American Teens Found Crushed by Belgian Cows."

"The Waterloo Stampede," Jess returned. God it was hot. Sweat poured down his neck; his knees were stiff, from standing so still. When Toast shuffled sideways and then laid a pie, the stench of it spreading through the thick air, Neal went white, turned, and barfed on the red dirt by the wall. Jess fought the sound by clenching his throat and making himself breathe.

"What the fuck are we doing here? That's what I want to know. What the fuck are we doing?"

"You wanted to play soccer, remember?"

"Oh, yeah. *Le football.* That's a good line, isn't it? America's got such lousy coaches, you have to go to the armpit of Europe to work up your game."

"So that's not the deal?"

"Shit, no. Christ, look at those flies. Look at Sugar, she's got a dozen of 'em in one eye, is that gross or what?"

"Well, what's the deal, then?"

"The deal, the deal. Oh, Bateson, you don't really want to know."

"C'mon man. We're standing here like a pair of goofs, hemmed in by a bunch of udders on legs. Might as well talk." Though Jess realized, even as he said it, that he'd have to take a turn at this; he shuddered, in the heat. "I know you by now," he went on, not looking at Neal but keeping an eye on Bossy. She'd started to nibble the grass around his feet, that was how close she'd gotten. Evil lurked in the sheer dullness of her eyes, the blunt unseeing forehead between them. "You don't do drugs or cheat or anything that'd get you booted. You love all this international stuff. Look how you went at the language."

"Yeah, sure. Hell, I had five years of it already."

"Five?"

"I'm not seventeen, Bateson. I'm eighteen. I graduated in June."

Bossy had turned from the grass to Jess' feet, tasting the sneaker leather with her lips, and the other cows moved forward another few inches. "That's a dumb thing to lie about," said Jess, though what he was thinking about was three years. Three years' difference, not two.

"Yeah, well, it's pretty lame, going on a high-school exchange when you're out already! But I couldn't get into the top league, you know how it is, and the school counselor said something like this'd spice up my file. My dad said go for it. Jesus, six months of your life for a line on a transcript, can you believe it works like this?"

"I can't believe you waited this long to tell me."

"I shouldn't have told you at all, you'll probably unload it on that porkpie Russell."

This wasn't worth answering. Bossy had turned her attention to Jess' jeans, was sticking out her enormous tongue and licking at the side where the brambles had torn the skin underneath. Shitface had moved in on Neal, her long tongue lolling out, sniffing at the backpack. They both smelled of regurgitated grass. "Take a look, I'm getting cleaned," Jess said. Sugar had followed Bossy's lead, was bumping his hand with her nose. "You sure they don't eat meat?"

"You wanted to go to the windmill. Jesus. What the fuck are we doing here?"

Jess took a step backward from Sugar and Bossy, his back now almost against the wall that there was no way to scale. The sun had sunk to where it shone in their faces and bounced off the brick. They were completely surrounded by tough-hided dumb animals weighing maybe a ton each. No one at the school knew where they were, the program leader was in Düsseldorf. Neal was saying something. "What?"

"I said, what's your real story?"

"Oh, I don't have one."

"You just decided to pick up from Columbus, Ohio, and come live with a bunch of monks in Belgium for six months?"

"Well, that's what Russell did."

"Russell's from Florida, he doesn't count."

"I came," Jess said, the impossible words spilling into the hot air, "because my mother's dying. They didn't want me to see it, so they sent me here."

"Jesus! That's rough!" Neal's words came out at different pitches. It wasn't the story he'd wanted. From here on, he could be saying—assuming they ever got away from these treacherous cows—they wouldn't be such a pair any more.

Hold it in, Jess thought. Something was ticking, in his belly. You held it in, that's what you did, you swallowed it down. You'd known people were assholes, that's why you hadn't ever come clean.

Then Neal asked, "She going to die before you get home?"

The bomb burst. A punch, that was what Neal needed, a hard cut to his soft eighteen-year-old jaw. Blood from skin. "The way we're going here," Jess managed, after a minute, "I'll beat her to it." And he shut his eyes, to shut Neal out.

When he saw her—in his closed sunstreaked lids, his nostrils full of the acrid odor of cow drool—she was lying as she had all summer, on the chaise longue on the screened porch. Only she'd reached the next stage, where she must be now. He saw her skin peopled with lesions, her eyes sunk in her head. Her speech had slowed—there was a virus in her brain as well, eating away at her language and memory, the immune system totally failed there. Everyone had agreed, everyone— witnessing such a thing could do a boy no good.

Senseless as it was, the stigma would pass to him if he stayed. And still he wouldn't have gone; would have run from home and lived in alleyways near the hospital's revolving door, if she hadn't asked him to sign on for this. Because she loved him, she said. Such a good program, and so much to distract him, a language to learn, something besides those furious computer games he kept playing. Said she'd call him home, if it came to that, and he'd believed her then but he didn't now. Not now, standing in the hot muddy field with Neal and the pea-brained cows. She'd die without calling him back, and if he came back before she called him she'd die faster from being so upset.

"Well, praise Jesus," came Neal's voice, behind him. When he snapped his eyes open they were looking straight into Toast's; her delicate lashes curled like springs. Then, miraculously, she took a step backwards, keeping her brown gaze on him. The others were moving, too, shuffling dancelike toward other pursuits. When even Shitface had turned her rump toward him, Jess looked around. Neal had sunk down on the weeds fringing the wall. "Party's over."

"How long've we been here?" asked Jess, sitting beside him. His knees shook; he had to hold them still with his hands. Inside he cried,

Mother!—knowing she couldn't hear, there was no telepathy between them.

"God, an hour at least."

"What about the windmill?"

"Oh, forget that, buddy boy!" The cows were cantering away, now. Neal laughed and dug out the coffee-iced biscuits, but Jess shook his head; his throat was a desert. "What fucking idiots we are," he said.

"City boys," said Jess.

"We probably could've pelted those fuckers with biscuits, and they'd of run off."

"I don't know," said Jess. "They're fucking big, and they—"

"Well, I'll never be a farmer, that's for sure. C'mon, let's head back." Neal pushed himself up and moved down along the wall toward the spot where they'd jumped over. Jess sat. "You coming?" Neal said finally, from a dozen yards away.

"They were curious about us," finished Jess, but he pulled himself up and followed. Where the wall made a corner, at the far end, past where they'd climbed and jumped, they found a pile of old crumbling bricks that they managed to stack into a stoop. Being taller, Jess hoisted himself up first, then took the backpack to toss over and straddled the wall while he helped pull Neal to the top. When Neal had leaped down on the safe side, Jess said he'd be a sec, and he sat in the breeze that gathered high up, watching the cows move away, their hindquarters swaying flirtatiously, up toward the cluster of farmhouses and barns at the top of the far rise. When his eyes finally came to rest on the windmill in the distance—this was the closest view, now, that he would ever have of it—he saw that its blades had begun to move. Not fast, but regularly enough that you could see it had been powered or unlocked or whatever it was you did to get a windmill going in a rising breeze. Shutting his eyes, Jess saw where he'd be a year from now, back in an American school, his mother dead. Her dying would always feel hot to him, full of the smell of hay and the sight of swarming flies, the gentle irresistible nudging of cows. He started to call down, to Neal, but Neal was already halfway up the hill, moving back to the school that promised them showers and a few more Pipps from the machine.

Lucy Ferriss' fourth novel, *The Misconceiver,* was nominated for the National Book Award.

WHERE NATIVE GRASS GROWS LOUD
IF WE LISTEN / *Walt McDonald*

Out here, cactus is the skyline, a hundred miles of flat.
Turn in a circle and never know you're back,
except for the neighbor's ranch, barns like specks of mica
in the dust, his windmill a semaphore of warning, *Go away*.

East Texas is a myth, black loam and heritage and trees.
The one road into town has highway signs boys use
as targets. The asphalt's cracked, dandelions thriving
as if crews planted them. Rattlesnakes nap

on the shoulders, no trucks along for months.
Jackrabbits limp along like dogs, nibbling grass
and careless weeds, no need to hurry from nothing
that can hide. Slumped on an aging appaloosa,

I roll a smoke that may take half a day to lick,
to get it right. I dig in deep shirt pockets for a match,
and bite it like a toothpick. I stick the unlit
cigarette like a feather in my hat. I kicked the habit

four years ago after the last grass fire
some trucker started. The butt's for practice,
in case I'm ever bored. My wife saves rattles
for the grandkids, flint arrowheads she finds,

digging strawberry gardens, prying out rocks
for the fish pond, scooping iron and umber
for sand paintings on the patio. Rocking at dusk
that starts at dinnertime and lasts past Halloween,

we talk softly about a coyote a mile away,
one drop of water bulging at sundown from the pipe
over the brimming-full horse trough, the stretch
and shimmer of the drop before it falls.

THAT SILENCE WHEN A MOUNTAIN LION
ATTACKS/*Walt McDonald*

Those puffy clouds in the Rocky Mountains
could be gunfire, another time and place.
Before this planet spins us back home to the plains,
dozens will die by rockets or cannon fire,

puffs like clouds the last skies they will see.
I heard explosions often in Saigon
and the rapid pop of rifles, but high over jungles
I saw only distant puffs and fire, silence

except my own breath and chatter in my headset.
Even when Kelly exploded in mid-air, no others heard,
only a blip that disappeared on radar screens
back at Da Nang. The earth turns green again,

no matter what. Outside our cabin, magpies clown
and crazy hop for worms and lazy bugs, sluggish
under a thawing, Colorado sun. Last week,
two campers had their throats slit in their tent

not ten miles east. We never heard a scream.
The world will be the world, springtime or not.
Our oldest daughter's forty and a day, and we are wiser
only by repute. The cost of living past a war

is personal. Feelings are cash stashed in cigar boxes
and not invested, no access by the Internet.
Only an elk calf knows how its neck feels
pierced by a puma, how nothing matters when fangs

bend it staggering back, unable to scream
or breathe. Nobody needs to know, but if they could,
they'd trade. Nobody's degree of pain has been felt
anywhere, nobody's loss is ever this severe.

CATARACTS/*Walt McDonald*

Clouds over Long's Peak, the sky blue everywhere but there,
and when I glance away and back, they're gone. Imagine:
I make the highest mountain disappear by tipping my head,
even by shifting my eyes. Watch that herd of mule deer

on the slope, floppy ears like semaphore: gone, a blur
like TV reception in the fifties. When I blink left
or right, they're back, magic. In night flight,
they taught that staring at a light too long

would saturate the rods or cones, a blind spot
we could find by sweeping left to right like radar.
A few more years, the specialist will pluck them out
like pearls, *presto*, bringing my vision back

like a picture tube, the world once more in focus.
If it works, that is, no procedure perfect.
Here from the cabin deck, I watch the river
cascade left to right, flowing to nothing but a roar,

then a shimmer twisting away downhill. For years,
we watched our son come rafting with his friends,
a bucking, rubber float jolting them into shrieks, so close
we could snap them as they passed, mouths open, holding on

in white-water rapids flinging them hard downriver
past the trees. I've turned old photo albums right to left,
a blur of portraits and snapshots. I've helped my wife
tidy his room, storing trophies, giving away good clothes.

I watched the car towed back, glass and metal
mangled out of focus, a scarred blur almost a car
that didn't burn. I've been to the scene, walked down
the ledge and lowered myself by roots and boulders

where his car careened. I've stood there where it crashed.
I've turned my eyes to focus far as I could see downstream,
even twisted in my chair, thinking I could hear
his voice behind me, not merely the river's roar.

TWINS AND ORAL HISTORY/Walt McDonald

> *If you think ground squirrels are fun,*
> *wait till you see a coyote.*

I'd never say that to grandsons,
but even coyotes have to eat. So what do I tell
their taped school project tomorrow?
What idealistic teacher makes historians of kids
in the second grade? With a flourish of her tongue

and simple Xeroxed lists of questions,
she'll flick us back to Saigon or Da Nang,
memories static as paper weights with winter scenes.
What did you do in the war, Grandpa? Shake us
with cassette tapes and watch snow flurries swirl.

What do I say about native kids their age?
They were hungry but cute, with tangled hair and eyes.
Did they play? Yes, I think they ran a lot. No,
they didn't believe in Santa Claus, but Halloween
was all year long. The tarmac track where I jogged

outside Saigon was hot. Yes, I sunburned
and others, most in jogging shorts and tennis shoes
or boots. No, I killed nobody on the track.
No, men jogged in the jungle with backpacks
and rifles. No, boys, I never saw tigers

eating people on the battlefield,
but if your teacher's daddy was there,
I guess they did. No, I don't have a gun to show you,
no enemy's teeth or dried ears in my duffle bag.
Have I been back to Vietnam? Do I have nightmares

still? [What's next on this teacher's list?
Have you stopped beating Grandma?]
It was a long time ago, and boys, you know
what happens when you sleep. You never know
what might trot by inside your mind—a friend

from school who moved away you'll never see
again, a tiger in a Disney show, a coyote
gnawing on a bone. But that's enough. Come,
hug me, both of you, then race me to the swing set
before your mother calls us to wash up.

FISHING WITH UNCLE WALTER IN WORLD WAR TWO/ *Walt McDonald*

I remember the first tub of red racers I saw in a walled shed
in Arkansas, down by the Ouachita. My uncle led us there
when I was nine, my father, and another man with some
    4-F condition
or too old. We drove five hundred miles in World War Two
over bumpy roads at night to see my aunt and uncle

who lost their only son at Pearl Harbor, to grieve again
about what happened two years ago, to fish the river
my father trawled and trapped when he was a boy in
    poverty Arkansas,
Granddaddy dead, his scattered brothers fretting for their boys
flung out across the world like dice and black bones,

a mystery of fate. My older brother was in jungles of Saipan
or Guam, pinheads on a map my mother kept back home.
    But here was rot,
real darkness in some back-swamp bait shop, a dozen washtubs
of rotting crawdads, eels, and fish heads, the hot shed
squishing under my Keds as I ducked in mud under cobwebs

long as nets. My uncle punched me in the ribs and kidded
what my girl friends would think of this. I mumbled something
and my uncle laughed. What all this rot and splash of slime
in barrels had to do with fish I didn't know, the perch and bass
we caught back on the Brazos suckers for worms and grubs

the size of snot. I wondered if this was one of those places
we whispered about at night behind the barn, where men
went to women, where boys were lucky if they came back alive,
bleeding, part of their things chopped off, circumcised
or sick for weeks. I shuddered, that odd, familiar swelling

in my pants and taste of alum. My father walked behind me
like a guard, and I followed my distant uncle and a
    one-armed man

who hobbled to a row of tubs and buckets. *My God*,
my Uncle Walter said, stepping back and clapping
as if he'd found the manger, always one to make the best

of everything. I stopped nose level with the tub, nothing
but fifty pounds of straw and dirt. My father bowed down
    to smell,
big-knuckled fists on the nicked and rusted rim. The one-
    armed man
who owned it all reached around my back and tapped the tub
with a hammer. Chaos swarmed, enormous worms twelve
    inches long,

swirling out of black dirt and squirming over each other,
gone in the blink of my eyes, the fastest motion I'd ever seen.
His nub still around me, the unshaved owner banged again,
and out they wound and slithered, red racers fat and slimy
    naked.
I imagined the fish these would catch, the sharks or alligator gar

it would take to swallow them, the meat hooks we'd have
    to squish
and impale them on, if any of us could hold them writhing
like fire hoses. I don't know how many gar and big-mouthed
    bass
we caught that week, what bait we used. I remember my uncle
suddenly weeping against the wall, sunlight odd on his
    balding head

in the bait shop. I remember my father clearing his throat
and staring at worms with unusual interest, big knuckles white
on the tub. Now that I've been to war, now that I've
    watched TV
around the clock and worried about one son under Iraqi rockets,
I can hear my Uncle Walter beating his fist against the wall

of that bait shop, there to fish with only his brother
and a distant nephew. I can't remember much about that day,
but my father's face sunburned. Out on the lake, I drank
my first half-bottle of beer. I got to pee from the boat,
standing up, a long-arched splash and ripple my uncle
    promised

would draw fish. I know we carried two canoes over a crust
of mud that shuddered like dough, and fished the river
past midnight. I remember Uncle Walter cursing, clubbing
alligator gars with his oar, trash fish he hated, head down,
shaking, smashing them in the moonlight with his fists.

WITH HORSEHAIRS DIPPED IN OILS/
Walt McDonald

My wife's green eyes are jade and rainbows.
With horsehairs dipped in oils,
she brushes corrals and cattle on canvas,
the burnt sienna sand and pastures of our boots.
Combing October lawns like yarn,
we heap dry leaves on flames that float away.
Friends disappear, and nothing we do
could save them. We store the rakes
away from pups gnawing our gloves.

Rocking, we watch them sniff the yard
for bones the old dog buried. We watch smoke
drifting east toward slow whirlpools of wings.
A neighbor's tin roof shimmers.
Prairie cattle go mad when the wind dies.
They stomp, lashing their tails at horseflies.
We survive hardscrabble drought
like spiders that spin their webs in wind
and anchor them to thorns.

AFTER THE FIRES WE ONCE CALLED
VIETNAM/*Walt McDonald*

Here on these flat fields I remember napalm,
that lavish charcoal lighter of a fat man's barbecue.
I'm like a pitcher with eyes in the back of his head
who wore his ball cap backward, ignoring the signs
his catcher gave, the finger between his thighs.
Often, he saw the runner leading too far off and whirled
and picked him off. Amazing, how hindsight made him hard
to steal on. He scrolled mistakes in his mind

like a three-inch roll of tape, adding them up,
the total always the same, like calling for a fly ball
in the infield, *my fault, mine.* Saigon was lost
before I got there, fortunes stashed in Swiss banks,
French plantation rubber and raw silk. I flew off to war
and came back home alone. These are the facts.
I have a fence to mend, cattle to keep, or give up all
we've worked for. My wife depends on my saddle, ten miles

from any mesa, from any town, ten thousand miles
from jungles that once burned. Those villages were theirs,
and these flat pastures mine, a flat field not on fire
but shimmering in the sun, my herd of Angus burned
as black as toast in the sun that heats the wind,
that turns the windmill, that pumps cold water to the troughs
and faucet I bow to, splashing my face to cool my neck
until I'm sober. I know this patient appaloosa is my horse,

those barbed wires sagging a mile away are mine,
and only I can twist and tighten them to save these steers
needing alfalfa and water from a well, not a lake
less tangible than guilt, a shimmer, a trick my eyes ignore
while I ride there on a trotting horse. The sun will blaze

tomorrow like most days on the plains, a mirage
fat Angus wade before the slaughterhouse. But now,
dismounting at the wires, when I glance back, it's gone.

Walt McDonald is the author of sixteen collections of poetry and fiction, including *Counting Survivors* and *Night Landings*.

"I read 'The Hidden Life of Dogs' last
year, so this doesn't come as a complete
surprise to me."

FLAME/*Ha Jin*

A LETTER WAS lying on Nimei's desk. She was puzzled because the envelope did not give a return address. The postmark showed the letter came from Harbin, but she knew nobody in that city. When she opened the envelope, the squarish handwriting looked familiar to her, and she turned the first page to see who the sender was. As she saw the name Hsu Peng, her heart began palpitating, and a surge of emotion overcame her. She had not heard from him for seventeen years.

He wrote that through an acquaintance of his he had learned that Nimei worked in the Central Hospital. How glad he was that he had at last found her. He was going to attend a conference at the headquarters of Muji Military Sub-Command at the end of September. "For old time's sake," he said, "I hope you will allow me to visit you and your family." Without mentioning his wife, he told Nimei that he had three children now—two girls and one boy—and that he was the commissar of an armored division garrisoned in the suburbs of Harbin. In the bottom left-hand corner of the second page, he gave her the address of his office.

Nimei locked away the letter in the middle drawer of her desk. She glanced across the office and saw nobody, so she stretched up her arms. Again a pain tightened the small of her back, and she let out a moan.

It was already early September. If she wanted to meet Hsu Peng, she should write him back soon, but she was unsure why he wanted to see her.

The door opened and Wanyan, a young nurse, came in. "Nimei," she said, "the patient in Ward 3 wants to see you."

"What happened?" Nimei asked in alarm.

"I've no idea. He just wants to see the head nurse."

The patient in Ward 3 was the director of the Cadre Department at the Prefecture Administration, who had been operated on for gastric perforation two weeks ago. Although he no longer needed special care, he had to stick to a soft diet for at least another week. Nimei got up and walked to the door while slipping on her white robe. She stopped to pat her bobbed hair, then went out.

When she arrived at Ward 3, the patient was sitting up in bed, his shoulders hunched over a magazine, a marking pencil between his fingers. "Director Liao, how are you today?" Nimei asked pleasantly.

"Fine." He put the magazine and the pencil on the bedside cabinet, on which stood two scarlet thermoses and four white teacups with landscapes painted on their sides.

"Did you have a good nap?" she asked, resting her hand on the brass knob of a bedpost.

"Yes, I slept two hours after lunch."

"How is your appetite?"

"My appetite is all right, but I'm tired of the liquid stuff."

She smiled. "Rice porridge and egg-drop soup don't taste very good."

"They're not bad, but it's hard to eat them every day. Can I have something else for a change?"

"What would you like?"

"Fish—a soup or a stew."

Nimei looked at her wristwatch. "It's almost four. It may be too late for today, but I'll go and tell the kitchen manager."

Director Liao thanked her, but he didn't look happy; his thick-lidded eyes glinted as the muscles of his face suddenly hardened. Nimei noticed, but she pretended she had seen nothing. Although one of the hospital leaders had informed her that the nurses should show special attention to Liao, she couldn't bother too much about him. There were too many patients here. From the ward she went directly downstairs to the kitchen and told the manager to have a fish stew made for the patient the next day. Meanwhile, she couldn't help thinking of Hsu Peng's letter. She returned to the office, took it out of the drawer, and read it again before she left for home.

Walking along Peace Avenue, she was thinking of Hsu Peng. On the street dozens of trucks and tractors traveled north and south, transporting lumber, cement, pupils, tomatoes, pumpkins. Even the vehicles' blasting horns and the explosive snarls of their exhaust pipes couldn't interrupt Nimei's thoughts. Her mind had again slipped into the quagmire of the past. She and Hsu Peng had been in love once. That was seventeen years ago, in her home village. After her father had died of tetanus contracted in an accident at the village quarry, many matchmakers came to see her mother, intending to persuade her to marry off Nimei inexpensively. The widow, however, declined their offers, declaring that her daughter had already lost her heart to a man. Most people believed her, because they often saw Jiang Zhen, a young mess officer in the nearby barracks, visit her house on weekends. Every time, he'd arrive with a parcel under his arm, which the villagers knew must contain tasty stuff from the army's kitchen. Behind dusty windowpanes numerous eyes observed this small man emerge in the dusk, as though he were a deity of sorts, knowing the secret of abundance and harvest.

The villagers were hungry. For two years in a row, floods had drowned most of their crops. Dozens of people had died of dropsy in the village, where wails often burst out like cock-a-doodle-doos in broad daylight. So people thought Nimei was a lucky girl; she was going to marry an officer with infinite access to food.

Indeed Nimei had lost her heart to a man, but not the mess officer. In secret she had been meeting Hsu Peng at the bank of Snake Mouth Reservoir on Tuesday afternoons when she was off work from the commune's clinic. He was a platoon leader and had graduated from high school—much better educated than most of the army men. Later, when her mother wanted her to marry Jiang Zhen, Nimei opposed her wish, saying she hardly knew him. She revealed to her that she loved another man, also an officer, but her mother was adamant and gruffed, "What's love? You'll learn how to love your man after you marry him. I never met your father before our wedding."

Nimei showed her mother a photograph of Hsu Peng and begged her to meet the platoon leader in person, hoping his good manners and manly looks might help dissuade her, but her mother refused. Meanwhile, the small mess officer came at least twice a week, as though he had become a part of the family. Every Saturday evening the widow expected him, and waited to find out what he had brought. Sometimes his parcel contained a braised pig's foot, sometimes a bunch of dried mushrooms, sometimes a string of raw peanuts, sometimes two or three pounds of millet or sorghum. While most cauldrons in the village had rusted because there was little to cook, and while hundreds of people had faces bloated like white lanterns because they had eaten too many locust blossoms, Nimei and her mother never starved. Their chimney puffed out smoke on Sunday mornings, the fragrance of food drifting away from their yard, and children would gather along the high fence, sniffing the delicious air.

Fully content, the widow was determined to give Jiang Zhen her daughter. One evening she wept, begging Nimei, "You must marry this man who can save us!" Out of pity and filial duty, Nimei finally yielded.

When she told Hsu Peng that she couldn't disobey her mother and had to marry the other man, he spat a willow leaf to the ground and said with a ferocious light in his eyes, "I hate you! I'll get my revenge."

She turned and ran away, tears stinging her cheeks in the autumn wind. Those were his last words for her.

Nimei had been married to Jiang Zhen for sixteen years, and had left the countryside when he was demobilized, but she had never forgotten Hsu Peng's angry words and his maddened, lozenged eyes. At night, awake and lonesome, she'd wonder where Hsu Peng was and what he was like. Was his wife kindhearted and pretty? Did he still serve in the army? Had he forgotten her?

Despite often thinking of him, she had dreamed of him only twice. Once he appeared in her dream as a farmer raising hundreds of white rabbits; he looked robust and owned a five-room house with a red tiled roof. In her other dream he was gray-mustached and bald, teaching geography in an elementary school, spinning a huge globe. Afterwards she was a little saddened by his aged appearance. But who wouldn't change in seventeen years? Her own body was thick and roundish now, the shape of a giant date stone. There was no trace of her slender waist, admired so much by the girls in her home village. Her chin had grown almost double, and she wore glasses. What hadn't changed was her sighing and murmuring in the small hours when her husband wheezed softly on the other bed in their room. What remained with her were Hsu Peng's last words, which had somehow grown more resonant in her mind each year.

"Want some tea?" Jiang Zhen asked Nimei.

"Yes." She was lying on her bed with both hands under her neck. The room still smelled musty, although the windows had been open since she came home two hours ago.

"Here you are." He put a cup of tea on the glass tabletop and walked out with a stoop. He went back to their daughter's room to help her prepare for language and chemistry exams. The girl had not passed the admission standard for business school the previous year, so this fall she would take exams for nursing school. In the living room Nimei's mother and her eleven-year-old son, Songshan, were watching a kung fu movie, made in Hong Kong, on TV. Their hearty laughter and the bleating music echoed through the house. Outside, a pair of caged grasshoppers were chirping languidly under the eaves, and the night air smelled of boiled corn and potato.

Why does Hsu Peng want to see me? Nimei wondered. Didn't he hate me? Even if he no longer hates me, he must surely hate my mother and Jiang Zhen. It's good that they have never met. Why is he eager to visit me and my family after so many years? Does this mean he still has feelings for me? Eager to fan the old flame? If he knew what I look like now . . .

She turned from side to side, wondering what Hsu Peng's motivation was, but unable to guess. Then a thought, which had lurked at the back of her mind, came to the fore. Hadn't he said he was a divisional commissar? He must be a general, a VIP. Did this mean he was going to flaunt his high rank in her face? Always so imposing, he'd never change.

The image of such an important officer's presence in her shabby house troubled her. In her mind's eye she saw a brand-new jeep parked by their front gate. While the commissar was sitting inside the house, his chauffeur and bodyguards were chatting noisily with the men and children from the neighborhood, who gathered around the vehicle. This was awful, too shameful for her to stand. Her own husband was merely a senior clerk in the General Service Section of the hospital, his civilian rank at most equal to a battalion commander's. If only Jiang Zhen had held a position one or two ranks higher. Such a useless man.

On the other hand, Hsu Peng's presence in her house could produce a positive effect. After he left, she would reveal to her mother who this general was. His visit would impress the old woman and make her understand what an unforgivable mistake she had made in forcing Nimei to marry Jiang Zhen. It was time to teach the crone a lesson, so as to restrain her from nagging incessantly.

Without telling anybody, Nimei wrote Hsu Peng back the next day, saying she and her family would be glad to see him. She gave him her home address, the directions, and a tentative date. She even wrote, "For old time's sake, please come to see me. I miss you." On the lavender envelope she pasted a special stamp, issued to celebrate Youth Day, on which a young man tapped a tambourine and kicked the heels of his boots while a girl whirled around, her head thrown back and her numerous braids flying.

At noon Nimei observed her face in the bathroom mirror on the third floor of the medical building. Gazing at her dim, myopic eyes, she sighed, wiping her glasses with a piece of tissue. Somebody flushed a toilet in a stall, the throaty noise drowning out the mechanical hum of the ventilators. You have to do something about yourself, she thought. Remember to dye your hair. Also, you must lose some weight. You look puffy.

The young nurse Wanyan reported that the patient in Ward 3 had complained about the fish stew at lunch. She said with a pout, "He's so hard to please. I wonder why his family doesn't come to see him."

"His family's not in town," said Nimei. "I guess his wife must be too busy to care about him. She's an official in Tianjin."

"What should I say if he grumbles at me again?"

"Don't worry. I'll talk with him and see what I can do. By the way, Wanyan, can I ask you a favor? Can you help me buy five hundred bricks from your brother's brickyard?"

"Are you going to build a coal bunker or something?"

"No. My yard always turns muddy when it rains. I want to have it paved before National Day."

"All right, I'll ask my brother."

"Could you ask him to give me a discount?"

"You can probably use some half-baked bricks. Much cheaper, you know—just four fen apiece."

"Wonderful. Ask him to get me five hundred of those."

Nimei went to Ward 3. At the sight of her, Director Liao blew his nose into a crumpled handkerchief and began complaining about the mackerel stew, which he hadn't been able to eat. He disliked saltwater fish except for shrimp and crab. Nimei explained that the kitchen manager had said only mackerel and yellow croaker were available. But she assured Director Liao that she'd try her best to find freshwater fish for him.

Shaking his balding head, the patient snorted, "I can't believe this. Muji City is right on the Songhua River and there are no freshwater fish here."

"I promise I'll find fish for you, Director Liao," Nimei told him.

"Well, I don't mean to claim any special privilege."

"I understand."

That evening Nimei talked with her husband about the patient in Ward 3. She wanted him to go to the riverbank the next morning and buy a carp, not too big, just a three- or four-pounder. Jiang Zhen felt uneasy about her suggestion because carp were expensive these days and few people could afford them. A four-pounder would cost a fifth of his monthly salary. But Nimei said that he shouldn't worry too much about the money, and that whatever he spent for the fish would come back to him eventually.

"Trust me," she told him. "Go buy a carp. Stew it tomorrow afternoon and take it to my office. It's for yourself, not for me."

He dared not argue more, remembering that she had once burned three ten-yuan notes because he was going to buy her mother an expensive fur coat. He'd had to wrestle with her to rescue the rest of the sum. So he promised to get the fish.

The next morning Nimei got up early and went jogging on the playground at the middle school nearby. For the first time she put on the rubber sneakers her husband had bought her three years ago. Jiang Zhen was pleased to see that at last she was beginning to take care of her health. Time and again he had advised her to join him in practicing *tai chi* on the riverbank in the morning with a group of old people, but she disliked the "shadowboxing," which looked silly to her, like catching fish in the air. That morning Jiang Zhen went to the riverbank with an enamel basin and stayed there for almost an hour exercising and chatting with friends, but he didn't find any carp for sale. Instead, he bought a three-pound whitefish, which he carried home and kept alive in a vat of rainwater. Songshan fed the fish a piece of pancake before setting out for school.

Jiang Zhen didn't take a break at noon. After lunch he returned to his office immediately and resumed working at account books. He left work an hour and a half early. The moment he reached home, he put on his purple apron and began cooking the fish. He scooped it out of the vat and laid it on the chopping board. It writhed, its tail slapping the board noisily, its mouth wide open, as though it were trying to disgorge its innards. He struck it three times with the side of a cleaver. Instantly the fish stopped wiggling.

Having scaled and gutted it, he rinsed it twice with clean water. He heated half a wok of vegetable oil on a kerosene stove and put in the fish to fry for a few minutes. Meanwhile, he chopped its gills and innards to bits for the chickens and then washed clean the knife and the board.

The deep-frying had got rid of the fish's earthy smell. Next he boiled it in plain water. As the pot was bubbling, he sliced a chunk of peeled ginger, diced a thick scallion, crushed four large cloves of garlic, poured half a cup of cooking wine, and took out the sugar jar and the sesame oil bottle. He used a scrap of newspaper to get a fire from the stove and lit a cigarette. Sitting on a bench and waving a bamboo fan, he gave a toothy smile to his mother-in-law, who had been watching the boiling pot with bulging eyes. Not until the broth turned milky did he put in the spices and the vegetables, all at once. After adding a touch of salt and a spoon of sesame oil, he turned off the fire, ladled up a bit of the soup, and tasted it. "Yummy," he said and smacked his thin lips.

The old woman asked, "It's not a holiday today, why cook the fish in such a fancy way?"

"My job, Mother. I'm helping Nimei."

"She's forgotten who she is, totally spoiled. She has a princess's heart but a maid's fortune."

At five-thirty Jiang Zhen arrived at Nimei's office with a dinner pail. Together the couple went to Ward 3. The patient gave them a lukewarm greeting, but at the sight of the fish soup, his eyes brightened. Having tried two spoonfuls, he exclaimed, "I'll be damned, who made this? What a beautiful job!"

"He did." Nimei pointed at her husband. "He used to be a mess officer in the army, so he knows how to cook fish. I'm so glad you like the soup."

"Thank you, Young Jiang." The patient stretched out his right hand while chewing noisily. Gingerly Jiang Zhen held Liao's thick thumb and gave it a shake.

Nimei said, "Be careful, Director Liao. Don't eat the head or suck the bones, and don't eat too much for the time being. Your stomach needs time to recover."

"I know, or this wouldn't be enough." The patient gave a hearty laugh.

Every morning from then on, Jiang Zhen got up early and went to the riverbank to buy fish. Sometimes he bought a silver carp, sometimes a pike, sometimes a catfish; once he got a two-pound crucian, which he smoked. Every day he cooked the fish in a different way, and his dishes pleased the director greatly. Soon Jiang Zhen ran out of money. When he told Nimei he had spent all their wages, she suggested he withdraw two hundred yuan from their savings account. He did, and day after day he continued to make the fancy dishes. In the meantime, Nimei kept jogging for half an hour every morning. She even borrowed from the hospital's gym (the supervisor was a friend of hers) a pair of small dumbbells, with which she exercised at home. Although she had lost little weight, ten days later her muscles were firmer and her face less flabby. Her jaw had begun to show a fine contour. She said to herself, You should've started to exercise long ago. That would've kept you tighter and smaller. A healthy body surely makes the heart feel younger.

A few times Director Liao wanted to pay Nimei for the fish, but she refused to accept any money from him, saying, "It's my job to take care of my patients."

Gradually the director and Jiang Zhen got to know each other. Every day after Liao finished dinner, Jiang would stay an hour or two, chatting with the leader, who unfailingly turned talkative after a good meal. The nurses were amazed that the patient in Ward 3 had mellowed so much. When they asked Nimei why her husband came at dinnertime every day, she said that Liao and Jiang Zhen had known each other before. Of course, nobody believed her, but the nurses were glad when the patient's manners and attitudes became wholesome and even avuncular. Nimei claimed Director Liao paid for the fish he ate.

The bricks arrived, a cartful of them, drawn over by three Mongolian ponies. Nimei paid for them promptly and gave the driver two packs of Great Production cigarettes.

For an entire weekend the couple leveled the ground and laid the bricks. Nimei wanted the yard to be paved neatly, so Jiang Zhen hammered wooden stakes into the dirt and tied white string to them to make sure the bricks would be set in straight lines. It was an unusually hot day for the fall, and the couple were soaked with sweat. Nimei's mother cooked a large pot of mung bean soup for them to drink, to relieve their inner heat and prevent sunstroke. She put white sugar into the soup and ladled it into five bowls, which were placed on a long bench to cool.

When the work was done, Nimei felt pleased despite her painful back. But her mother tottered around on bound feet, muttering, "What a waste of money! We've never used such good bricks for a house."

Nimei ignored her, too exhausted to talk, while Jiang Zhen sipped a bowl of soup, his bony shoulders stooping more than before. A lock of hair, sweaty and gray, stuck to his flat forehead. The sweat-stained back of his shirt looked like a map. A few maple seeds swirled in the air like helicopter blades while a pair of magpies clamored atop the ridge of the gable roof. Nimei's mother kept saying, "We'll have to spend a lot of money for winter vegetables, and we ought to save for the Spring Festival."

Save your breath, old hag! thought Nimei.

The next day she bought two large pots of wild roses and had them placed on both sides of the front gate. She assigned her daughter to water the flowers every morning.

Director Liao was going to leave the hospital in two days. He was grateful to the couple and even said they had treated him better than his family.

On Tuesday afternoon he had the head nurse called in. He said, "Nimei, how can I thank you enough!"

"It's my job. Please don't mention it."

"I've told the hospital's leaders that they should elect you a model nurse this year. Is there anything else I can do for you?"

"No, I don't need anything," she said. "Jiang Zhen and I are very happy that you've recovered so soon."

"Ah yes, how about Young Jiang? Can I do something for him?"

She pretended to think for a minute. "Well, maybe. He has worked in the same office for almost ten years. He may want a change. But don't tell him I said this, or he'll be mad at me."

"I won't say a word. Do you think he wants to leave the hospital?"

"No, he likes it here. Just moving to another office would be enough."

"Is there a position open?"

"Yes, there are two," Nimei told him. "The Personnel and the Security sections haven't had directors for months."

"I'm going to write a note to the hospital leaders," promised Liao. "They'll take my suggestion seriously. Tell Young Jiang I'll miss his fish."

They both laughed.

Everything seemed to be going as Nimei had planned. Hsu Peng had written back and said he would be happy to come to her house for tea. She was certain Jiang Zhen's promotion would work out, because none of the hospital leaders would dare disobey Director Liao, whose department decided their promotions and demotions. If Jiang Zhen became the chief of a section, he'd hold a rank equal to a vice-regimental commander's, which, although still several ranks lower than Hsu Peng's, shouldn't be too unpresentable. True, the promotion hadn't materialized yet, but she could say it was already definite. In addition, her daughter had just been notified that a nursing school in Jilin City had admitted her. Nimei felt she could finally meet Hsu Peng without embarrassment.

On the evening of September 29, a Beijing jeep pulled up at the Jiangs' gate. At the sound of the motor Nimei got up, patting her permed hair, and went to receive the guest. But to her surprise, two soldiers walked in, one shouldering a kraft paper parcel and the other holding a large, green plastic gasoline can. "Is this Head Nurse Nimei's home?" one of them asked.

"Yes," she said eagerly, her left hand fingering the belt of her chemise, which was flowered and brand-new. Her husband came out and joined her.

The taller soldier declared, "Our commissar cannot come this evening. He's very sorry. He has to accompany Commander Chen of Shenyang Military Region to a party."

"Oh." Nimei was too flustered to say another word.

The man went on, "Commissar Hsu ordered us to deliver the fish and the soy oil to you for National Day." With two thuds they dropped the parcel and the can on a low table in the yard.

"Will he come to see us?" she asked.

"No. We're leaving for Harbin on the earliest train tomorrow morning."

"Who's this commissar?" Jiang Zhen asked his wife.

"A former patient of mine, as I told you," she managed to reply. She turned to the soldiers. "Tell your leader we thank him."

"How much?" Jiang Zhen asked them, still puzzled.

"Our commissar said not to take any money."

The young men turned and went out. Then came a long honk and children's cries; the jeep was drawing away.

The parcel was unwrapped and four salmon emerged, each weighing at least fifteen pounds. One of them still had a three-inch hook stuck through its nostril, with a short piece of fishing line attached to the hook's eye. "Oh my, what fish are these?" asked Nimei's mother, mouthing a long pipe and smiling broadly. The boy and the girl gathered at the table, watching their father spread the gills to see the scarlet color inside.

"These are salmon, Mother," said Jiang Zhen. Then he announced with a thrill in his voice, "They're as fresh as if they were alive! Too bad Director Liao has left the hospital. These are the best fish, but he doesn't have the luck." He asked his wife, "How come I've never met this commissar?"

"He commands an armored division somewhere in Harbin. The fish and the oil probably didn't cost him anything." She felt like weeping.

"Of course not. If you have power, you can always get the best stuff free." He flicked a bluebottle away with his fingers. "Songshan, get me the largest basin, quick."

The boy turned with a half-eaten peach in his hand, running toward their shack to fetch the washbasin.

Nimei couldn't suppress her tears anymore. She hurried into the house and threw herself on her bed. She broke out sobbing, unsure whether Hsu Peng had ever intended to visit her.

Ha Jin has published two books of poems and two story collections which have won the PEN/Hemingway Award and the Flannery O'Connor Award for Short Fiction.

UNDERGROUND MUSIC/*H. E. Francis*

ON WEEKDAY mornings in Madrid any number of músicos go down into the Metro to play. Toni Valero plays the guitar at the Velázquez station. Marcos Medina plays the recorder at La Latina. Victor Salcedo plays a harmonium at Núñez de Balboa. Pepe Castillo plays the guitar and Juan Ramos sings with him at Banco de España. Luis Manzanero plays the electric guitar and Silvero Ortega the guitar and Juanca Navarro the violin and Carlitos Sanz the flute in the narrow exit to the park at Retiro. Pablo Zamorano plays the guitar at the exit to the wax museum at Colón. Pedro Galicia sings as he plays his guitar at Alonso Martínez. Raúl Ontalba boards a train at Puente de Vallecas with his accordion and like many others goes playing from car to car from one end of a line to the other and back.

Weeks ago Justo Severano claimed this spot at the Fuencarral exit of Bilboa station. Justo loves loud music. He thinks of nothing but the sound of pesetas dropped into his metal cup. He empties the coins into his mochila, always leaving a couple of veinte duro coins to suggest dig deep, the bigger the better. At first he paid no mind to the far strains of strings in the overriding sounds of footsteps and the turnstiles and the voices of the marroquíes and nigerianos hawking cigarettes, belts, purses, bandanas; but in any lull it took no listening to hear it, a stream of strings, fucking classical shit. He kids with the gang, his own pandilla that hangs around, But never put, no, not a fucking finger on my guitar, you hijosdeputa, understand? and them always hoping for enough cash he'll maybe share a bocadillo, beer, vino. Pensión, no, he doesn't need—he has a mattress in his sick tía's house—and why?—when she's tight as a virgin cunt the bitch his mother's sister. Why? Because she's so afraid of dying alone she gives him a tiny mattress in the fucking closet, but at least that colchón, food— even sometimes on her saint's day she's all guilt or shame and begs intercession from the Virgin or prays to the Son, and she gets off her dead ass and goes out and comes home with a shirt, maybe vaqueros and if it's the Son's birthday Noche Buena or Reyes even shoes. Those nights she cries and says You're my sister's son and you've got the one thing burying her gave enough money for, that guitar, it's a living if you know what to do with it. Lucky? Mierda! He's her only blood, the only body, only life in the house when she's down and crying she's dying, Call the clínica, go to the far-macia, get this filled, *go*, quick, you want me to die? What made him decide *here*, this spot at the foot of the second stairs as you enter, by the public phone, was one Saturday he's there above, outside, and teens crowd every bar *a tope* and on the streets off Bilbao circle all the restaurants, German Egyptian Mexican Chinese, a flood weekends, and he thinks My age, they'll go crazy for my stuff, look at their clothes, smell them, money and thinks And weekdays there's the cafeteria by the turnstiles, the busy Café Comercial, and Bilbao has access to five streets. What more! Coño!

Toni Valero plays at Velázquez because the neighborhood's classy—well-dressed, expensively perfumed women, businessmen with gold watches like on Serrano or Goya or the Castellana. Marcos Medina plays the recorder at La Latina because he's a punk, black leather, points, wrist cords, shaved head with a coxcomb dyed orange and knows the bohemians of Lavapiés sympathize with what it's like living his way and may fork over five duros, even one, or some abuela longing for her dope-addict grandson maybe or some madre for her son.

Benigno de la Fuente has his spot at Bilbao. It's not far from the mouth of the Malasaña access to the underground labyrinth, cool in summer and very damp and cold in winter. His is the corner sit-uated at the foot of seven steps on one side of a raised level, where the tunnel makes a sharp right turn to a long passageway to the street and the Café Comercial. All year long the wind sucked through the passages is strong here. Why he chose this corner, who knows?—if because the Café Comercial is famous for the high cultural level of its customers, who are generous because they appreciate his classical music, or from some sentimental, nos-talgic, or whatever other personal reason. Anyway he's there. You may find him, or hear him, there during the city's business hours from eleven to near lunch hour at one-thirty or two, his case open at his feet, where people passing sometimes toss a coin. It is not something he originally came to do; and though he has been here many years, perhaps only two or three people know that, passersby who have stopped often to talk and have developed that casual affection which comes of everyday familiarity and ex-pectation.

Pepe Castillo plays the guitar and Juan Ramos sings with him at Banco de España. Pepe Castillo knows it's not his playing but Juan Ramos' singing which brings in the coins, and Juan Ramos knows this too but loves Pepe Castillo and has to be with him and never wants to leave him. Pepe Castillo depends on him. Juan needs somebody to depend on him. He wants Pepe Castillo to depend on him completely. And Pepe Castillo knows this and doesn't give a shit. It's easy.

Now between songs Justo, curious, crosses the tunnel up five steps to the rise with its low ceiling, then down the other side, seven steps, to the corner—the old man, that one. He should've known. Who else'd play such shit? He looks tall because thin, but he's small, his violin clamped under his chin, playing with his eyes open but like blind he looks, not seeing—not him, anything. Justo descends and stands and makes like listening but *more* looks down—because the bottom of the violin case—look at those coins!—more than littered, is almost covered. Holychrist! How can that be? The bastard's old and decently dressed and clean, yes—but *him* need money? If he did, he'd empty it, hoard it, leave a few bits for bait, not make such a show of pesetas. It rankles. Justo's fingers itch for the coins. He should batter the bastard and steal, but it's day, there's traffic. He goes back to his guitar. All morning he knows how he's playing—with no heart, no desire— from despair and a lingering fury; but won't quit—waits—till he sees the old man cross the corridor and pass slowly, standing straight with his black case, straight like El Rey or don Felipe—he thinks he's young!—and go through the turnstile. Viejo de mierda!

Carlitos Sanz plays the flute at the narrow exit to the park at Retiro. It is such a high, lonely seductive sound, above all the other sounds that come from the Metro, that people can't help stopping and looking and perhaps wondering how he ever got a flute because he's so ragged and thin and tall but with a face so idyllically young and eyes which fix on no one but always up and out; so people stop from admiration, awe, or maybe a longing for *the time when*—who knows?—and few pass without yielding up a bit of homage to—who knows?

Benigno turns seventy-four this year. He is small and neat in his dark suit and vest and keeps his mustache and beard trimmed. In his youth A genius you'll be, you *are,* his teachers told him. He dreamed *music,* dreamed *sounds never heard from strings,* dreamed. A new Paganini. He practiced and practiced, perfected. He pursued tortuous passages till his bow and his fingers made them flow. He felt himself floating, transported. He loved the transport, the travel in infinite sound. Madrid counted on two State orchestras. You applied, auditioned, awaited a vacancy. It came. His mother, father, sister were delirious: for their sacri-fice and his— the Opera! But he failed—not the music, not the composers, not himself. He failed the conductor, and the orchestra. He failed the discipline of submergence in sounds collective but not his. Oh, he could—he did—discipline, worked at it, but came moments when his will went its way. Wild it must have seemed to those in the orchestra at critical moments when he was suddenly singular, alone. That *cannot be,* the conductor reiterated. He himself knew, but knew too that some will in him willed itself into his fingers, heart, spirit; and his mind gave way to it. Whatever heights he gained were his loss: he felt unfit, but felt free—too free, the conductor said. He had no argument against. Discipline! How he knew years of it! But submission to the whole symphonic, submerged, would be failure. Sink when he wanted to rise? He could not explain the *other* submission. Madness the conductor would say. Something like that he did say and, with some legal difficulties, broke the contract, released him, with appropriate indemnity.

Pablo Zamorano plays the guitar at the exit to the wax museum at Colón because he has a sister fifteen who's so hot to go he worries day and night, until now sure that her part-time work at a clothes boutique and his part-time as a waiter and what he can earn in-between times with the guitar will keep them till—he dreams this miracle—one of his own songs he can convince a major band to introduce or some group to play at a club or concert or benefit and make enough money for the brands of perfumes, clothes, shoes she keeps mentioning, sorry he didn't study and hoping she will—he dreams that miracle too—she's young, smart, so pretty, but impatient.

The days Justo gets Blas to sing with him he makes more but coño he half the time gets fucked, he has to decide *Blas or no Blas?* but some days comes a killing like yesterday and then the Bar Ronda half the night and waking with a curda, even now his head splitting, all his body slumped, such a curda, every yell or each click of the turnstile or horn from the street drives a nail in his head, all the morning irritated, even the music an infection, his eyeballs ache, his eyes burn. And sometimes, like a scratching scratching over his skin, an abuse of his head, that scratch of strings. That prick won't let up. He burns. He thrums to drive out the least sound of the fucking violin—sure, yes, sure the old bastard's doing it just to annoy him because he's seen him now and again spy on him, stop, eyeball him—so the old goat *does* see, the old fox, he doesn't miss what's going on around him; sure the old goat *knows* he's aching from the curda he'd pulled last night and is determined to drive it into him, make him suffer, like his fucking tía always trying to teach him a lesson, Serve you right, you should know better.

Pedro Galicia sings as he plays his guitar at Alonso Martínez because he's a lazy son of a bitch like his father, his mother says, but he knows his mother will go on keeping him—she has for thirty-three years—because he's the spit and image of his father and he knows she still loves his father, who knocked her up and ran off and never came back. And you, she says—she says it fiercely, furiously, but never without a quiver of affection—you're just like him, you never worked but one year in your life.

Benigno loves his violin, not only its music—his passion—but the instrument itself. The violin is his wife that once stood in the way of a wife—because Rosaura, the daughter of the patrona of the pensión he then lived in, fell in love with him. First, it was for the music—Play, don Benigno, play—and he was so attracted by her attraction to the music and his playing that he thought Rosaura, ideal she'll be, she'll always stand by me, my ambition, my life of sound; and under this impulse his desire for her became inseparable from her appreciation of his music. He traveled to Barcelona, Zaragoza, Valladolid, Valencia, Bilboa—but what in this music-loving country with such a dictatorial dearth of orchestras, state money, or any Maecenas could he do but return to Madrid jobless. He never deceived Rosaura, told her all—his failure with the orchestra, the why, his temperament, what (if they married) inconstancy in work but constancy to the violin she might have to bear. Bear? She couldn't. Music she enjoyed, but for *him:* For you, Benigno, with or without music, but with a living, a good living—and why not from the violin and submission? Submission, he said, or repression. Look what repression did to this country, Rosaura—and for decades! It's a miracle its near-cadaver was saved at least by the death of Franco, who clung too long to his own cadaver and ours. Then what's a group for? Rosaura said. Oh, it's not for the money itself, Benigno, but we must live, eat, have our own piso and furniture and things because I won't, won't—will you leave me to that?—won't be a slave in a pensión all my life, with the pittance—yes, she said that, *pittance* your family's provided—that's your making and your ruin. But I tried, he said, tried. One horse can pull a surrey, but for every wagon here there are fifty horses and more, he said. But you're special—of one breed, she meant. At this moment, he said, Spain cares nothing for the breed though the country's starving—and for more than food. I cannot—oh, Benigno—cannot, she said it even knowing what he meant. That was decades ago. So he went on. He changed pensiones. He played, he plays, he carries his case to his corner in the corridor at the Manuela Malasaña exit and opens it and gently takes out his love, and he stands and he plays and hours he plays and hears only the music, his.

Victor Salcedo plays a harmonium at Núñez de Balboa. It's heavy. It sits on a metal frame. Here he's close to Clínica El Rosario and is sure people are worried or fretting or nervous or fearful and lonely because their loved ones at the clinic are sick or maybe dying or have contracted a deadly disease, so he counts on the music appealing to their sympathy in a weak moment and their remembering his soft God give you grace when the coin hits the cloth he's laid down.

Justo, some days now after the long morning, pretends to go through the tunnel past Benigno, but he spies the take in the old man's violin case, on the worst day always twice his at least. Sometimes he sends Blas: Sit on the steps by the exit. Listen. See what gives. Bored, Blas comes back. Nothing. People listen. A man stops, talks. Benigno—his name's Benigno. One asks for a Mozart—what's that?—talking high and waving his hands like a maricón. What more? says Justo. Not a thing, nada—that's what the old goat is, nothing. Why waste time? But Justo now and then, but for days and days, sends him. Be like natural, just go past, don't stop, don't let him see you're up to something, see *what*. And some days *he* goes but stops just before where the corridor ascends; from this side he can see only the old man's head and shoulders, the raised arm holding the violin and the arm riding the bow over the strings. He looks, listens, hoards the tidbits he learns, not even sure yet what he wants, why he wants it, but something—it stirs— some finest chafe almost too vague to feel. Only one thing from Blas he hears, a fragment his mind at the time tosses aside, but later he spits it out like phlegm against a wind that blows it back in his face, and it sticks—a pensión on Romanones.

On weekends there are few músicos in the Metro. Like the beggars, they either rest or go to the parks or fairs or wherever the crowds are. In July and August almost no músicos play in the Metro though, despite the heat and the musty smell of standing water, there is a relative comfort in the subterranean rush of wind from the trains trundling in and from the suction of air from the street and the underground ventilation system. There are almost no músicos in summer because virtually half of Madrid goes on a month's vacation in July and the other half in August, so most restaurants are closed, hospitals and clinics and public offices operate at half staff, and lawyers, doctors, politicians, businessmen virtually vanish. The streets are fairly empty. Dogs abandoned by madrileños on vacation run loose. Only tourism flourishes; but, as the músicos know from experience, tourists are tight, they have to do some heavy fishing for a few pesetas.

Nights for Benigno there is nothing like the opera at the Teatro Lírico now since the Opera's being remodeled, not for the voices alone, great as they are, but for the orchestra and especially for the strings and particularly for solitary passages, their solos—he thrills then though he knows that beyond is a possible sound, single, which no group can attain. But some days, rare, when a strange gray sky or a long dark rain covers Madrid, he himself takes line 2 or 5 or 4 or 9, simply to listen to the sounds other músicos make. He makes his little tour of the sounds in the Metro, thinking how, if he could stand above the Metro and hear it all at one time, he would hear what is one human music that contains the hopes and dreams, sufferings and joys, of all who have ever passed through and experienced them, and he himself would feel the beat of the blood, the rush, the sadness, the joy. He laughs. Nonsense, of course. Still, he thinks it. He wishes it. But what he finds is that most he is lured to Avenida de América: there is a long corridor cut off by a sharp turn at each end, and midway there sits a boy with a guitar—young and dark and in that long passageway small, so alone—and lonely. Benigno does not even have to enter that tunnel which reverberates sonorously with the strings and his singing to know *lonely*—and, no, it is not the guitar but the boy's voice that touches with its loneliness, an infinite sadness too young, a love lost, a girl gone or dead, some great yearning unfulfilled, a place he can't know. As if there is a melancholy he cannot stop uttering, he plays when there is no one, even in those hours of siesta and meals when few pass through the Metro. It was during one of those moments that Benigno himself first passed through and was struck by the tone of the boy's voice. And though Benigno has never stopped before the boy, never spoken to him, often enough merely standing out of sight in the connecting corridor, something comes from the music and the voice, their coupled sound, which makes him feel he is hearing himself with a strange understanding, and going up, out, into the long dark rain over the city, he feels impervious to cold and rain and the darkness.

Feliciano Castillo plays the guitar at Atocha. Feliciano Castillo plays the guitar because his brother is an invalid. His brother has shriveled legs and is in a wheelchair. He carves tiny wood animals that Feliciano sets beside his guitar case to sell. His mother is a cleaning woman nights in the Hotel Francisco I on Arenal. That's good—it's not far from their piso. So nights he stays with Gregorio, and days his mother stays while he plays. Every peseta she needs. You, Feliciano, you the blessed Virgin gave to me. Since your father . . . how'd we live without you? His father drowned in the Jarama, slipped, couldn't swim, a guardia civil found him floating. Sometimes, he says, playing soft he sees water moving softly, carrying his father floating up over the empty rails, over the andén, up the stairs, floating on the music, over the crowd, back to him. He does not tell his mother he sees his father. It would hurt her too much.

Benigno knows that for the regulars who pass every weekday he is a local fame, a fixture, an unknown friend, just as his eyes raised or lowered as if blind recognize the configurations of years, figures who stop frequently only an instant to listen and sometimes to talk or who after passing halt for a note or two or who feel into their pockets or purses for a coin, their thanks or respect or pity or grace or even guilt or self-satisfaction, whatever. The first day—with his case open at his feet—the sound of a coin startled. Almost he said I'm no beggar, but quickly thought But none of us músicos is, we're all earning. It still surprises—how like confession a coin is; though never since the first day has he felt urgent need, posted himself there for a living but to play to his heart's content, uncensored, undisturbing. Uninterrupted—no pensión, no authorities, no police—he can play a whole piece through—Vivaldi, Mozart, Schumann, all his loves, company, old friends. No, no, not for money he plays, but for sound, passion channeled and powerful—beauty, that is. But *that* he can't explain. Who would believe? So he plays and each day leaves the case open so as not to confuse them or be interrupted and have to explain. Why should he? But they come, and keep coming, the pesetas—and he thinks of Rosaura, but time has too quickly swept over him, that possibility has vanished, and the years have left only this old body, face, the gray beard, and the balding head his cap neatly covers.

Nobody ever plays at Puente de Vallecas or Lavapiés or Antón Martín or Embajadores. Nobody plays at stations like San Blas, plagued by beggars, drogadictos, and alcohólicos living in miserable chabolas notorious for camellos selling drugs. Nobody ever plays at Campamento because they know soldiers have little enough to share among themselves. Nobody ever plays at Ciudad Universitaria because many students have barely money enough to buy books or are simply comfortable and because others have guitars and instruments and have their own fiestas and celebrations and opportunities, and because they buy tickets to plays and films and operas but mostly bands from England and the U.S. and other countries, and invite friends to horchatas or beer for talk in the bars or on the terrazas. But in the Centro people seldom pass without turning a head or listening; and there's no end to the variety of portable instruments, even harmonicas, a zither, a concertina, a rare bagpipe, in winter or cold weather sometimes a group, mariachis.

A *pensión. On Romanones.* So the old fucker lives in the Centro, two blocks from Sol—and takes line 1 to his pensión. Justo thinks and thinks *the old man, that corner, pesetas;* thinks *violin;* thinks *Romanones,* not sure yet of *how* but, yes, of *why*—that corner, exclusive, for me. Drive out the cabrón. And one night he follows that Benigno down the steps to line 1, keeping distance, but when the old man enters a car, he enters the next. Yes, at Tirso the old man descends and goes up the Romanones exit and crosses and turns right straight up the street several doors and takes out his key under that small green neon sign four storeys up, *Hostal Residencia Rubio.* Justo's thinking begins to come easy then: And in this barrio loaded with *negros, moros, árabes, ilegales, drogadictos* everything happens. He's on some kind of threshold, almost giddy, feels he could touch the answer, it's so close—But *what?*— and back at his tía's he's so quiet and soft with her she says Some girl or what? startling him. Silent, he smiles, thinking *what.* I thought so, she says.

Raúl Ontalba with his accordion boards the train at Puente de Valleca and goes from car to car from one end of the line to the other, giving his appeal and then playing a couple of fragments. Raúl Ontalba has learned his little speech by heart, though sometimes half-drunk he stumbles Forgive the molestia, señores and señoras, but I'm married and I have two children, I'm without work and with no other income, any small help you can give me will be truly appreciated and God bless you.

Benigno this day plays bits from de Falla. Some stop to listen to the whole of "La Andaluza" because, he knows, we love our own music, what country doesn't? You need motion this cold fall morning and music makes you faster, your blood moves. He is all verve. He captures more listeners this morning. Some usuals he recognizes. During an interval he has a chat with Ginés, the set designer for the production of *El Sombrero de Tres Picos* he saw last night, and they spend some talk on *La Vida Breve.* Ginés leaves him hearty. He feels life arace this morning, not breve. Only once, playing at a busy moment, much noise and many passing and a few standing there, the shadow of a boy intervenes. At the sight of the boy—in the look of him, the face so obviously rankled, he knows hate in the eyes—the eyes drive into him, into the music, and nearly falter his fingers. And all morning it imposes, that face—he has seen it before, it has passed, and it has come and stood at some distance before—dark, surly, filled with some fire, and fuming—against what? And what has it to do with him, who, as he comes and goes twice each day, sees the boy playing just beyond the entrance to the turnstiles. Or is it, today, the de Falla that makes him imagine. But, then, weren't there other days? Did he imagine them too?

Delmiro Toribio likes to play his guitar when he feels up to it. Life's easy. He knows he's handsome, very macho. He's a mujeriego, who loves drinking and fucking so he drinks and fucks and keeps his own hours.

The violin's the answer, of course. Without it old Benigno can't play and Justo will have his corner, the coins, no competition. But steal? No. What would he do with it? The way the old bastard plays, from its sound, the violin's quality stuff like—he hates to admit it, hate classical music as he does—the stuff he plays: you'd have to be deaf not to hear that. And he, Justo, hasn't he got the ear! No, not steal—not to hide or sell or keep, no evidence to do himself in. But—too easy now it comes—*destroy.* How many times has he raised his hands to crush, his fury turned on that viejo de mierda, cabrón, hideputa! *That!* Smash it! *How* and *when* will come—like this his decision. Easy, Justo, easy, he says to himself. But who could stop the head from spinning and spinning? There's Blas, he says, or one of the others, or two. Not himself—that won't do—not for him to touch the thing, be guilty of smashing it. And Blas—or one of the others—what could they say? what prove? How'd Blas dare say, defend himself, prove innocent if accused, caught, arrested: But Justo gave me the job, so Justo did it, Justo's responsible? Blas, yes, always hard up, on the streets, sometimes in the rattiest pensión, hungry, experienced holyjesus at what *not*—in such a state what police would believe what story he'd tell? But if Blas did it alone, with not a sign to the others, and none know but him, Justo, Blas wouldn't talk. And the old man would never identify *him,* Justo, no matter what claim he could make, and surely not Blas unless he gets stupid: Blas may be ditched by his family, down and out, but no, never's so stupid he'd be caught. Track the old man home when dark, the best hour—and clobber—and kill his violin, take his living for good. I'll get his corner.

There are no women who play music in the Metro. There are women who pass the cup. There are women who sell contraband Winstons and Marlboros and other brands or single roses rolled in plastic or the lottery, and there are women who tend newsstands and work in the underground boutiques and cafés or who are custodians or who sell *La Farola*, especially printed for the poor and the homeless to live off the proceeds, but there are no women músicos in the Metro.

On a late fall night, his feet stone after standing so long, trembling with cold, Benigno closes his violin case, crosses the tunnel, goes through the turnstile and leaves—straight—as always past the blue Miguel Hernández sign with the stations listed in white and down the steps—and, half-asleep in the trundle and sway and the warmth of the car, rides the four stops home. At Tirso, he crosses. Halfway up, in the dark, and nobody in sight, he feels something sudden—his head—and then nothing—and remembers nothing after to tell the police, the hospital—he spends the night, no concussion, he's released, he's back in his pensión. My violin! Where's my violin? He sees their faces—what's wrong?—apprehensive, evasive, ashamed, fearful. What— My violin! he cries. Where's my violin? But he's relieved when he sees the case by his chair. Still there is a hang to their faces—no relief, comfort, assurance. He stoops—his head bolts under the strain—and picks up the case. Too light. Empty! Where *is* it? My violin! What— And then he goes dumb—it strikes him—he understands. Stolen. But no, not stolen, doña Manuela the patrona hesitantly tells him, but—ay, don Benigno—broken to bits, nothing but pieces and strings. Then he knows: attacked from behind and his violin smashed. *Why?* Why? He's dizzy. He can't fathom. I must go the the comisaría, make my denuncia. Tomorrow, tomorrow, don Benigno, right now to your bed. Bed? No, give me— But he can't stop wondering From what low meanness, cowardice, jealousy, hate, fear—he can't think *meannesses* fast enough. He is faint. My violin. No violin. My. No music. Then nothing.

Luis Manzanero plays the electric guitar at the narrow exit to the park at Retiro. Luis Manzanero plays so loud you can hear it even above the trains trundling below. He plays it loud to drown out Silvero Ortega and Juan Navarro and Carlitos Sanz and drive them to the end of the corridor or into Retiro Park. Silvero Ortega plays the guitar at Retiro because he's lonely and likes to sit with boys his age and feel he's part of their talk with the illusion that he's even a fellow músico in a club or sindicato and even for a while deceives himself that they are friends, but always goes home alone to hear his brother, who hates him, say So what today, more shitty noise? Juanca Navarro plays the violin at Retiro because he'll be a pro—he swears it—and can practice as long as he likes with no family and neighbors shouting Cut the noise or criticizing him for playing the same difficult passages over and over and nobody to say Give us something popular, current, the latest songs, not that whining.

Justo waits. Don't be a fool, don't get nervy, he says to himself, wait a few days. He waits to occupy the old man's place—he wants nothing obvious, no confrontation, condemnation—so stays. But it's Blas who streaks breathless. Coño! He whispers You won't believe this—the bastard's back! Back? And with no violin, the case open, and him with a face so yellow, dead he looks. Justo says Me cago en Dios! He's got a new one already? Nothing. Not a trace of a violin. Just stands there and stares. At the end of the morning, the old man, leaving, stops in the corridor and gazes their way, only an instant—he never has before—and goes on. Jesús, you see that? You think— No, I don't, I don't think, I don't think about anything, I don't think. Don't *you*.

Músicos are seldom seen in some central arteries like Gran Vía and Callao and Opera and Sevilla because these are the oldest areas of the Metro so are small even after being reconstructed, and traffic and tourist movement there are not merely heavy but too fast, and vendors both outside and in crowd out the músicos. And the number of músicos dwindles in the stations farther out in the tentacles of the Metro.

Some days Benigno goes to one line or other of the Metro—4, 2, 5, but most often to 9, where the boy alone, lonely, plays out his pain in those songs in English; and he courses the complex of other corridors and stops and sits on a wooden bench and listens to the music, and listens too to the trains and the people, their own music. And again on this day—he can't explain what will moves him—the habit his body's dictated for so many years?—like the ghost of another life, he returns to Bilbao. He reaches the foot of the raised level before his old corner, but someone is there now— that boy, the dark shadow he knew always passing, too young, the shadow of what rankles and divides and plants the seed of some death before dying. He moves out of sight. He stands and listens and ponders. His thoughts race. He stands long, still hardly believing, stands till he has to give in since he's not playing. The stone is too cold, and the wind blowing down from the street.

At Carabanchel it is perhaps the jail, perhaps the military hospital and the barracks, or perhaps the fame of the three cemeteries with no other need than the silent and inviolable music of the tombs and the tall beautiful cypresses which también *creen en Dios*, rooted in the land of the dead and rising from the hillside in a reaching beyond death, which keep the músicos from playing underground there.

What *is* this? Justo's nervous. He keeps looking up, expectant. He can't figure it. He waited long enough, didn't he? After the lull—five work days, count two weekends, so nine days—there's no sight of the old man. So he's won! Without lifting a finger he's won, and he moves. It's his corner. At first coins come, like with anybody new, but the take falls off—his playing is shoddy, he knows it. Blas, sing. And Blas sings and now when he sings Justo feels like a partner, trapped. And just when all's going well and he's feeling free, he's escaped—this one day—who can believe?—as if no man but a ghost from *when* down the steps from Malasaña comes the dark shadow in black, the old man with his black case. He walks straight up close and stands and he looks—long. His gaze is not far. He stares straight at Justo as he listens. And Justo plays and plays. He's afraid to stop—he looks down—the song ends, twice. The old man comes close and—what the fuck!—tosses a coin into the cup. And the same time every day now the old man comes with his case. Justo's irritated. It's his time—here he comes, the old bastard. He halts and he looks—long—right at him—listening, then tosses twenty duros into the cup and goes on. Blas laughs and picks up the coin. Blas laughs again. That stupid viejo de mierda! he says, laughing. Shut up! Justo says. He's sweating. This could go on day after day. What's the fucker up to? Justo's confused. Blas laughs. Shut up! Shut up and sing, you bastard, sing. Me cago en Dios!

Nights at 9:40 at each station at least one of the gates is closed, at 1:30 the Metro closes, and by 2:00 the regular rhythm of trains trundling and the click-clack of escalators and the complex rhythms of footsteps and voices cease. There is only the sound the wind makes and the whirr of the ventilators and the reverberation of night traffic, the horns, police sirens and ambulances from the streets above; and the felt sound of silence itself pervades until six in the morning when, like a mammoth creature whose blood stirs its deep organs, the body of the city trembles with its first deep motions.

H.E. Francis' new collection, *The Sudden Trees*, will be published in 1998.

WITH RESPECT TO THE PALMER
METHOD/*Sandra McPherson*

handwriting course, 1920s

useless useless useless useless

—a studious life would practice this
enough to please the flintiest judge.
Why not **badge, ridge, hedge,**
fudge, pledge (should a quill fledge).
A girl might splurge, in private,
and round a strict stroke; a boy
might coach himself in the feminine
-ess of **use**. She might become
the feminine stress of **úseless**.

One day they're charged with coiling
ink bales of wire. Hands roll so fast
they don't see the barbs.
Is part of them verb? Is all?
A tumbleweed's botanical grandstand,
a scribble's wonderland penned on wind.
Make ten revolutions in one place:
Can they embrace such politics
and still compose a civil invitation?

Never channel a heavy line.
Light lines, light lines.
Tremblers need speed.
Stern ideals ask allegiance:
If your fingers pinch the penholder,
scold them, say "Naughty fingers,
stop pinching, just hold it,"
until they behave.
Be earnest, be faithful.
Tremblers need speed.

Clean hands will not smudge.
Glide on your fingernails.
I write with my large muscles.
Quebec is a very quaint city.
Write well by sitting well.
Youth is the time to learn.

Acquiescent and principled,
each child agrees to entirely slant,
in ways one would never walk.
Script's the defense umbrellas grant
against a shove of squall.
But more than that, the safety of the several:
The letters from head to tail
join hands and bear each other up. None fall.

That's what connects us.

DEAR DIARY, BETTY OFFIELD, 1925/
Sandra McPherson

There *is* a world of lemonade and swans,
the young girls resting out the heat on lawns
beside Parisian water and its ferrying skiffs.
They have been out dancing and they're
only thirteen. They were, of course,
politely, firmly told to stop, in Paris,
in public, two girls *are not allowed to dance
together* even if they're both named Betty.
Even if on other days they play
Duck on a Rock, want dolls for a birthday,
take goat rides down the Champs Elysées.
You need to understand girls
who understand a beautiful life
with the depth of Rembrandt's
conversancy with darkness, how
it is really mixed into a climactic mist
on the shimmering moon's palette of eclipse.

Betty draws and paints too. Shelled
French village homes make awful lace,
look like Pompeii. Near Villa d'Este
a view *looks just like Catalina,*
which her family owns. (On
Catalina, a boulder in the sun appears
as though it had glass spears through it.)
Horses with suits of silver. Venetian lanterns.
A funeral procession in Verona carries voices
of so many children, she gathers the dead's
a girl. In Belgian battlefields *the trenches
are full of water and the trees nothing
but stumps.* A man with palsy treads
in wooden shoes. These subjects serve
in place of school though she loves her teacher
in America with a galvanizing crush,
and without blush, enrapturing *Dear Diary*
with how beautiful is divine Miss Bell,

every scolding word coming from her mouth
she adores, can't bear to miss her when Miss
Bell is ill, so delivers her a concert ticket
as pretext to see *my darling* open her door.
She knows she's overblazing but trusts
this watermarked confessor, this linen page.

With girlfriends she plays cards without
her clothes, until a rap from the delivery man.
But likes clothes too: those bridesmaids
dressed in pink, with brown straw hats,
bunching roses on the side, pink satin bags
with orchids and ferns. And there are
other colors: *In the afternoon,*
we saw a dead man, killed in a taxi,
his face was purple and smashed in.

Out of a letter from Elsa Armour II
slips a news shot of Betty's grandparents,
Wrigleys—*thought you'd want to know.*
Under spring trees, with the Kellogg Betty
and an unsmiling English girl—*predictably!*—
she's reading *Dracula.* Caught in
their own spell, they pick the hotel
flowers, buy lavender ribbon in Evian,
make bouquets to give their moms
about to leave them with a governess
who teaches leather crafts.
Betty beats Betty at tennis.
They're noticed by *The Prince.*
He asked if we wanted to go for a walk.
It was only about 8:30 and not dark
so we went. We went through woods
two or three miles. I thought we would never
get home. He kept taking my hands
and Betty's. I walked ahead, left him with her.
(I try to scan his exiled Russian autograph.
All its many names are of another world
and that world's hand.)

The night Betty Offield turns fourteen,
she watches mounted Cossacks

jump through flame. Another night,
a naughty play where none of the women
wore any clothes. She sizes up, in one
chateau they tour, *the skeleton*
of the famous race horse Flying Fox
and *great big stones from horses' stomachs.*
She weighs 88 pounds dressed, with chocolate
an almost daily inner beauty regimen.

There's nothing frantic or zany in her voice.
Consummately without guilt or defiance
of the testy kind. No sense of failing
at anything. Nor stress to prove herself
resplendent with success. Guided through
dungeons, she doesn't know she didn't learn,
in Miss Harris' school in Illinois, how to spell
torchur.

                    Last week she visited
the house where Dante lived when he was a poet.
On a lone page without a date—it's oddly
the book's first leaf and not the last—
she floats a summary:

> *Orange blossoms picked at Sorrento.*
> *Laurel leaves at Pompeii.*
> *The candle given at the Catacombs.*
> *The lava (black) saved from Vesuvius.*
> *Sulphur discovered at Little Vesuvius,*
> *Statue of St. Francis, at the church, Assisi.*
> *Sea shells: the Lido.*

The bay leaves from Pompeii
still prickle between blank pages.
I try to woo back their cool aroma but it's gone.
That's why we need her words, how at the Doge's palace
We saw the largest picture in the world, of Paradise.

DIARY WITH FISHHOOKS / *Sandra McPherson*

GEORGE W. GROW, NORTHEASTERN
PENNSYLVANIA, 1876–1880

My own words, no two
lists alike, rosters
of what you owe
on goods edible, drapeable,
hammerable, accounts
payable.
You know me,
my name is Grow.

A large fishhook sunk through October
emerges timeworked pages later
among the celebratory year's eclipses,
two suns, two moons.
Every few days a further barb—
a lock on the stream of the diary—
anchors the writer in keen seclusion.
They more than do for paper clips.
Wounded, we whine
(but why should we?)
of finding no prized secrets.
He lives, labors, balances
where people keep up
on each other, where accounts
and not confessions, worths
not sins, are tallied in patience
until settled and signed off.
Cloistered or caught?—the wriggling
purchases: potash, shoes, lemons
and coffee, maple sugar and shirting,
bushels of potatoes, nails, hinges,
bushels of oats, a bar of soap,
vest buttons, shoe buttons,
21 pounds pork, 3 yards gingham,
butter and the wife's expensive hat,

tin pail, belt strings, and beans.
Here, lying in wait, tied flies on hooks,
one with unfaded red hair,
a fox's or a wiry child's reared now, now sleep's.
Hook through the combs
of his bee garden, his horn of smoke.
Through flow and slow overflow
of honey . . .

              Trim to go on
Anny Strowbridge Coffin. Poor fish, *the man*
that drowned last Monday was found today.
Uncovered with a stab.
Hidden behind this peril, his order
for a dozen Sunday School songbooks.
Secreted under others, all the weeks
he fashioned his skiff and its oars.
He never says what he loves
or what he shuns, just what he does.
Impaled, verses of Paul, Matthew, John,
the temperance meeting and the Centennial train
riding the excursion of our history.
Snagged for a hundred years
until I release them—pages of
dinner squirrels and sawn board feet;
gaffed on the backward tine
until it releases me—
these nosing fingertips.
The probe is patchable,
the quest not harmed.
Leader with dried river running it
curled up in this creel of time spent
stairs-building and church-painting,
bringing provision to the handmade table.
Pierced, with an original idea,
no office boy he,
George Grow, thorny for privacy.

              Of course: They're
my own words. I set them true
        on this new patented page surface
erasable with dew

or spangle off a well's bucket.
Some are God's own words:
"And Jesus when he was baptized
went up straight out of the water . . . "
Remove a fishhook to continue.
I launched the boat.
Long ago for breakfast
there were trout.

SPECIALTY / *Sandra McPherson*

With the uninvited need to draw
the human body, he was conversant,
for he bought and sold estates
of those who drew it privately then died.

His guests, collectors of such an artist, arrived
out of the public world, their eyes
lowered from the sharp edifice of city sun.
It hurt the way it cut corners of stone.

He held ready the photograph
from their wedding announcement
and compared the steady image of the groom
with the real man in several motions

of the head, glance down, gaze up
to the more flushed true skin
(the photo from winter shows him dispositioned
on a rainy radius of evergreens).

A pretty good likeness
he hadn't, before this facing,
been able to set ticking with heartbeat
or murmur, off the beat.

His original patron and friend, the bride,
stirred about his loft. He turned to her:
Even the cartoons were sexy,
didn't she think? Sketched in the thirties,

with—in the line—workman's labor
to be . . . not racy but racy enough.
"Not naughty and not nice. Just him,"
he says of the artist. In one, a stripper

walks naked, wan, for the first time
in front of the guys

who roil behind a little orchestra
shivering at her feet,

her tippy (like hardening
stems on two downed maple leaves) high heels.
She's freezing with stage fright.
Her shoulders squeeze together.

If flesh, she would be a very old woman now,
but surely she'd remember that first undressing.
He points to another aspiringly
libertine work, a deepening

oil, of a nickelodeon—
one way or another the lights go out
and you have this recollection
burning ahead of you

of a drawable body.
Make an initial contour.
And don't miss the gawking men's girlfriends'
faces at the burlesque, how they look carefully

expressionless. The host notices
every finespun detail, bend and crescent.
This practice of his, a client can see, whets real love,
exposed love, every particular saved into feeling.

The debuting stripper,
though not yet up to her full savor,
throws no protective shadow over her shyness.
As the couple scan her

in the home of her frame
and choose to take her home—
pull the thread of her ink line out through
the keyhole eye of afternoon—

the dealer shakes the husband's
real, round, and roseate hand
and kisses the wife in caricature
good-bye.

SURFACES, CENTRAL VALLEY, 109°/ *Sandra McPherson*

haibun

The electric fan revamps old air over old, lasting
quilts, yellow and white against dark wood, a lenient,
murmuring condolence. Long summer brightness eats
down through dark leaves. Hedges veil farms.
Porcelain, old print, ancient picture frame profit this
shop a dollar. After their useful life, the objects have in-
somnia until some soul returns their gaze and makes
them the picture of use again, decorated for their service at the ceremony of their purchase.

Down the side street the cheaper, more "flea,"
more anthropological shop's framed O.
J. Simpson in a Hertz ad.
Antiquities everywhere . . .

Here in the apollonian, peaceable, cottage-roomed
emporium called Bon Marché the shopkeeper polishes a
crowded quietness. No dust, no apparent worm at
work. A reupholstered hush becalms completed lives.
The ottoman says with rested regard, "One life, it's
done, the rest is honorarium." With voice in reserve, "A
little something."

A plate's
a plate to go home with you. Cup by cup
cups leave the rooms. None means
to remain this time next year.

At the produce stand, there's sulfur in the well.
Backyard obliges hanging grapes and crawling squash.
A forgotten onion from another year blossoms up

through strawberries against a fence. Inside our home
the glass on all the paintings turns to window screens.
The hatracked, full length mirror mimics a screen door.
The creak. The latch. The threshold. Look out to olean-
ders spilling onto shoulders of subliminal country
roads. The pines are cracking, crackling at their tops.
Pine nuts small and black snap off, fling out. They line
the ditches. I walk—it feels like creekfording—to a
neighbor's to get a trout.

Distant big-city radio: "Super Equis."
When we choose
music in tongues other than our own
the mood is clearer. We do not pretend
we know the words for how we feel.
Burning pine nuts and dented objects
say things we feel too.
A shimmer becomes

one more screen
over the screens.
One more degree and there are
no surfaces.

Sandra McPherson has published eight collections of poems including *The Spaces Between Birds: Mother/Daughter Poems 1967–1995.*

© Bradford Veley

Bobbie Ann Mason

© Marion Ettlinger

Bobbie Ann Mason's short stories have appeared in the *New Yorker*, the *Atlantic Monthly*, *Harper's* and the *Paris Review*, among others. Her published fiction includes three novels: *In Country* (1985), *Spence + Lila* (1988) and *Feather Crowns* (1993), along with two short story collections: *Shiloh and Other Stories* (1982) and *Love Life* (1989). She has been a finalist for the National Book Critics Circle Award, the American Book Award and the PEN/Faulkner Fiction Award. Her other honors include the Southern Book Award, the Ernest Hemingway Foundation Award for best first fiction, a Guggenheim Fellowship, and grants from the National Endowment for the Arts and the Pennsylvania Arts Council. She is currently finishing a nonfiction book about her family's farm, to be published in 1998. She lives and writes in Kentucky.

This interview was conducted by correspondence over a period of several months during 1997 by *The Missouri Review* staff.

An Interview with Bobbie Ann Mason

Interviewer: How did your background, growing up on a Kentucky dairy farm in the forties and fifties, contribute to your becoming a writer?

Mason: It was a somewhat isolated social setting, although we lived close enough to town that its pleasures and privileges seemed within easy reach. I suppose the desire to go to town helped make me ambitious, and the allure of the worlds that came in over the radio also helped. But the rewards of growing up on a farm were far greater in many ways than life in town. There is nothing that compares to the familiarity with natural detail: with knowing about grasshoppers, the anatomy of a leaf, the texture of high weeds, the color of a robin's egg.

Interviewer: Is that part of the reason you returned to Kentucky, after living in the Northeast for a while?

Mason: I moved back to Kentucky eventually for family and cultural reasons. I'd returned to nature, so to speak, during graduate school, when I was writing my dissertation about the nature imagery in Nabokov's *Ada*. I moved to the country in Connecticut and planted my own garden then. Most of the time I was in the Northeast I lived in the country, and I think that helped me to discover my material for writing.

Interviewer: So your home, the place you came from, and your interest in nature gave you a lot of material. Were there also ways in which these things gave you the motivation to write?

Mason: My motivation to write was complicated: for some reason, probably because I was the first-born, I was treated as special. I lived on the farm with my parents and grandparents. I had no playmates as a young child, and I was indulged. I helped my grandmother piece quilts, and we made pretty albums, an old-fashioned pastime. We cut poems and pictures out of magazines. I suppose I had the sensibility of a writer—the attentiveness to texture and detail and sound, and the desire to learn. But in order to become a writer, I had to rebel against the limits of my surroundings. We weren't poor, but we were well defined, circumscribed by generations of folkways and the rigid expectations of a farm culture. I wanted to get out. I wanted to go places, see the world. This ambitiousness developed at a time historically when it was first possible to leave—to go to college, to seek a livelihood other than farm wife. So you could say the early ambition to write was part natural sensibility and part idealism.

Interviewer: Was the feeling of being constricted more intense, do you think, because you're female? Gender roles seem to be a concern in your early work especially. Sam Hughes, for example, is disgusted by her friend Dawn's pregnancy and her own mother's new baby, and she's very aware of the limited—and limiting—potential of her relationship with her boyfriend. Norma Jean, in "Shiloh," is discovering her capabilities in a way that Leroy doesn't understand; he's worried that it's "some Women's Lib thing." Would you say that was true of you and your ambition? Was part of your desire to achieve, and get out, a feminist desire?

Mason: I rejected the traditional notion of "women's work," but I never thought of my early ambitions in a feminist way, exactly. Primarily I rebelled against apathy and limited education. I was rejecting a whole way of life that I thought trapped everyone. I didn't see women doing much of anything in my region except having babies and slaving away on the farm. They might work in stores or factories or teach school, but none of that was for me. But I didn't see men doing anything I wanted to do either. When I went to college, all the intellectuals and writers were men, so I aspired to crash into that world. I never had that feminist sense of wanting to prove myself by having a job. I didn't know of any women trapped at home in a fifties paradise with nothing to do. The idea of working outside the home as a matter of principle was a middle-class notion that I had little knowledge of. My mother worked in a factory some of the time, and she didn't do it to make a point. She did it for money. I was trying to get an education so I could escape from the labor force.

"I was trying to get an education so I could escape from the labor force."

Interviewer: You've said elsewhere that your early reading was typical: children's series like the Bobbsey Twins and Nancy Drew. You've even written a book about female detectives in some of those books, *The Girl Sleuth*. How, if at all, did those series influence you?

Mason: The Bobbsey Twins and Nancy Drew fed my aspirations to see the world, to become something else. The Bobbsey Twins always went on vacations, and of course a dairy farmer does not take a vacation, not even a day off, because the cows have to be milked. The Bobbseys frustrated me with their endless travels. The girl detectives' adventures made me long for something exciting to happen. I got the notion that everything exciting happened elsewhere, so I was filled with desire to go places and find out things. I tried to write stories patterned after the girl detectives, and that was the first thrill of writing—finding adventure through it.

Interviewer: How has the traditional farm culture that you came out of changed in the past fifty years or so? If you were growing up on the farm now, how might your trajectory be different from what it's been?

Mason: Growing up on a farm nowadays is not that isolated or autonomous, and the family farm as I knew it hardly exists. You couldn't feed a family on fifty-four acres now. Anyway, the wide world is much closer and more accessible than it was when I was little, so a kid today would have more choices. My ambitions were fed mostly by illusions and lack of information. I had little to go on except the movies and songs on the radio. I often dwell on that impossible question—what would my life have been like if I had had more advantages? Or what if I'd had fewer; what if I had lived in my grandmother's time? That's the personal question underlying *Feather Crowns*. I can't really answer it.

"My ambitions were fed mostly by illusions and lack of information."

Interviewer: You made a foray into academia before becoming a writer. You went to graduate school at SUNY–Binghamton and the University of Connecticut. Did you plan to teach literature?

Mason: I went to graduate school in literature because I wanted to read and write and didn't want to work at a meaningless job. I had no plans for a teaching career. I was just trying to find a situation where I could read and write for as long as possible. I had wanted to go to a writing program, but there were only a few of them then. In fact, I had applied to the Stanford creative writing program but I wasn't accepted. So I went into literature. I was a graduate assistant, and I taught freshman English, but the class wasn't only composition. It was a survey of Western literature course.

Interviewer: What was teaching like for you?

Mason: Frightening. At Binghamton all the students were smart, sophisticated kids from New York City, and as a quiet Southerner I was terrified. I look back on that time with a shudder because it was so embarrassing, difficult, and scary—that classic situation where you feel everybody else in the room seems suave and articulate. That was what visiting a professor's house was like, too. At one such gathering at the University of Connecticut I found myself seated next to the poet John Berryman, a genuine luminary who had just given a reading at the there. I was nobody, with nothing in my head, unable to speak. Poets lived on another plane. What would you say to a poet? I found myself catapulted into situations like this, where I felt I didn't belong, and I had neither the confidence nor the social graces to manage.

Interviewer: How did the experience of living in the North affect your notion of regional differences?

Mason: The North was, in our Southern mythology, the land of arrogant Yankees. They were the authorities. We felt inferior; we were losers. When I lived up there, I subscribed to that notion so completely that it was years before I could begin to get out from under it. Jimmy Carter had to be elected before the South in general could get ahold of its shame and start to turn it around. In the North, I was in few situations where I could tell about things like my Granny wringing a chicken's neck or how my chore was washing the milk cans twice a day. If I did tell people a little about my background, they tended to misinterpret it in terms of quaint stereotypes, something out of *Ma and Pa Kettle*. There was a yawning cultural gap between North and South in those days, and bridging it seemed almost impossible for somebody as bashful as I was.

Interviewer: Do you think of yourself as a Southern writer?

Mason: I'm a writer from the South and I write out of a Southern culture, but I'm not immersed in the South. I think my exile in the North gave me a sense of detachment, a way of looking in two directions at once. It's an advantage. I don't want to celebrate the South more than it deserves—which it does to a great extent, of course, but I'm wary of too much regional pride. It's important to pick a place and be there, but not to be provincial about it. So much country music wallows in that provinciality—like saying "I'm ignorant and proud of it."

Interviewer: Did you "pick your place" early on, or did your subject come to you over time?

Mason: I think, given my background and my earnest endeavor to lose my Southern accent—to find my place in the North—that it was unlikely that I would know early on what my material was. I started writing fiction in college, but it took me a number of years to get the right perspective on my material. I hadn't really recognized what I had to write about. I was looking outside. In the late sixties I wrote a novel about the Beatles, inspired by Donald Barthelme's *Snow White*. Finally, in the early seventies I wrote the obligatory autobiographical, coming-of-age novel. These were great practice and got me started, but I was slow to get into focus.

Interviewer: It's hard to imagine the Bobbie Ann Mason who wrote "Shiloh" and *In Country* being inspired by an experimental, satirical book like *Snow White*.

Mason: *Snow White* was right up my alley. Early on, I was interested in stylists, writers who loved language and played with words. In college, I loved Max Shulman ("Rally Round the Flag, Boys"); his writing was sophomoric, but then I went straight to James Joyce. Barthelme's story "Robert Kennedy Saved from Drowning" gave me the idea that you could write fiction about somebody famous. *Snow White* was written in short bursts and had a sustained tone of disconnectedness. The technique was very alluring. Nothing had to be explained, no full context and development—just hits. It looked easy and revolutionary. I wrote most of the Beatles book in 1967, the summer of "Sergeant Pepper's Lonely Hearts Club Band." It was a time to throw the graduate school reading list out the window and just go with the times.

Interviewer: Were you also writing short stories during this period?

Mason: I wrote short stories in college, published one in the college literary magazine, but I didn't write any more stories to speak of for fifteen years.

Interviewer: But then you started writing them again, and you made an immediate impact with the stories in *Shiloh*. How did that come about?

Mason: In the late seventies, as I neared the mid-life identity-crisis time, I decided it was now or never. I think the crisis went back to my childhood conviction that I was special, and I followed the notion, picked up in college, that writing was a calling, that writers were different and could indulge their sense of apartness by writing. All that seems a little silly to me now, but at the time it helped give me the determination I needed. When I realized that I hadn't yet done anything of note, I got busy. I wrote a story that was about five pages long and took it to a writers' workshop. I got some inspiration from seeing that people were actually writing and it looked possible, so I wrote a couple of other stories and immediately sent them to the *New Yorker*. Do you see the ten-year-old child there answering the Famous Writers School ad in the back of a magazine? What was I thinking? To my surprise, I got encouraging responses from Roger Angell, one of the *New Yorker*'s most illustrious editors and writers. He took me under his wing, responded to all my submissions with great care and interest, and gave me the first real encouragement I had ever had.

"I think my exile in the North gave me a way of looking in two directions at once."

Interviewer: What was the writers' workshop you attended?

Mason: For three summers in the late seventies I went to a week-long workshop run by Joe David Bellamy from St. Lawrence University. It was at Saranac Lake in the Adirondacks. It was pleasant, a chance to hang out with some writers. I attended workshops run by Gail Godwin, Charles Simmons and Margaret Atwood. They were all encouraging, but I think what charged me up most was the rediscovery of a notion I had gotten in college that writing was a passionate commitment and an honorable thing to do. I had always believed that, but my writing ambition had gotten so dissipated by lack of confidence and various diversions. The typical story for women writers seems to be that they spend twenty years raising children and then they go back to their original ambition of writing. I didn't raise children, but it took twenty years just to get my head together.

Interviewer: *Love Life* is dedicated to Roger Angell. What was that writer editor relationship like?

Mason: Roger Angell was the first person who said, "You are a writer." His encouragement brought me to life as a writer. Finally, I believed I could do it. As an editor he has always been very professional, yet he deals with a story on the level of emotions; in those early stories he helped me understand that I should go deeper into the characters' lives. His responses were subjective, never prescriptive. I heard how the story made him feel. He was always very careful not to tell me how to do it. He said he didn't know, but he made me think that I did. The story "Offerings" was the first story he accepted—the twentieth one I sent in. He telephoned me and said he liked the story but thought there was something lacking in the portrayal of the absent husband. It needed something a little darker. I studied the story for a long time

"You can hack off an image and examine it, but it would be like trying to cut away light and shadow."

and worked on some revisions. I was going to New York about three weeks later and I was going to meet Roger for the first time—November, 1979. I took the revisions with me—only about three sentences' worth—and met him in his office. He passed the story along to William Shawn, the editor, who made the ultimate decisions. The next day, a Friday, I met Roger for a drink at the Algonquin Hotel. I still did not have a story accepted—I would know on Monday—but there I was, being entertained at the celebrated Algonquin. It was awkward, but exciting. I kept looking for the Algonquin cat, Hamlet. On Monday I was to call about one o'clock, which was when the messages ordinarily came back from Mr. Shawn. I phoned from some place on Fifth Avenue, and Roger said the word hadn't come yet. He said to call again in fifteen minutes. I called again. Still no word. Then I had another appointment and couldn't call until 3:15. I called from the ladies' room phone at Saks Fifth Avenue and learned that the story was accepted. Roger wanted to know my social security number. I spouted out some numbers, but realized later they were wrong. The rest of the day is quite unclear in my mind. I was probably never so thrilled in my life.

Interviewer: What about the editing of your books? Do you have any insights into the working relationship between a novelist and her editor?

Mason: I have been fortunate to have had some of the great editors—Roger Angell, William Shawn, and Ted Solotaroff. I was spoiled by the *New Yorker,* and so I expect careful, close editing that serves the work. Ted Solotaroff's great quality is his ability to penetrate the heart of a work and to push for something deeper. In the early stages of writing *In Country,* he pushed me to confront the subject of Vietnam. I'd worked on the novel for some time before I realized it really was about the effects of the Vietnam War. When I did realize it, I felt somewhat intimidated. How could I write about such a big subject? What authority did I have? But Ted helped give me the confidence to stay with it.

Interviewer: Critics said of your first book something to the effect of your being, already, a full-fledged master of the short story form. *Shiloh and Other Stories* was nominated for the National Book Critics Circle Award and the American Book Award, and received several other honors. With the exception of the Nancy Culpepper stories, the characters are all ordinary, small-town people who work at ordinary jobs—the "K-Mart crowd" as they've been stereotyped. You were obviously well on the way to developing your vision by the time that collection was published. How did that happen?

Mason: I don't know how I developed a cohesive "vision," if that's what it is. The subject matter is a given. The vision is something internal, and writing helps me find it and bring it out. For me, the process of writing is a matter of dealing with inhibitions, to find out what I have hidden down inside; if I can get it out, it seems to fall loosely into shape, and then I help it along in a more deliberate way. My stories typically start out very rough. But if I see there's something in a story, I'll work and rework it over and over, making small improvements with each draft until it finally reaches its finished shape. In writing most of the pieces in *Shiloh*, I just fooled around with what randomly came to mind. In that way I made discoveries that I could work with. I wrote about fifty stories, of which sixteen went into the collection.

Interviewer: Most of your early short stories are told in third person, and they're almost all in the present tense. You use present tense and the same center-of-consciousness viewpoint in your first two novels, also. Why is that natural for you, and what do you think are the respective advantages and disadvantages?

Mason: The later stories moved into the past tense—stories like "Memphis" and "Coyotes"—when I got really tired of that convention of present tense. Present tense seems quite natural for characters meandering through a vague situation. It prevents the author from overtly asserting *authority*, the privilege of saying "Once upon a time . . . this happened, and I know how it is going to end and I'm going to tell you how it was."

Interviewer: Critics and readers have commented, too, on the consciousness, in your early work, of popular culture and of the media, especially film and TV.

Mason: I'm a little sensitive about being reduced to the terms of "popular culture," since it's often a pejorative term. I don't think the culture of the people ought to be dismissed like that. Their lives are just as important as the lives of those who read the *New York Times* and go to the opera. I often write about characters who happen to watch TV. Most Americans do watch TV. It's a big deal in their lives, especially if they work hard at some mind-numbing job. I try to write what is appropriate to the characters, the attributes and interests that are meaningful to them. For most of them, the TV is not a malignant force droning in the background, as it might be in a Cheever story. For many of my characters, it's a source of pleasure and escape, although that's changing now, as they get cable and find fifty-seven channels with nothing on. As a writer I can maintain a bit of detachment from the characters, showing them in their world and seeing a little bit more than they do. But I'm not looking down at them.

Interviewer: You've had some magazine writing experience, also. You've written quite a bit of nonfiction for the *New Yorker.*

Mason: Since I began publishing fiction in the *New Yorker* in 1980, I've been contributing occasional nonfiction pieces as well. I've done a couple of dozen "Talk of the Town" pieces, some humor pieces, and some reporting. I had a little background in journalism—writing columns for my college paper, and teaching journalism for a while during the seventies. In certain ways, I was influenced by Tom Wolfe and Lillian Ross and some of those "new journalists" anthologized by Wolfe.

Interviewer: How did those writers influence you?

Mason: I absorbed them because I had to deal with them so much in teaching journalism: Tom Wolfe's use of point of view—"the downstage narrator"—and his accumulation of what he called "status detail." Lillian Ross' wonderful deadpan reporting. Those writers wrote about real events by using techniques of fiction. It was the techniques of fiction I was most interested in, and so I picked up on some of them.

Interviewer: What would you say are your literary "roots"?

"I often think many of us are misfits who achieve some kind of mystique by virtue of our quirks."

Mason: I think my aesthetic principles derive from James Joyce and Vladimir Nabokov. From Joyce I learned about how a work is organic—how sound, for instance, is meaning, how the language is appropriate to the subject. If the story is *about* a journey, then it should *be* a journey. From Nabokov I learned that the surfaces are not symbolic representations, but the thing itself, irreducible. Rather than depending on an underlying idea, an image or set of images should be infinitely complex—just the opposite of what we're sometimes taught about symbols and themes as hidden treasures. You can hack off an image and examine it, but it would be like trying to cut away light and shadow. The work should shimmer.

Interviewer: You mention Joyce as an influence, but you generally eschew the Joycean epiphany as a way of ending a short story. In your stories, because we're so much in the minds of characters who aren't necessarily all that self-aware, the "recognition"—if there is one—is left up to the reader. How deliberate is that?

Mason: The goal is to leave the story at the most appropriate point, with the fullest sense of what it comes to, with a passage that has resonance and brings into focus the whole story. It has to sound right and seem right, even if its meaning isn't obvious.

Interviewer: How, in your mind, is that different from what a novel does?

Mason: It's principally scale, the size of the canvas. I write novels in much the same way as I write stories—that is, the process is the same, but the effect is larger, more developed. In either case, though, I revise and revise. I fuss over every word.

"Writers belong on the edge, not in the center of the action."

Interviewer: While we're on the subject of what fiction does, perhaps I should ask what you see as the role of the writer in society. How does literary writing matter—other than, obviously, as a sort of catharsis for the person doing it?

Mason: It is tempting to say that writing does serve the writers first; I often think many of us are misfits who can't hold a job and who achieve, at best, some kind of mystique by virtue of our quirks. But I look back to Emerson and Thoreau when I think about why literary writing matters. It's easier to see the writer's role in the smaller world of Concord, Massachusetts, in the mid-nineteenth century. Thoreau was certainly a quirky misfit, but *Walden* comes down to us as an instruction manual for the heart and soul, as well as for getting a crop out. Emerson was famous, a very public figure, but both of them were quite visible in their community. In Concord, a town of two thousand, they could simply go to the Lyceum and give lectures. They engaged their neighbors in their discoveries. As writers, Thoreau and Emerson were lively and curious and demanding. They took on the world and tried to figure it out and then to translate what they found to the public, all in terms of the deepest questions about the nature of reality and morality and aesthetics. They led with their genius, turning their observations of nature into poetry and essays. They were standing on the verge of our time and they could almost see what was going to happen to us. They were leading their readers and listeners into the future. Writers belong on the edge, not in the center of the action. Nowadays we don't have leaders who are worth much when it comes to the heart and soul, but if writers can make us feel and appreciate and explore the world, then I think that's an extremely valuable function; it goes far beyond entertainment and steers well clear of politics.

Interviewer: How do you see your own role as a writer?

Mason: I don't make any claims for myself. I'm sitting on the toe of Thoreau's boot. I'm not a natural storyteller. I see writing as a way of finding words to fashion a design, to discover a vision, not as a way of chronicling or championing or documenting. In other words, it is to applaud the creative imagination as it acts upon whatever materials are at hand. Creative writing is not to me primarily theme, subject, topic, region, class, or any ideas. It has more to do with feeling, imagination, suggestiveness, subtlety, complexity, richness of perception— all of which are found through fooling around with language and observations.

Interviewer: You've written two story collections, two full-length novels, and *Spence + Lila*, which is really more of a novella. Your work has been pretty much equally divided between long and short fiction. Do you consider yourself a novelist first, or a short story writer first?

Mason: I don't know. I've written only eight or nine stories in this decade. In the eighties, I wrote about seventy-five stories. I have been busier with novels and nonfiction in the nineties. But in the future, it could go either way. There's more of an immediate gratification in writing a story, but in the long run, writing a novel is more deeply gratifying. It's not really something I can consciously control. But I try to be wary of jumping into a novel too casually. Some notion has to really grab me hard for me to get into a novel. Stories come and go. If a story doesn't work, it's no great loss to throw it away. But a novel . . . that's years of my life.

Interviewer: And a bigger challenge?

Mason: Yes. The challenges keep getting more and more complicated, as you become more aware as a writer. Committing to a novel is so risky and uncertain, and there is so little to go on when you begin. With *In Country* I couldn't find the story that held those characters together; with *Feather Crowns* I had to sustain a long narrative on a subject that threatened to be grotesque. I had to show how the characters' actions were justifiable in the terms of their world.

Interviewer: That novel was quite a departure for you. Like your other fiction, it's set in Kentucky but it's Kentucky of the turn of the century. What made you turn to historical fiction?

Mason: I don't think *Feather Crowns* was a major departure. It's the same people, the same landscape I have been preoccupied with since the start. The contemporary characters in my stories are the descendants of the rural people who were rooted on the farm for generations. On the farm, they were independent, land-owning yeoman farmers—in rural terms, the middle class. The Depression, the decline of the farm and the lure of cash sent them out of their culture into what they called "public work." In many ways, it was a demotion. In working for a boss, they lost their autonomy. That transition since the Depression has had profound effects on rural and small-town culture. It formed my expectations that I would have to work in a factory or at a clerical job. I dreaded and feared the loss of independence. Writing was my way of keeping my own life.

Interviewer: Can you say something about the genesis and writing of *Feather Crowns*?

Mason: The book was inspired by a true story, the birth of quintuplets in 1896. It happened in my hometown—in fact, across the field from where I grew up. I did not hear the story until 1988, and there wasn't much information about it, but it was enough to inspire me. I had been wanting to go back into the world of my grandparents when they were young, and that true story was just right for the journey. I seized on it for my own, as a chance to get into the language and folkways of the rural culture of the turn of the century. These things have a deep connection to the present, because the old ways are still hanging on; change is much slower than we imagine. So I see continuity between *Feather Crowns* and *Shiloh* more than I see a radical juxtaposition.

Interviewer: The project itself was somewhat different, though. For one thing, it must have required a lot of research. It's also a bigger novel than any that you've written so far—longer, more characters, richer and more complex thematically. Did you feel at all like Christie, at the start of the book, who fears that the baby inside her—which is actually five—is so big and wild that it must be a monster?

Mason: The historical research wasn't as extensive as you might think because I knew that world intimately, through my parents and grandparents. The language, superstitions, landscape, farming methods—all of it came down to me in my lifetime. The rural community didn't change that much from the turn of the century to the nineteen-forties. Much of my research involved asking my mother questions, and much

"Nowadays we don't have leaders who are worth much when it comes to the heart and soul."

---

of it I simply knew firsthand. I spent about the same amount of time writing it as I did writing *In Country*. The story was clear to me from the beginning, whereas with *In Country* there was so much I didn't know about what was going on. I actually spent more concentrated time writing *Feather Crowns*, whereas with *In Country* I spent most of the time searching and trying out various directions for the characters.

No, I didn't feel quite like Christie. I knew from the beginning that it was a big book, and I could see what it required in terms of pacing and emotion and goal. I had to invent most of it—the characters and their world—but I had a clear sense of direction.

Interviewer: Among other things, the novel is about the loss of privacy, and Christie and James' inability to defend themselves against the damaging effects of the public's curiosity. The babies are the product of a very intimate kind of desire, but they thrust the Wheelers' personal lives into public view. Christie is referred to by someone as having "dropped a litter," and James is leered at by other women, who assume he's extremely virile. Eventually the Wheelers' grief, too, becomes a public affair. Was that part of the real story you learned, of the 1896 quintuplets? Or is that your imagination, operating on the historical incident?

Mason: Some of it was true, but there was very little information on the 1896 quintuplets. I know they were besieged by the public. I think the litter-dropping and a sense of the public invasion was also part of the reports surrounding the Dionne Quintuplets. Everything else I had to imagine.

Interviewer: One of the very significant events in the book, which actually takes place prior to the main action, is Christie's trip with her friend Amanda to the revival at Reelfoot Lake. It becomes a sort of

"Sometimes it seems I'm working mostly with sounds and rhythms, the voice in my head."

---

focal point for Christie—and not just because it's one of the only times she's ever been away from James and her children. What, in your own mind, is the importance of that event in the novel?

Mason: The focal point had to do with guilt—Christie has impure thoughts about that sexy evangelist, Brother Cornett. So she builds on this guilt when she realizes her pregnancy is unusual. She imagines she's carrying a monster, a devil. But the true monster turns out to be the public response. Also, in her attraction to Brother Cornett and the sideshow atmosphere of the camp meeting, we have the seeds of her vulnerability to celebrity that she encounters later. Her innocent desire to experience something new also leads her into danger.

Interviewer: Can you comment on your current writing project?

Mason: I don't quite know what to say about it, as I'm still in the midst of it as we speak. It's called *Clear Springs* and I hope it will come out sometime in 1998. It is a personal story of the fate of the family farm—my family's farm. It includes a lot of memory of childhood and some autobiography, but I don't think of it as a memoir. It's less about me than about my family, especially my mother. By extension, it's about a way of life that's disappearing—the small family farm, the small rural community, that was once seen as the ideal for American civilization.

Interviewer: How does your notion of what Bobbie Ann Mason, the writer, is about differ, do you think, from the public and/or critical perception of your work?

Mason: I don't think of myself as the K-mart realist. I hope that what I'm trying to do is more than document patterns of discount shopping in the late twentieth century! Many teachers and scholars seem primarily concerned with themes and ideas, but that's not the way I think. If that was what I was after, I'd write a term paper. I think more in terms of literal details and images, as well as sound and tone—all the textures that bring a story to life. Sometimes it seems I'm working mostly with sounds and rhythms, the voice in my head. I write a story over and over until it sounds right. If it works, then the themes will be there. I don't plant them.

Interviewer: So you're more concerned with character and place than with any overriding theme in your work.

Mason: I'm not saying I'm uninterested in what a story means, it's just that I find it hard to isolate that, either during the process of writing or in the final analysis. I think theme sometimes gets separated out too much from a work. The themes are important, but the artistry is just as important. Ideally, form and function are inseparable. That's what I read for most: writing that can't be torn apart, a story that can't be told any other way. I read a writer for the *way* he tells the story. And when the substance and style are perfectly wedded, you can't reduce the story to a set of abstractions.

Advertising in the post-literate era.

"The Search After Happiness"
by
Charlotte Brontë

THE SEARCH AFTER 2
HAPINESS
A TALE BY
CHARLOTTE
BRONTE

PRINTED BY HERSELF
AND
SOLD BY
NOBODY &c &c

AUGUST
THE
SEVENTEENTH

EIGHTEEN HUNDRED
AND ~~ODD~~
~~TWENTY EIGHT~~
Twenty nine

THE SEARCH AFTER HAPPINESS/
Charlotte Brontë

Introduction

THE BRONTËS—Charlotte, Emily, and Anne—were a literary family whose accomplishments streaked across the sky of the 1840s, but only Charlotte lived long enough to briefly enjoy celebrity. The sisters began publishing their poetry and fiction at a time when life at home was dismal. Brother Branwell was declining into alcohol and opium addiction. An attempt by Emily and Charlotte to start a school had failed, and Charlotte had apparently had an unhappy love affair with a married man while under his tutelage in Belgium. Back at home, Charlotte happened to discover Emily's poetry, then Anne got out hers, and the sisters published a combined volume under the pseudonyms Currer, Ellis, and Acton Bell. Soon Emily's novel, *Wuthering Heights*, and Anne's *Agnes Grey* were published together. *The Professor*, by Charlotte, was initially rejected, but *Jane Eyre* was published in 1847. When Charlotte published *Shirley* in 1849, the true identities of the authors were made public, but by then tuberculosis had left only Charlotte and her father in what had been a family of eight.

During their brief period of publishing, Charlotte and Emily wrote two of the most important novels of mid-nineteenth-century English literature. They absorbed the animus of the Romantic period and sang its swan song in passionate, violent, distinctly female voices. Even Anne's *Agnes Grey* is a sturdy book—an unadorned, realistic story of the life of a governess. Of the four Brontë children who survived beyond childhood, only Branwell achieved no literary recognition, despite early promise and a lifetime of trying.

Their successes were not accidents of publishing. From the time they were quite young, the Brontë children had been at play, dramatizing and eventually writing a vast and intricately connected saga of romantic characters and landscapes. The early writings of the Brontë children are a fascinating study in literary precocity and the development of young writers' minds. Jane Austen rendered her own equally interesting juvenilia into fair, self-edited copies when she was a mature author, in three neatly done volumes, but the Brontë material remained in the condition that the children left it. This made it a more authentic record of their early writing than Jane Austen's, but it also made it less accessible.

The lack of fair copies is one of the reasons that the Brontë juvenilia long resisted the efforts of scholars.* The intriguing manuscripts were initially noted in 1857, when Charlotte's first biographer, Mrs. Gaskell, visited the author's widower, Reverend Arthur Bell Nicholls (Charlotte had been briefly married to her father's curate, before dying of pregnancy toxemia). Nicholls refused to part with her manuscripts, but Sir James Kay-Shuttleworth, who had accompanied the biographer, purloined a bundle of them under the reluctant widower's nose. The material, while too extensive for her to absorb, forced Mrs. Gaskell to rewrite the early parts of her biography before returning the manuscripts to Reverend Nicholls.

In the biography she notes, "I have had a curious packet confided to me, containing an immense amount of manuscript, in an inconceivably small space; tales, dramas, poems, romances, written principally by Charlotte, in a hand which it is almost impossible to decipher without the aid of a magnifying glass." These early childhood stories had been composed in miniature, in tiny booklets scarcely larger than postage stamps. They disappeared from notice for forty years and eventually were scattered among collectors and libraries. The shape of the manuscripts, the challenge of reading them, the complexity of authorship (Charlotte, Branwell, Emily, and Anne)—all conspired to make them a daunting job to comprehend and edit.

Unlike most children of their time, particularly girls, the Brontës were allowed full access to their father's library, including the writings of Byron. Their father, Patrick Brontë, was a poor clergyman at Haworth, West Riding of Yorkshire, who had gone to St. John's College, Cambridge, a few years after Wordsworth. Patrick read widely, wrote three books, and contributed often to magazines. He ascribed to the romantic idea of the healing and moral powers of nature and, uncharacteristically for the time, allowed his children to roam outdoors. Early portraits of Mr. Brontë, including Mrs. Gaskell's, depicted him as a hypochondriacal and negligent father. However, the children's writing belies that portrait. Their first title pages look much like the title page of one of their father's books, implying their

---

*Christine Alexander's *The Early Writings of Charlotte Brontë* (Prometheus, 1983) is the most comprehensive book on Charlotte Brontë's juvenilia. Alexander provides a brief history of scholarly commentary and explicates all the major known juvenilia, including "The Search After Happiness." We have relied heavily on Alexander and on Frances Beer's introduction to *The Juvenilia of Jane Austen and Charlotte Brontë* (Penguin, 1986).

admiration, and their writings are spilling over with excitement and imaginative boldness.

The Brontës' lives, nevertheless, had been marked by tragedy, beginning with the death of their mother and, four years later, the deaths of the older sisters, Maria and Elizabeth, who contracted TB at the Cowan Bridge School for the daughters of poor clergymen. Charlotte and Emily, also at the school, were brought home, and the four children lived for several years in the isolated Haworth parsonage—with its formidable cemetery of raised tombs nearby—as each other's chief companions. The remarkable unfolding of their imaginary worlds at first took shape through "plays," dramatic play-acting described by Charlotte, with characteristic flair, three years after they began, in her second earliest surviving manuscript:

> Our plays were established: *Young Men*, June 1826; *Our Fellows*, July 1827; *Islanders*, December 1827. These are our three great plays that are not kept secret. Emily's and my bed plays were established December 1, 1827; the others March 1828. Bed plays mean secret plays; they are very nice ones. All our plays are very strange ones. Their nature I need not write on paper, for I think I shall always remember them.

The plays had started when Mr. Brontë went to a clerical conference in Leeds and returned home with gifts for all his children. Toy soldiers intended for Branwell were a big hit among all the children, and each of them immediately took a soldier and named it. The two eldest, Charlotte and Branwell, chose "Bonaparte" and "Wellington," the two great adversaries of the age. Napoleon had recently died, in May 1827, and Wellington became British Prime Minister the following year. At first their plays went unrecorded, but around the time of the above description, Charlotte started writing down the stories on little scraps of paper, and from ages twelve through twenty-three, she continued to write the ongoing saga.

Their early plays included the Young Men's and the Islanders' plays. The Islanders' drew heavily on politics and important characters in the news of the day, although the island itself soon metamorphosed into Vision Island, a place of children ruled by adults. The Young Men's plays concerned an imaginary African colony. Gradually the differences between the two resolved. Elements of both overlapped, merging into the remarkably long-lived soap opera of Glass Town, an imaginary city in Africa.

The "Search After Happiness," which Charlotte started writing on July 29, 1829, is the first story that weds the two settings of the Islanders' and Glass Town plays. The Chief of the City and his sons are similar to the Duke of Wellington and his sons of the Islanders' plays. The African setting is evoked by the descriptions of the city. Although not referred to by name in the story, the characters are identified in Charlotte's Preface, which was seemingly added as an afterthought, as if the young writer was confirming to herself that the chief characters, originally Islanders, were now in Africa:

> The persons meant by the Chief of the city and his
> Sons are the Duke of Wellington, the Marquis of
> Duoro and Lord Wellesley. The city is the Glass Town.

The Glass Town saga changed over time, as the children grew up. Their interests changed, and the first generation of characters gave way to another. The Duke is replaced as protagonist by his son, Arthur, who later becomes the Duke of Zamorna and King of Angria; the narrative voice, too, changes from one of naïve idealism to a more adult perspective, as the Duke of Zamorna duels with court intrigue and rebellion, and himself goes through wives and lovers. Wellington had started as a mighty warrior and would ultimately become an arrogant, amoral, even demonic figure of destruction and depravity. Branwell conjured the military engagements and business deals, while Charlotte apparently wrote the bedroom scenes. Illicit love affairs made the plots go wild. Much of this was influenced by the newspaper accounts of Byron.

Charlotte—and indeed all the Brontës—had an abiding fascination with the Byronic hero. In her early work, she tended to emphasize his better sides, the solitary exile and lonely traveler in sublime nature, but as time went by the Brontës' Byronic characters became bored, misanthropic, prideful, and often destructive.

"The Search After Happiness" was written in a script so tiny that it requires a magnifying lens, in some places a microscope, to read. How it was made in such a small hand is a mystery of childhood dexterity. It was written by a twelve-year-old girl who hadn't the slightest idea about punctuation—Charlotte never mastered the mysteries of punctuation even as an adult—and little room on the page to make emendations and corrections. Reading it, however, one has an uncanny sense of seeing through a little window into the early development of a literary genius and of the tremendous osmotic and transformative potential of a young writer's mind.

This is an edited version of "The Search After Happiness." While we have attempted to preserve the flavor of Brontë's original text, we have employed standard capitalization, spelling and punctuation wherever necessary for the sake of clarity. In a few cases "an" or "a" has been substituted for "the," and ampersands have been replaced by "and." Some phrases and sentences have been left out because of illegible words and non sequiturs, and the table of contents has been placed at the beginning rather than at the end, where it appears in the original. The manuscript of "The Search after Happiness" resides at the British Library, Ashley 156.

THE SEARCH AFTER HAPPINESS CB July 28 1829

Contents

Chapter I

Not many years ago there lived in a certain city a person of the name of Henry O Donell. In figure he was tall, of a dark complexion and searching black eye. His mind was strong and unbending, his disposition unsociable, and, though respected by many, he was loved by few. The city where he resided was very great and magnificent. It was governed by a warrior, a mighty man of valor, whose deeds had resounded to the ends of the earth. The soldier had two sons who were at that time of the ages of 6 and 7 years. Henry O Donell was a nobleman of great consequence in the city and a peculiar favorite with the governor, before whose glance his stern mind would bow . . . . While playing with the young princes, he would forget his usual sullenness of demeanor, the days of his childhood returned upon him, and he would be as merry as the youngest, who was gay indeed.

One day at court, a quarrel ensued between him and another noble. Words came to blows, and O Donell struck his opponent a violent blow on the left cheek. At this the military king started up and commanded O Donell to apologize. This he immediately did, but from that hour a spell seemed to have been cast over him, and he resolved to quit the city.

The evening before he put this resolution into practice, he had an interview with the king and returned quite an altered man. Before, he seemed stern and intractable; now he was only meditative and sorrowful. As he was passing the inner court of the palace, he perceived the two young princes at play. He called them and they came running to him.

"I am going far from this city and shall most likely never see you again," said O Donell.

"Where are you going?"

"I cannot tell."

"Then why do you go away from us? Why do you go from your own house and lands, from this great and splendid city to you know not where?"

"Because I am not happy here."

"And if you are not happy here, where you have everything for which you can wish, do you expect to be happy when you are dying of hunger or thirst in a desert, or longing for the society of men when you are thousands of miles from any human being?"

"How do you know that will be my case?"

"It is very likely that it will."

"And if it was, I am determined to go."

"Take this then, that you may sometimes remember us when you dwell with only the wild beast of the desert and the great eagle of the mountain," said they, as they each gave him a curling lock of their hair.

"Yes I will take it, my princes. I shall remember you and the mighty warrior king, your father, even when the angel of death has stretched forth his bony arm against me and I am within the confines of his dreary kingdom, the cold damp grave," replied O Donell, as the tears rushed to his eyes and he once more embraced the little princes and then quitted them, it might be forever.

Chapter the II

The dawn of the next morning found O Donell on the summit of a high mountain which overlooked the city. He had stopped to take a farewell view of the place of his nativity. All along the eastern horizon there was a rich glowing light which as it rose gradually melted into the pale blue of the sky, in which, just over the light, there was visible the silver crescent of the moon. In a short time the sun began to rise in golden glory, casting his splendid radiance over all the face of nature and illuminating the magnificent city, in the midst of which, towering in silent grandeur, there appeared the palace where dwelt the mighty prince of that great and beautiful city.

All around the gated and massive walls there flowed the majestic stream of the Guadima, whose banks were bordered by splendid palaces and magnificent gardens. Behind these, stretching for many a league, were fruitful plains and forests, whose shade seemed almost impenetrable to a single ray of light, while in the distance blue mountains were seen raising their heads to the skies and forming a misty girdle to the plains of Dahomey.

O Donell's gaze was long and fixed, but his last look was to the palace of the king, and a tear stood in his eye as he said earnestly, "May he be preserved from all evil, may good attend him, and may the chief Geni spread his broad shield of protection over him all the time of his sojourn in this wearisome world."

Then turning around, he began to descend the mountain. He pursued his way till the sun began to wax hot. He stopped and, sitting down, took out some provisions which he had brought with him, which consisted of a few biscuits and dates. While he was eating, a tall man came up and accosted him. O Donell requested him to sit beside him and offered him a biscuit. . . .

He sat down, and they began to talk. In the course of conversation, O Donell learnt that this man's name was Alexander Delancy, that he was a native of France, and that he was engaged in the same pursuit as himself—the search for happiness. They talked for a long time and at last agreed to travel together. Then rising, they pursued their journey towards nightfall.

They lay down in the open air and slept soundly till morning, when they again set off, and thus they continued till the third day when, about two hours after noon, they approached an old castle, which they entered.

As they were examining it, they discovered a subterranean passage, which they could not see the end of. "Let us follow where this passage leads us, and perhaps we may find happiness here," said O Donell.

Delancy agreed. The two stepped into the opening. Immediately a great stone was rolled to the mouth of the passage with a noise like thunder which shut out all but a single ray of daylight.

"What is that?" exclaimed O Donell.

"I cannot tell," replied Delancy. "But never mind, I suppose it is only some genius playing tricks."

"Well it may be so returned," O Donell said, and they proceeded on their way. After traveling for a long time—as near as they could reckon about two days—they perceived a silvery streak of light on the walls of the passage something like the light of the moon.

In a short time they came to the end of the passage. Leaping out of the opening which it formed, they entered a new world, where they were at first so much bewildered by the different objects which struck their senses that they almost fainted. At length recovering, they had time to see everything around them.

They were upon the top of a rock, which was more than a thousand fathoms high, and all beneath them was liquid mountains tossed to and fro with horrible confusion, roaring and raging with a tremendous noise. Crowned with waves of foam all above them was a mighty firmament in one part covered with black clouds from which darted huge and terrible sheets of lightning. In another part an immense globe of light like silver was hanging in the sky, and several smaller globes surrounded it.

In a short time the tempest, which was dreadful beyond description, ceased. The black clouds cleared away, the silver globes vanished, and another globe whose light was of a gold color appeared. In a little time it became so intensely bright that they could no longer gaze on it. After looking around them for some time, they rose and pursued their journey. They had traveled a long way when they came on an immense forest, the trees of which bore a large fruit of a deep purple color, of which they tasted and found that it was fit for food.

They journeyed in this forest for three days, and on the third day they entered a valley, or rather a deep glen, surrounded on each side by tremendous rocks whose tops were lost in the clouds. In this glen they continued for some time and at last came in sight of a mountain, which rose so high that they could not see the summit, though the sky was quite clear.

At the foot of the mountain there flowed a river of pure water, bordered by trees, which had flowers of a beautiful rose color. Except these trees, nothing was to be seen but black forest and huge rocks rising out of a wilderness, which bore the terrible aspect of devastation and which stretched as far as the eye could reach. In this desolate land no sound was to be heard, not even the cry of the eagle, but a silence like the silence of the grave reigned over all the face of nature, unbroken except by the murmur of the river, as it slowly wound its course through the desert.

Chapter the III

After they had contemplated this scene some time, O Donell exclaimed, "Alexander, let us abide here. What need have we to travel farther? Let us make this our place of rest."

"We will," replied Delancy. "This shall be our abode." He pointed to a cave at the foot of the mountain.

"It shall," returned O Donell, as they entered it.

In this country they remained for many long years and passed their time in a manner which made them completely happy. Sometimes they would sit upon a high rock and listen to the hoarse thunder rolling through the sky and making the mountains to echo and the desert to ring with its awful voice. Sometimes they would watch the lightning darting across black clouds and shivering huge fragments of rock in its terrible passage. Sometimes they would witness the great glorious orb of gold sink behind the far, distant mountains which girded the horizon and then watch the advance of gray twilight and the little stars coming forth in beauty and the silver moon arising in her splendor till the cold dews of night began to fall, and then they would retire to their bed in the cave with hearts full of joy and thankfulness.

One evening they were sealed in this cave by a large blazing fire, which cast its lurid light to the high, arched roof and illuminated the tall and stately pillars cut by the hand of nature out the rock with a cheerful red glare. It appeared strange in this desolate land, where no fires had ever before visited except those flames of death which flash from the heavens when robed in the dreadful majesty of their thunder.

They were seated in this cave then, listening to the howling night wind, as it swept in mournful cadence through the trees of the forest which encircled the foot of the mount and bordered the stream which flowed round it. They were quite silent, and their thoughts were occupied by those that were far off, and whom it was their fate most likely never more to behold.

O Donell was thinking of his noble master and his young princes, of the thousands of miles which intervened between him and them, and the sad, silent tear gushed forth. He ruminated on the happiness of those times when his master frowned not, when the gloom of care gave place to the smile of friendship, when he would talk to him, and laugh with him, and be not as a brother, no, but as a mighty warrior who, relaxing from his haughtiness, would now and then converse with his high officers in a strain of vivacity and playful humor.

He viewed him in his mind's eye at the head of his army, he heard in the ears of his imagination the buzz of expectation, of hope and supposition which hummed round him, as his penetrating eye, with a still expression, was fixed on the distant ranks of the enemy. Then he heard his authoritative voice exclaim, "Onward, brave sons of freedom, onward to the battle." His parting words to him—"In misery, in sorrow, or in joy, in populous cities and in desolate wildernesses, my prayer shall go with you"—darted across his mind with such painful distinctness that he, at length, gave way to his uncontrollable grief at the thought that he should never behold his beloved and mighty commander more, and he burst into a flood of tears.

"What is the matter Henry?" exclaimed Delancy.

"Oh nothing, nothing," was the reply. They were resuming their tacit thinking when a voice was heard outside the cavern, which broke strangely upon the desolate silence of that land, which for thousands of years had heard no sound save the howling of the wind through the forest, the echoing of the thunder among mountains or the solitary murmuring of the river, except the presence of O Donell and Delancy.

"Listen!" cried Alexander. "Listen! What is that?"

"It is the sound of a man's voice," replied Henry, and then snatching up a burning torch, he rushed to the mouth of the cave, followed by Delancy. When they had got there, they saw the figure of a very old man sitting on the damp wet ground, moaning and complaining bitterly.

They went up to him. At their approach, he rose and said, "Are you human or supernatural beings?"

They assured him that they were human. He went on, "Then why have you taken up your abode in this land of the grave?"

O Donell answered that he would relate to him all the particulars if he would take shelter for the night with them. The old man consented, and, when they were all assembled around the cheerful fire, O Donell fulfilled his promise and then requested the old man to tell them how he came to be traveling, then he complied and began as follows.

Chapter the IV

"I was the son of a respectable merchant in Moussoul. My father intended to bring me up to his own trade, but I was idle and did not like it. One day, as I was playing in the street, a weary old man came up to me and asked me if I would go with him. I asked him where. He replied that if I would go with him he would show me very wonderful things.

"This raised my curiosity and I consented. He immediately took me by the hand and hurried me out of the city of Moussoul so quickly that my breath was almost stopped. It seemed as if we glided along in the air, for I could hear no sound of our footsteps. We continued on our course for a long time, till we came to a glen surrounded by very high mountains. How we passed over those mountains I could never tell.

"In the middle of the glen there was a small fountain of very clear water. My conductor directed me to drink of this. I did, and immediately I found myself in a palace, the glory of which far exceeds any description which I can give. The tall stately pillars reaching from heaven to earth were formed of the finest pure diamonds, the pavement sparkling with gold and precious stones, and the mighty dome, made solemn and awful by its stupendous magnificence, was of 1 single emerald. In the midst of this grand magnificent palace was a lamp like the sun, the radiance of which made all the palace to flash and glitter with an almost fearful grandeur. The ruby sent forth a stream of crimson light, the topaz gold, the sapphire purple. The dome poured a flood of deep clear splendor which overcame all the other gaudy lights by its wild triumphant glory. In this palace were thousands and tens of thousands of fairies and geni some of whom flitted lightly among the blazing lamps to the sound of unearthly music, which died and swelled in wild grandeur suited to the words they sung—

In this fairy land of light
no mortal ere has been,
and the dreadful grandeur of this sight
by them hath not been seen.

T'would strike them shuddering to the earth
like the flash from a thunder cloud,
it would quench their light and joyous mirth
and fit them for the shroud.

The rising of our palaces,
like visions of the deep,
and the glory of their structure
no mortal voice can speak.

The music of our songs
and our mighty trumpets swell,
and the sounding of our silver harps
no mortal tongue can tell.

Of us they know but little,
save when the storm doth rise,
and the mighty waves are tossing
against the arched skies.

Then oft they see us striding
o'er the billows' snow white foam,
or hear us speak in thunder
when we stand in grandeur lone.

On the darkest of the mighty clouds
which veil the pearly moon,
around us lightning flashing
night's blackness to illume.

Carries the music of our songs,
and our mighty trumpets
swell, and the sounding of our silver
harp no mortal tongue can tell.

"When they had finished, there was a dead silence for about half an hour, and then the palace began slowly and gradually to vanish, till it disappeared entirely. And I found myself in the glen, surrounded by high mountains, the fountain illuminated by the cold light of the moon springing up in the middle of the valley. And standing close by was the old man who had conducted me to this enchanted place.

"He turned round and I could see that his countenance had an expression of strange severity, which I had not before observed. 'Follow me,' he said.

"I obeyed, and we began to ascend the mountain.

"It would be needless to trouble you with a repetition of all my adventures. Suffice it to say that after two months' time we arrived at a large temple. We entered it. The interior, as well as the outside, had a very gloomy and ominous aspect, being built of black marble.

"The old man suddenly seized me and dragged me to an altar at the upper end of the temple, then, forcing me down to my knees, he made me swear that I would be his servant forever. This promise I faithfully kept, notwithstanding the dreadful scenes of magic of which every day of my life I was forced to be a witness.

"One day he told me that he would discharge me from the oath I had taken and commanded me to leave his service. I obeyed and, after wandering about the world for many years, I one evening laid myself down on a little bank by the roadside, intending to pass the night there. Suddenly I felt myself raised in the air by invisible hands. In a short time, I lost sight of the earth and continued on my course through the clouds till I became insensible and, when I recovered from my swoon, I found myself lying outside this cave. What may be my future destiny I know not."

Chapter the V

When the old man had finished his tale, O Donell and Delancy thanked him for the relation, adding that they had never heard anything half so wonderful. As it was very late, they all retired to rest.

Next morning, O Donell awoke very early and, looking round the cave, he perceived the bed of leaves on which the old man had lain to be empty. Rising, he went out of the cave.

The sky was covered with red clouds except those in the east, whose edges were tinged with the bright rays of the sun, as they strove to hide its glory with their dark morning veil of vapors. The golden line of light streaked their gloomy surface. Beneath this storm-portending sky, far off to the west, rose two tremendous rocks whose summits were enveloped with black clouds rolling one above another. In the air between these two rocks was a chariot of light. In the chariot sat a figure whose countenance was that of an old man armed with the majesty and might of a spirit. O Donell stood at the mouth of the cave watching it till it vanished, and then, calling Delancy, he related the circumstances to him.

Some years after this Alexander went out one morning in search of the fruit on which they subsisted. Noon came and he had not returned. Evening and still no tiding of him. O Donell began to be alarmed and set out in search of him but could nowhere find him. One whole day he spent in wandering about the rocks and mountain, and in the evening he came back to his cave weary and faint with hunger and thirst. Days, weeks, months passed away, and no Delancy appeared.

O Donell might now be said to be truly miserable. He would sit on a rock for hours together and cry out, "Alexander, Alexander," but receive no answer except the distant echoing of his voice among the rocks. Sometimes he fancied it was another person answering him, and he would listen earnestly till it died away, then, sinking into utter despair, again he would sit till the dews of night began to fall, when he would retire to his cave to pass the night in unquiet, broken slumbers or in thinking of his beloved commander, whom he could never see more.

In one of these dreadful intervals he took up a small parcel and, opening it, he saw lying before him two locks of softly shining hair like burnished gold. He gazed on them for a time and thought of the words of those who gave the charge to him: "Take this, then, that you may remember us when you dwell with the wild beast of the desert, the great eagle of the mountain."

He burst in a flood of tears and wrung his hands in sorrow. In the anguish of the moment, he wished that he could once more see them and the mighty warrior king, their father, if it cost him his life.

Just at that instant, a loud clap of thunder shook the roof of the cave, a sound like the rushing of the wind was heard, and a mighty genius stood before him. "I know thy wish," cried he with a loud and terrible voice. "I will grant it if thou returnest to the castle whence thou camest and surrender thyself into my power."

O Donell promised that he would, and instantly he found himself at the door of the old castle and in the land of his birth. He pursued his journey for three days and on the third day he arrived at the mountain which overlooked the city.

It was a beautiful evening in the month of September, and the full moon was shedding her tranquil light on all the face of nature. The city was lying in its splendor and magnificence, surrounded by the broad stream of the Guadima. The palace was majestically towering in the midst of it and all its pillars and battlements in the calm light of the moon, as if they were transformed into silver by the touch of a fairy's wand.

O Donell stayed not long to contemplate this beautiful scene, but, descending the mountain, he soon crossed the fertile plain which led to the city. Entering the gates, he quickly arrived at the palace without speaking to anyone. He entered the palace by a secret way, and then, going up the flight of steps and crossing a long gallery, he arrived at the king's private apartment. The door was half open. He looked and beheld two very handsome young men sitting together and reading. He instantly recognized them and was going to step forward when the door opened and the great Duke entered.

O Donell could contain himself no longer but rushing in he threw himself at the feet of his Grace. "O Donell, is this you?" exclaimed the Duke.

"It is, my most noble master," answered O Donell, almost choking with joy. The young princes embraced him while he almost smothered them with caresses.

After a while they became tranquil, and then O Donell, at the request of the Duke, related all his adventures since he parted with them, not omitting the condition on which he was now in the palace. When he had ended, a loud voice was heard, saying that he was free from his promise and might spend the rest of his days in his native city.

Some time after this, as O Donell was walking in the streets, he met a gentleman who he thought he had seen before but could not recollect where or under what circumstances. After a little conversation, he discovered that he was Alexander Delancy, that he was now a rich merchant in the city of Paris and high in favor with the Emperor Napoleon. As may be supposed, they both were delighted at the discovery.

They ever after lived happily in their separate cities, and so ends my little tale.

C. Brontë August the 17
1829

FINIS

TULSA SNOW / *Edward Falco*

S HE SAID, "You have no character. I see right through you." She leaned across the table, closer to me, her eyes glittering a little, as if she had just told me I was cute.

I tried hard to appear amused. We were seated in a high-backed booth in a Tulsa, Oklahoma café. I hardly knew this woman. I had met her maybe an hour earlier in the airport coffee shop, where we were both killing time, drinking coffee, stranded by a snowstorm—and beyond the café's big plateglass windows, snow continued falling thick and slow, floating to the ground in big flakes that seemed almost to rock like little boats as they descended. I looked around the café, embarrassed by the turn in the conversation. There were five other people in the place. Three old guys with big guts and gray hair, in cowboy hats, were seated at one of the round tables in the center of the room. They were silent, looking down at their coffee cups. Behind the counter, a waitress in a black uniform with a white nametag pinned to her breast wiped a saucer with a dishrag. Behind her, the cook stood over the grill with his arms crossed, looking down at the metal surface as if something were cooking there, which nothing was. They were listening to us. They had been watching us and listening to us since we walked through the door. I said, "What do you mean I have no character? What kind of a thing is that to say?"

"The truth," she said. She pushed her hair back off her face. She had crimped blonde hair that fell over her forehead and cheeks. She was young, maybe twenty-five, twenty-six. I figured about ten years younger than me.

"Why is it the truth?"

"Why?"

"I mean," I said, "why do you think I have no character?"

"Just listen to yourself." She crossed her arms under her breasts and leaned back. She still had that bright look in her eyes that seemed to say she didn't really mean any harm: she was just noting something fascinating. "You're talking like me," she said. "You're picking up my inflections, my tone, even my mannerisms. You're a blank slate. It's as if you're turning into my image as I watch."

I laughed, but it was an obviously uncomfortable laugh. I thought about just getting up and walking out. Unfortunately, there was no place to go. We had taken a taxi from the airport, and I'd have to walk over to the phone, which was in plain view against the opposite wall, call a cab, and then wait. Meanwhile, the place was still as a closet. The cook was a big, heavy guy and you could hear him breathing. I said, "You're an interesting woman, Jessie. Here we were, talking amiably about things—and then suddenly: I have no character. Did I say something wrong?"

She looked at me a long moment, as if deciding how she should continue, as if measuring me and trying to determine what she could tell me and what she couldn't. At the airport, I had joined her at her table because she was pretty and seemed nice, an ordinary attractive blonde with crimped hair, wearing bright sneakers and blue jeans and a green suede shirt with the top two buttons open, looking dreamily out the window at falling snow. I knew myself to be a good-looking man. I had been told so all my life by women and by men. I was tall and muscular, with a squarish, rugged-looking face. I knew I could walk up to most unattached women and start up a conversation and my advances would be welcome. As a salesman, my looks were my chief asset, and for that reason I kept myself in good shape, working out an hour every day with weights, jogging two miles every morning.

From a distance, Jessie had seemed nice—attractive and nice. And she had acted that way too, sharing pleasant, friendly conversation with a stranger stuck in an airport during a snowstorm, though her eyes did seem to probe, and she had hesitated often before responding, as if feeling me out. Still, it had all been good until the character remark. There was something about her that I liked and I was hoping we might get back on that easy-going track. I sat quietly on my side of the table and watched her watching me. Finally, she said, "Didn't you ever meet someone and have the urge to tell the truth? I look at you and I see someone without any real identity beyond what can be absorbed from others. You're like a sponge, an absence waiting to be filled. You're—"

"Excuse me, Jessie," I said. "I'm not interested in this conversation." I picked up my coat from the bench and tried to take the bill off the table, but she pulled it away.

"On me," she said.

"No thank you," I said. "I'll buy my own breakfast." I went to the counter and paid for my meal. I wanted to strike up a conversation with the waitress, but she wouldn't meet my eyes. Nor would anyone else in the room. The cook was looking at the back wall, and the three cowboys were still staring at their coffee. I thought, "The hell with this," and went to the wall phone and dialed the airport taxi, only to find the taxis weren't running. Too much snow. I asked, "How am I supposed to get back to the airport?" and the voice on the other end suggested I should worry about how to get to a motel, since I was certainly going to be in Tulsa at least another twenty-four hours. "Oh, great," I said, and hung up. I looked toward the waitress. "No taxis," I said. "You allow camping here?"

One of the cowboys looked up from his coffee and tipped his hat in my direction. He said, "I'll give you a ride, Pardner. If you don't mind waiting till I finish my coffee."

My first thought was, given the rate at which he was drinking that coffee, waiting out the snowstorm might be the better bet. My second thought was that he really looked like an asshole in that cowboy hat. I said, "Thanks. That's very kind of you." And then, there I was, just as I had feared: standing next to the phone with my coat over my arm in a room that was like an empty stage—and I felt like I was on stage. I felt as though Jessie and I were actors in an impromptu theatrical production, and everyone was waiting for the climax. In a few seconds the silence grew overwhelming. I thought about joining the three cowboys, but that would have been like walking off the stage and taking a seat in the audience.

The quiet wasn't broken until Jessie shifted around in her booth. She turned to face me and stretched her legs out across the bench. She spoke as if I were still sitting across the table from her. "Tell me if I'm wrong," she said. "You had a parent who overwhelmed you as a child. Someone who crushed the character out of you."

The cowboys, the waitress, and the cook all looked at Jessie for a moment and then turned and looked at me. It was beginning to occur to me that I had found myself a genuine crazy woman. I thought, "The bitch, the cunt, she's a lunatic." I put my coat on, taking my time sliding my arms into the sleeves, and then crossed the room to Jessie, not really knowing what I was going to do until I did it. I walked to her table with my eyes on her eyes and I leaned into the booth and put my lips close to her ear. "Jessie," I whispered. "Fuck you." Then I walked out of the café and into the snow.

Except for a single pickup truck, the parking lot was empty. A couple of inches of snow had accumulated already, erasing the yellow lines that divided the blacktop surface into parking spaces. As I crossed the lot to the truck, flakes of snow stuck to my hair. I jammed my hands deep in the pockets of my overcoat and waited by the passenger door of the pickup, where I had a clear view of the interior of the café. After only a minute or two, the cowboy said a few words to his buddies and then picked up his coat and came out to give me a ride. Jessie had turned around in the booth again, and was sipping her coffee as she stared out the side window toward a snow-covered field. I yelled "Thanks! I really appreciate this!" before the cowboy even reached the truck. He nodded and climbed into the driver's seat, and I climbed in alongside him.

"Name's Bob," I said. "Bob Resttler."

He nodded, without looking at me. "Pleased to meet you, Pardner."

I said, "Do you believe that woman? I never met her before in my life." I made a face that I hoped suggested my amused disbelief at her behavior.

"Don't know her at all?"

"I don't know that woman from Adam. I met her an hour ago in the airport coffee shop."

He seemed to think about that a moment and then shook his head.

"Unbelievable, isn't it?"

"Well," he said. "Women . . ." And he shook his head again, as if sorry for the state of the world.

I thought he might say more, but that turned out to be it. For the whole ride. When I got out at the airport, I thanked him again. I said, "I really appreciate this, Pardner. Thanks again." I slammed the door and walked away, and it wasn't until I was inside the airport and approaching the airline counter that I realized I had said Pardner and that was why he had given me such a funny look right before I closed the door. He had sort of stopped midway in a nod and given me this strange look. I tried to laugh at myself—but someplace not very deep at all under the surface I was bothered. I said aloud, "Fuck him." Then added, "Fuck her, too."

Luckily, the airline people were friendly. They arranged a decent motel room for me and even found me a ride—and I know I should have been more appreciative, but I was in a seriously sour mood. I think I might have been able to just laugh the whole thing off if I hadn't called that cowboy Pardner, a word I had never in my whole life ever even considered using. By the time I got to my motel room, I was wondering about the things Jessie had said to me, how much truth there was to them. It was the case, I was willing to grant, that I had a tendency to pick up other people's speech patterns. Put me in Mississippi for a few days, and I'd be talking with a drawl. Put me in Vermont and I'd become taciturn. But so what? That didn't mean I didn't have any character. I was a salesman. I sold financial software to mid-size businesses. I had probably just learned to pick up local speech characteristics as a way of relating to people. Why did it have to mean anything bigger than that?

Still, by the time I got settled into my motel room, my sour mood had only deepened. I made a quick phone call to my parents' house and left a message on their machine, telling them not to worry, I was stuck in Tulsa. I'd give them a call tomorrow. I didn't give them the motel number because I knew my mother would call as soon as she got the message, wanting to be sure I hadn't really been in a plane crash and just wasn't telling her. Then my father would bitch at her for making a long distance call for no good reason, and when I got back he'd bitch at me for not calling, for only leaving a message, knowing my mother would then have to call back. I'd tell him she didn't have to call, and we'd be off, at each other's throats, same as always. My life was nothing if not predictable.

For a while after I hung up the phone, I sat on the edge of the bed and debated calling back and leaving my number so that my mother wouldn't worry—but eventually I decided against it. I had other plans, which didn't involve talking to her. I got up and pulled the curtains. I stopped up the bathtub drain and ran the water nice and hot, and then stripped out of my clothes and popped open my suitcase and pulled out a brand-new, unopened bottle of Jack Daniel's. I unwrapped a tumbler from the bathroom sink, filled it halfway, and slid my body down into the hot water. There. I was feeling better already. The hell with Jessie I-Have-No-Character. I was in a nice warm motel room with a bottle of whiskey and cable TV—and nobody calling to check and make sure I wasn't drinking. Life was just fine.

I settled back in the tub and lifted the tumbler of whiskey to my lips, savoring the sharp aroma of the bourbon—and just as I was about to take my first sip, someone knocked at the door. I pulled myself up out of the tub, wrapped a motel towel around my waist, and went to the window, where I peeked out through the curtains. It was Jessie. She was standing in the snow without a jacket. I opened the door a crack. "You'll freeze," I said.

She moved closer to the door in order to get a better look. "Got more clothes on than you."

"That's because I was in the bathtub. Did you come to apologize?"

"No, not really," she said. "I came to take you up on your invitation."

"What invitation?"

"Right before you left the restaurant. Wasn't that an invitation you whispered in my ear?"

"I said, 'fuck you.'"

She nodded and smiled. "I've been looking forward to it ever since."

I opened the door and let her in. She came into the room and looked over the matching beds and then up at the fake oil paintings centered over each headboard. They were both seashore paintings, copies of some French painter, people in old-fashioned bathing suits carrying umbrellas, a crowded beach. I hadn't noticed them until I saw her looking at them. "Well," she said. "Which bed?"

I said, "I've got a feeling I'll regret this."

Her eyes brightened. "You don't need to fear," she said. "I'm not crazy, I promise. I've never been your standard-issue human being, sure. But I'm not dangerous."

I said, "And I don't have any condoms."

She pulled a crushed box of condoms out of the pocket of her jeans. "I had the driver stop at a pharmacy on the way here. Haven't the airline people been really nice?"

"Amazingly so," I said. "Did they just direct you to my room?"

"Same guy drove me as drove you." She tossed the condoms onto the center nightstand, and then sat on the bed closest to the far wall. "This one okay?" she asked.

"Fine," I said.

"Good, then . . ." She unbuttoned her blouse and undid her belt buckle. "Do you like to watch?" She patted the edge of the second bed, across from where she sat.

"You're very attractive," I said. I sat across from her.

She yanked the bottom of her shirt out of her jeans, undid the cuffs, and took it off. "I should be," she said. She took a strand of her hair between her thumb and forefinger. "The crimp is artificial, of course. So is the color. I'm naturally a dingy shade of blonde, a sort of sandy blonde. No luster at all. But, for a significant amount of money and with bimonthly treatments, we get this: pretty, bright blonde hair."

"Very nice," I said. "It's worth it." She had me feeling good again, as she had when we first met. The stuff about my character was fading out of memory. I was beginning to concentrate on the fact that I had an attractive, entertaining woman in my motel room getting undressed for me.

She took off her bra. Her breasts were lovely. "You like them?" she asked.

"I adore them," I said. I reached across the space between us to touch them, letting the warm flesh rest in the palm of one hand while my thumb traced the circle of her nipple.

"Umm," she said. "But they're not real unfortunately. Saline implants."

"No kidding?" I squished a breast in my hand. "Feels real to me."

"That's what counts," she said. She leaned forward and kissed me on the bridge of my nose. She pointed to her own nose: "This isn't the original model either: resized and reshaped." She pointed to her green eyes, which were one of the first things I had noticed about her, how strikingly the green of her eyes picked up the green of her suede shirt. "Contact lenses," she said. "They're really brown."

"Your eyes are brown?"

"Brown," she said. "Plain old. See? I should be attractive. Look at all the effort." She summed up for me: "Dyed hair, colored contacts, breast implants, redone nose." She stood up and kicked off her shoes and then shimmied half way out of her pants and underwear before falling back on the bed, onto her elbows, smiling wickedly and putting her feet in my lap. I pulled her pants off the rest of the way and then climbed onto the bed with her. She kissed my chest, hungrily. I kissed her breasts. They felt great. They felt like real breasts. She pulled back the blankets and slid under. I joined her. "One other thing," she said. "Before we commence."

"What?" I was worked up and breathing hard. I had only one thing on my mind.

"Nothing," she said. She smiled revealing perfect teeth, white and straight—but she looked, somehow, worried suddenly. A little frightened. "Condom," she said. She handed me the box from the nightstand. "Can't forget."

There had been something in her look that worried me, though I couldn't place it. It felt as if she had started to tell me something and then changed her mind. I said, "I don't have any diseases. You don't either, do you?"

"No," she said. "I'm healthy." She pointed to the condom, and the casual, playful look returned to her face. "But you still have to wear it."

"Sure," I said. I put on the condom and we made love. It took me maybe at most a minute and half and then I was finished. This had happened to me before, more than once. It was one of the reasons I wasn't really all that into sex. I pulled myself away from her. "I'm sorry," I said. "I . . . I just."

"What is it?" she said. She touched my chest, her eyes alive again with that sparkle.

I looked around the dark room. The curtains were pulled and the lights were off. I was tempted to reach for the remote control, which was bolted to the nightstand, and see what was on the tube. I thought about my tumbler of bourbon on the rim of the bathtub. "Excuse me," I said, and I scurried out of the bed, the condom dangling from my dick like a misplaced elf's cap. I peeled it off in the bathroom, flushed it down the commode, and then fortified myself with a couple of solid swigs of bourbon before returning to the bed.

Jessie was sitting up, her back cushioned with pillows. Her knees were pulled up to her chest and her arms were wrapped around her legs. She said, "Want to see a picture of me?"

I pulled the covers to my neck and lay on my side, my head propped on my elbow. "Sure," I said.

She reached down between the beds and pulled a slim wallet out of the back pocket of her jeans. From the wallet, she carefully extracted a photograph and handed it to me.

"Who's this?" I said. I dropped the photo on the bed, as if I were worried about catching something from it.

"It's me," she said. Same smile. Same sparkle.

I picked up the photo again. The girl pictured in it was terribly ugly. She had the flat, dingy hair of the poor, and a hooked beak of a nose that was just plain unnaturally long. Without question, the longest nose I had ever seen. It looked like it had to be a gag: a fake nose stuck on top of the real one. It made her look freakishly ugly.

Amazingly, that wasn't the worst feature of the girl's face. The worst feature was her teeth, which were gnarled and twisted in what appeared to be double rows. She looked like she had two rows of teeth and they were all fighting with each other for some space to grow. A couple of the teeth stuck out almost horizontally, useless and freakish. Several of the teeth were discolored and appeared to be rotting. "This is you?" I said. "Was you?"

"It's still me," she said. "Only with the benefit of cosmetic science and a lot of money."

I looked at the photo again. I studied it. It made me feel weird to think that this might really be the same woman I had just had sex with. "I don't believe you," I said. I tossed the photo to her. "Who are you? You are crazy, aren't you?"

She didn't answer for a moment. She watched me with that searching-out look again.

I said, "I just hope you're not dangerous."

That made her laugh. "Why don't you believe it's me?"

"Because!" I said. "Look at this!" I snatched the photo up off the bed. "Look at this girl's teeth!"

"Ah," she said. "Teeth." She smiled brightly, showing off her perfect teeth—and then she blew up her cheeks and made an odd motion with her jaw and she pulled her teeth out of her mouth with her thumb and forefinger. She placed the teeth on the nightstand beside her.

I got out of the bed. I stepped back, away from her.

"Teeth," she said, sounding suddenly like an old woman.

"Put them back in," I said. "Please." I turned my back to her.

"They're back in," she said, her voice normal again. "Turn around. Look at me."

When I turned around, she was posing. A sultry look about her face, a corner of the sheet held sexily to her breasts, hiding just enough to emphasize her beauty.

I touched my fingers to my forehead. "I'm feeling a little dizzy," I said. I sat down on the edge of the bed and dropped my head between my knees.

She knelt behind me and rubbed my back. "The teeth," she said. "They're a shocker, no?"

"Slightly," I said.

She leaned over me, shaping her body to mine, holding me in her arms. She kissed the back of my neck. She said, "Do you not find me attractive now . . . because of the teeth? Because you know how I used to look?"

"No," I said. "It's not that. But it is . . . disorienting."

"I can understand that," she said. She nuzzled against me. Her cheek was warm against the back of my neck.

We were both quiet for a while, me with my head between my legs and her with her body wrapped around me. For a while I kept seeing in my mind that picture of her looking so ugly, and then I kept going over the pure weirdness of seeing a young, attractive woman reach into her mouth and pull out her teeth and place them on a nightstand. Her body felt good against my body, and I knew if I turned around I'd see a beautiful young woman—and one generous enough to not make a big deal out of my pathetic sexual performance—but I was having trouble getting past the picture and the teeth. It was as if, somehow, she wasn't really who she appeared to be. I saw an attractive young woman—but it felt as if that were a mask, as if it weren't real. I tried to think of something to say, but no words came. Then she pulled away from me, and when I sat up and turned around I saw her peek out the curtains and then pull them open, filling the room with daylight. When she turned around she appeared solemn. She said, "Do you want me to leave now?"

Beyond the window, the snow was falling thick as fog. A moment earlier, I think I would have asked her to leave. But seeing her standing there by the window, her body so lovely, her face so attractive, I didn't want her to leave. "Not if you don't want to," I said.

She said, "I don't want to," and came and got into bed with me again.

I leaned back against the headboard and put my arm around her shoulder, and she laid her head against my chest. I said, "How come you showed me that picture? I mean . . . Why?"

"Because," she whispered. "I don't know. I just wanted to tell you. I don't really know why."

"You don't know?"

"Not really."

"Not really?"

She looked up at me, amused. Then I heard myself say, "I'm an alcoholic."

She said, "I'm not surprised. I figured something like that."

I didn't say anything right away. If she wasn't surprised, I was. I had never said those three words out loud.

Jessie turned her body toward mine and nuzzled up against me. "Do you mind if I go to sleep?" she said. "I'm deliciously tired."

I stroked her forehead. "But I'm curious about you," I said. "I want to know how . . ."

"We'll talk about it later," she said. "We'll go into details. Both of us. I'll tell you all about my transformation." She turned away and snuggled up with a pillow, and I watched her face relax and her eyes begin to move around under her closed eyelids. I kissed her on the shoulder, and then I went to the window and stood in front of it and watched the snow fall for a long time. In my head, there were words floating: transformation, Tulsa, *snow* . . . I could see the parking lot and a sloping hill and then beyond that the highway and a long line of trees—and all of it, except for the trunks of the trees, was covered with snow. Then, when I turned around and looked at the room again, everything was different. The colors, the textures . . . everything. It was as if something inside the substances of the room had been altered and now all the surfaces looked different. It was very strange. I kept staring at everything: the soft brown wood of the headboards, the blue cotton fabric of the blankets, the white sheets—and the surfaces seemed almost to glow. The colors appeared to pulse and shimmer. It was beautiful, but it was also frightening. I had no idea what was going on with me. Not really. I went to the big mirror over the bathroom sink and looked at myself. At first nothing seemed different. It was still me. Just me. Same muscular, healthy body. Same rugged looks. I stared at my own eyes staring back at myself and then I guess because I was staring so intensely, the room disappeared out of the background. I gazed into the mirror and it was just my body, with a kind of light around me, as if I were floating. I closed my eyes. I extended my arms and tilted my head down, and then I felt as though I were plummeting, flying. For a few moments it was as if I had no body at all. What I sensed, it was ominous. I was a dark spirit, dense and hard, rock-like, but soaring like a crow, gliding though a pitch-black place, looking for something . . . like hunting, like I was hunting.

When I opened my eyes again, everything was back to normal. I lay beside Jessie on the motel's mattress as if I were climbing into my own bed. I pressed against her. "Jessie?" I said, even though I knew she was sleeping. I looked at her face and tried to imagine under her attractive features the old face with the twisted teeth and a beak for a nose. I touched my face to her breasts and closed my eyes, and I settled toward sleep thinking not about Jessie, or how she had once looked so different, but about myself, my life, what there was of it, and just before I fell asleep that sense of being a small dark spirit returned, something hunting and angry. I lifted Jessie's arm from where it lay at her side and draped it over my shoulder. I pressed closer to her, pushing my body into hers, anxious to join her in her sleep and inexplicably grateful to be lying next to her in bed, in a Tulsa motel, with snow falling beyond the window.

Edward Falco's most recent book is *A Dream with Demons.*

"It must be a problem of interpretation. I've read this book dozens of times, and I keep winding up here!"

HER NEW LAST NAME/*Franklin Fisher*

1

NELL SLEEPS with her hand on her mother's breast until Mrs. Pope comes in, carrying chickens to pluck. Nell is put outside. She hears the door close behind her, and feels the wind warm on her back.

The wind whistles in the trees. Children down in the haystack yard climb the shed and jump into the haystack and vanish. A big boy tosses a little girl into the hay and she vanishes. Nell catches her dress on the barbs and the big boy comes and untangles her and throws her into the haystack, where she vanishes.

Her brothers have typhoid fever. Nell carries their food to them from the kitchen and eats what they leave on their plates.

Nell may die. Dr. Brownfield pulls up her nightgown, places a hand on her belly. She pushes his hand away.

Her brother Dave will give her marbles if he can cut her hair. She keeps her eyes closed and drifts inside her fever but holds the marbles tight in her hand as she feels the hair drop from one side of her head, then the other, and gather on the cot under her neck.

For a long time she is pulled everywhere in the little red wagon by her mother. Her mother takes her everywhere she goes. She is with her mother all the time.

She kneels in the potato cellar while her brothers pour potatoes down onto her from the kitchen floor. Her job is to push the potatoes aside as they pour in, to make room for more. Stink bugs crawl over her hands as she pushes the potatoes. Potatoes pour in so fast she is afraid of being smothered. They cover her thighs as she squats there; they strike her arms and shoulders.

2

A man the others call George sits at the table and rocks it back and forth on his knees while everyone laughs. He breaks his potatoes open with his fingers. When he comes again Nell runs to her mother in the kitchen and whispers: That big man who makes the table go back and forth is in the house.

That's your brother, her mother says.

Nell goes back and watches him from the doorway until her mother tells her to move.

A dark-haired man with a careless smile stays with them for a month. Nell falls in love with his teeth. She follows him around the house and into the yard, and would follow him into town if he didn't reach down from his horse and pick her up and carry her back to the yard. She learns his name is Gil and he's her brother too, but he has a different mother and she's dead. In the evening he plays I see you, I see you, hiding behind that chair for Nell on his harmonica while she peeks out and ducks her head again, dissolving in love for Gil. When he leaves he lifts her up for a kiss and tells her when he's a millionaire he'll buy her a silk dress.

An angry man her mother's age comes to town once and disappears with her father for the afternoon. Her sister Phebe tells her he is their brother Moroni, who hates their mother.

On Decoration Day they go into the fields and gather Johnny-jump-ups. The boys and men gather the lilies that cover Lily Hill and put bands of them around their hats.

3

From the back yard she hears Doc Pope swearing, and she knows his chickens have flown over the fence into his vegetable garden again, and he is throwing rocks at them.

Bishop's going to excommunicate you for swearing, Doc, a man Nell can't see says.

Anybody says I swear's a damn liar, Doc says.

Her mother visits Doc Pope at home, taking Nell. His house is a one-room cabin with a dirt roof. Inside, near the door, is a cobbler's bench. Old shoes and pieces of leather lie scattered on the floor. His bed is in a corner; his table with a chair in front of it is in the middle of the floor. A small stove stands against the wall with his coal bucket beside it.

Is there anything they can do for him, Nell's mother asks.

He don't need anything, he guesses. Thanks though.

He chops up potatoes in his frying pan while they watch, and sets the pan on the stove. When the potatoes become brown on the bottom he turns them onto his plate, brown side up, and eats them with a fork and a spoon, using the fork to hold them down and the spoon to tear them apart. When he finishes eating he turns the plate upside down on his table.

Would you like me to wash that for you, Brother Pope? Nell's mother asks.

I know what was in it, he says.

Doc Pope takes his eggs to the store and trades them for tobacco, shoes, collars, newspapers, magazines. He sends away for things he sees advertised, mostly pills and tonics, then peddles them in town. He goes door to door, beginning with Nell's mother's house.

Her mother sends Nell and her sisters over the fence into Doc Pope's vegetable garden to gather pig-weed. While they are there they eat his green peas, turnips, rutabagas and pie plant.

4

Her father cuts the ends off his eggs, gives one end to Dave, one to Nell. After breakfast she hears him outside, hammering nails into the cedar posts that hold up the barbed wire fence that surrounds the house. He's building cabinets for the hotel and doesn't want strangers walking into his yard while he works. In the afternoon it rains and he brings his sawhorses, saws and planes and other tools into the house. The shavings come off in ringlets as he works and Nell fastens them in her hair. After dinner he sits in a kitchen chair and tips it back against the wall, so it stands on two legs. She watches him to see if he will fall. He reads his paper, and when the children become noisy he looks at them over the top of his spectacles and they go silent.

They park the wagon in the woods across the road from the lake, and her father hangs up a mirror on the tree and shaves his throat, leaving his white beard sloppy with soap. They sleep in a tent, and in the morning run across the road and down to the lakeshore. They crawl under the upside-down boat on the sand and play babies and mothers. Nell swims in the lake with her sister Ruth, and feels her feet pass through a warm current. Her brother Dave, who can't swim, sits on the white-coated rocks and howls that he sees the monster coming up behind them. An animal with a head like a horse and a body like an alligator lives in Bear Lake and pulls people down to the bottom and eats them alive.

Her father is sick, but gets better. In April he dresses and goes outside. When he is in bed again, sicker than before, the doctor tells them he's got a pleurisy. Her mother and the neighbors fix Denver mud plasters to put on his chest. Nell likes the smell. They spread it on a piece of flannel like you would spread peanut butter on bread. In bed her father asks her mother to send Nell to him. Nell is shy, tries to pull away when he wants to kiss her. She and the other children stay all night with neighbors. In the morning they come home, where someone tells them that Pa is dead. There are lots of people around, and they hand her from one to the other and say, This is John's baby.

She wakes in Aunt Sarah Calder's house at Bear Lake, and no one is there. She doesn't hear any sounds anyplace and she peeks through the window and there is nobody outside the house either and she knows she has been left. Then she hears voices and runs to the back of the house. They are all there, picking raspberries early in the morning, before the sun is up.

5

Her mother, pregnant, cooks for the field hands and cowboys at the Jackson ranch north of town. Nell goes with her. One of the Jackson sons comes to the house before noon and stands around while Nell's mother turns the beans in the iron pot with a wooden spoon. He crumples his hat in his hands and puts it back on his head. Nell's mother tells him to bring her some apples from the root cellar if he hasn't got anything to do. The root cellar is away from the house, concealed by trees. Nell wants to go too.

Take her, her mother says.

Nell runs to catch up with him. At the steps he turns.

Want to come down? he asks. She remembers the stink bugs in the potato cellar and shakes her head. He goes down the steps to the cellar door and disappears inside. She sits on the top step. When he comes out he's holding a sack. When the sack moves he looks like her brother Marion when he pees in the haystack yard.

Know what I got? he asks.

Apples, she says.

He reaches under her dress and pulls her underpants, which are buttoned to her shirt. After a while he stops pulling and grins at her. He takes his hat off and wipes the side of his head with his arm. Nell runs ahead of him back to the house where her mother and the other men are waiting. She goes to a corner of the dining room and stands there while he comes in and hands her mother the bag of apples. He looks at her standing in the corner.

All the little girls in her book wear sunbonnets, hiding their faces. Nell lays her head down on the book and tries to see under their bonnets.

To punish students Miss Woolley makes a girl sit with a boy, or a boy with a girl. Nell has talked while Miss Woolley was writing the figure 4 on the board, and has to sit with one of the Henderson boys. The Henderson boy is not quite right. He's too big to be in her grade, and she cries in the double seat, pulling as far away from him as she can so their arms don't touch.

Her mother has the baby after Thanksgiving, and it dies on Christmas Eve. Nell is still the baby.

While her mother scrubs the scats and benches and floors in the schoolhouse, Nell draws angels on the blackboards her mother hasn't gotten to yet.

Her mother cleans houses and washes people's clothes. Doc Pope sits in a chair beside the machine and turns the wheel until he nods asleep, his hand still on the handle. I'll do it, Brother Pope, Nell's mother says, touching his hand. He jerks awake, throws her hand off, and turns the wheel furiously.

Doc Pope lives with them because he is sick. She lies awake and hears him coughing somewhere in the house, and in the morning sees bloody phlegm on the snow outside the kitchen door where it has frozen into terrible scabs.

Charley Pope comes to town to visit his sick father in Nell's mother's house. Charley is a sheep shearer; no one knows what he does when it's not shearing season. After Doc Pope dies Charley comes to town anyway. He stays in his father's cabin and comes through the fence and drinks coffee in Nell's mother's kitchen. He nails tin across the hole in her house that mice get in through. He puts up shelves in her ice house. He brings candy and takes Nell's mother to dances at Bear Lake. Nell is frightened when she and Dave are left alone in the house at night. She asks Dave to sleep in her room. Dave steals cigarettes from Charley's sack and smokes them in Nell's room before he takes off his shoes and stretches across the foot of her bed with his clothes on. Her mother marries Charley.

6

Brother Passey drives Nell and her mother home from cleaning his house. From the back of the wagon Nell sees a haystack moving along the lane from her mother's field. Her mother puts a hand on Brother Passey's arm and he stops. She climbs down and stands where the lane from her field enters the road. Nell climbs down too and stands with her mother. The man driving the wagon full of her hay stops when he reaches them. Brother Passey says goodbye and drives on.

I just paid Charley cash for the load, the man says.

It wasn't Charley's hay, Nell's mother says. And it isn't your hay now. And I don't expect I know you.

They see Charley, a long way off, standing in the field, watching them come. Charley and the man unload the hay without talking. Charley takes out his wallet, counts out the bills, puts them in the man's hand. The three of them watch the man turn his empty wagon around and head back out to the road.

Can I have some money, Mary Ann? Charley asks.

Nell cries over her arithmetic at the kitchen table because she doesn't understand arithmetic. Her mother is out of the house. Charley gets up from the sofa and pulls a chair over to the table and sits beside her. Let me help you, he says. He takes her pencil and subtracts a large number from a small one, explaining that he is taking away from the number next to the small one. He crosses out the neighboring number and writes a lesser number, in a tiny hand, above it, and puts a tiny number one beside the small number he is to subtract a larger number from. Nell stops bawling and watches the pencil move. Understand? Charley asks. She nods. She does not understand. Go ahead and do it, then, he says. He hands her the pencil and gets up. The paper is wet where his hand has been on it.

Brother Snowball calls her Nellie Pope when she goes to play at Elva's house.

My name is Nellie Smith, she says.

Your mother is married to Charley Pope, he says. That makes you Nellie Pope.

Her mother has a miscarriage. In the afternoon Nell sees Charley a long way off crossing the field on his horse leading another horse with two small girls on it. They're coming toward the house. From the corral Nell watches him lift the girls down in the dooryard and take them into the house. When she goes in she finds them sitting on a bench outside the pantry eating pie plant. Her mother and Charley are in the bedroom where she hears their voices sounding tight and angry. Before supper Charley's brother's wife comes to the house and takes one of the girls away. The one that is left cries under the stairs.

The girl in Nell's house eats with her fingers and smells bad, even after a bath. She backs away and hides in a corner if you walk into the room and she thinks you are going to speak to her. Her name is Blanca, but Nell's mother won't have that name in the house.

If she stays, her name is Blanche, she tells Charley.

Nell follows Blanche around to look at her because she has never seen anyone who looks like that. Dave follows her singing a song he has made up: Blanche Pope, without any hope.

Small things in the house disappear, a penny, a sliver of soap, half of one of Nell's broken marbles. Nell sees Blanche lying under the lilacs eating dirt. After a while Blanche is not in the house any more. Nell asks her mother where she is. She expects Blanche has gone home, her mother tells her.

Her mother goes with Dr. Reay whenever a baby is born in Randolph. She takes care of the mother and the baby.

7

Her mother is hanging the wash. Nell crouches under the steps with her hands over her ears and listens as Olaf Larsen makes her mother cry. Did Mary Ann know her son Joe left the gate open between their properties again last night? Did she know her son Dave has gotten into her shitass husband's cigarettes and liquor again and started a fire in Olaf's privy? When her husband went off to whores in Evanston and came back drunk and bloody in the middle of the day how did she think that looked to Olaf's children?

Nell's mother hangs her laundry and does not look at Olaf, so he can't see that her eyes are wet.

He sees that boy of hers smoking cigarettes on his property again, that boy's going to get the shit beat right out of him, Olaf says and rides away.

I seen Olaf beat his own horse nearly to death once, Uncle Ike tells Nell and her mother. Never seen a man that mad. Uncle Ike is Nell's dead father's brother.

At church Uncle Ike tells Olaf to go easy on Mary Ann. She hasn't got an easy row to hoe.

You doing the widow's business? Olaf asks Uncle Ike.

She's not a widow, Uncle Ike says.

Be better off if she was, Olaf says.

The next time Olaf rides to the house Nell runs to town and collapses, panting, in Uncle Ike's store. He gives her a phosphate and says he'll see about Olaf being mean to her mother.

At the next conference one of the apostles comes up from Salt Lake and Olaf is made bishop in Randolph. Uncle Ike expects he was wrong about Olaf.

8

Nell visits her sister Phebe at the ranch at Argyle, south of town, where the converts from Scotland have settled. Phebe's husband comes into Nell's room at night and reaches down the back of her nightgown as she lies curled in her bed and cups his hand against her hinder.

Nobody'll know, he says.

In the morning she watches Charley and the other shearers strip the wool from the struggling sheep; it drops to the ground and piles like nasty foam.

She sleeps at her best friend Clea's house. Clea lights a candle and reads under the blanket, holding the blanket away from the flame with her elbow. Her mother opens the door.

Put out that candle.

Through her eyelids Nell sees the light go out. She hears the door close and opens her eyes. She watches Clea light the candle and disappear under the blanket again. The door slams against the wall and Clea's mother is in the room pulling Clea from bed by the hair. The blanket is on the floor; Nell sees the candle, dead, spin and strike the headboard and drop onto a pillow. Clea screams, and her mother slaps her.

In the morning Clea says: I'll show you something. She takes Nell into her mother's bedroom and shows her some bloody rags. Nell does not know what they are.

When it happens to her, her mother starts to tell her about it.

Clea already told me, Nell says.

All right, her mother says.

Nell is standing behind her mother when the principal makes his visit. The principal is new; the state board has sent him up from Salt Lake City.

The teachers are putting on a melodrama, he tells her mother. Some of the good students will get to participate as well. We'd like Nell to be in it. Would that be all right with you?

My Nell? her mother says.

You'll be the heroine, he says to Nell. I'll have to kiss you. Will that be all right?

All right, Nell says.

9

In the fall the canal overflows onto the meadows, and when it freezes over they skate for miles. They are all friends: her brother

Dave; his best pal Jack Pierce, who doesn't have a girlfriend; Clifford Nichols, who doesn't have a girlfriend either; Otto McKinnon, who is Nell's boyfriend. After skating they go to Otto's house, where his mother has taken a batch of bread out of the oven. The oven door is down, and they all try to get their feet in the oven. Otto's mother breaks the loaves up and puts butter and honey on the hot, exposed bread, and passes it among them. They go sleigh riding in the afternoon and stay all night at Otto's house. Nell and Otto snuggle all night in a rocking chair.

She goes on a picnic with her best friend Eleeda's family. Eleeda's father is sheriff of Rich County and keeps a pistol in his car. He catches frogs out of the pond in the gravel pit, and tears off their legs on the grass. Nell watches him skin the legs and spit them on sharpened twigs over the fire. Everyone eats them, crisp and dripping, directly off the twigs except Nell, who gives hers to Eleeda.

When Eleeda's father is at the jail, Nell and Eleeda go into his office in the house and look at the pictures of men wanted for rape. Neither knows what rape is. They ask Eleeda's mother, who tells them to do their homework.

Her brothers Joe and Gil enlist when a recruiter comes to town. Dave wants to enlist, but his mother says he may not. He tells Nell he feels like a slacker.

Her mother moves uptown and manages the hotel, a big brick house beside the furniture store, with a widow's walk and an iron fence. Nell, Ruth, and Dave live there with her. Charley lives there too, but he is not around much. Sometimes they find him in bed in one of the empty rooms, his head lying in vomitus. Nell and Ruth share the cleaning. It's their job to bring the chamber pots out of each room in the morning and carry them outside to empty and clean with rags. Nell thinks one of the renters is sweet on her. He lives there all year and runs the dry-goods store. He's a handsome man, and he makes good money, but Nell has to empty his chamber pot and cannot think of him without revulsion.

Most of their guests are salesmen. They come through town selling saucepans, brooms, clothes from Paris, medicine, violins. A company of Hawaiians comes to town and performs at the bowery with their grass skirts and headdresses and little guitars. They stay at the hotel two nights. One of the Hawaiian men, wearing bib overalls to breakfast, asks Nell: What's a big girl like you doing in school?

Otto is stationed in New York. Nell writes to him every day and lets her tears fall on the paper.

Soldiers are billeted at the hotel. Charley brings Nell's mother a petition to sign.

It tells the War Office I'm helping you run the hotel.

Nell's mother is scrubbing walls in the back parlor while Nell sits on the piano bench and braids muslin for trim on the pillow shams.

I got a son and a stepson in France already, Nell's mother says, not looking at Charley.

I know that, Mary Ann, Charley says.

I got another son called as soon as his grain is in the sacks, Nell's mother says.

When Nell looks up her mother has started on the next wall and Charley isn't standing there any more. His petition is on the table. When she goes to get towels out of the closet in her mother's and Charley's bedroom she sees his razor gone and the mattress cut up and the stuffing falling out.

10

Her brother Joe comes home with a story about getting a shave and a haircut from a frightened little German barber who it turned out didn't know the war was over and thought he was shaving an enemy.

Her brother Gil was on a munitions train that was hit. They couldn't find enough to bury.

Otto is home from France. They sit in the rocker and cuddle and Nell coaxes him to give her back the letters she wrote to him in the army.

Hell no, he says. They made him happy and he's not about to give them back. He plans on reading them at least once every year.

Of course he wants to read them again and again, she says. She just wants to interleave her letters with his in an album. Wouldn't it be sweet to have them all together, hers and his, in an album that'd be just theirs and that she'd tie up with a ribbon, and they'd sit together and read them again and again forever?

He gets up out of the rocker and comes back with a tin box.

Just don't take too long putting that album together, he says.

They cuddle some more and then he takes her home. In the morning she burns all the letters in the fireplace in the front parlor.

Otto goes to work at his brother's ranch near Price.

Her brother Joe wraps his woolen army leggings around her legs and goes back to bed. Outside, the light is blue. Her dog, a gift from a boyfriend, tears ahead of her through the snow along Main Street and waits, panting and shivering, till she catches up with him at the cafe, then turns and bounds up the covered stairs. Nell feels her way up the stairs, holding tightly to the rail and unlocks the door to the telephone office. She hears her dog's toenails across the room and waves her hand till she finds the light hanging from the ceiling. She empties the ashes from the coal stove in the center of the room and builds a fire. She drinks the coffee, now cold, that she has brought with her in a preserve jar, and when the fire is well started she sits in the hard wooden chair in front of the switchboard. She listens to Edna Rex tell Elaine Kimball in Woodruff that Jane might be going to have a baby. She learns that Hank Rowberry may buy that little ranch outside Almy.

Nell dances at Bear Lake with boys back from the front, but only the ones who have cars. Boys from the ranches pull their wagons under the willows, and go in to look for girls from neighboring ranches. Young men from Garden City and Montpelier sit in open cars outside the dance hall passing a bottle around and smoking cigarettes, waiting for girls to come out. One of them takes Nell around to the pier side to look at the moon on the water. She turns her face away when he bends to kiss her, so he kisses her on the neck, below her ear. She turns and kisses him furiously, and then breaks away, sobbing. She waits till she hears his footsteps on the planks behind her before she buries her face in her hands. She feels his hands on her shoulders and the scrape of his jaw against her cheek. I have a boyfriend, she says. So what, the young man says.

Otto sends her a ticket to come to Price. She sees him waiting on the platform while she's still in her seat and concludes he looks ignorant since moving to Price. She lets him kiss her when she climbs down from the train and hold her elbow with one hand as he hefts her suitcase with the other to his car, which he has been burning to show her. The ground beside the tracks is heavy with coal dust and she tries to keep her shoulders from touching the people heading for the platform because she's afraid of being smeared. Otto points out groups of Greeks and Chinamen on the sidewalks and tells her there are niggers here too but you mostly don't see them on the streets. Nell has never seen a colored person and is afraid one might come up behind her as she stands at the hotel desk while Otto pays the clerk and holds out his hand for the key.

At supper, Otto's brother's wife nudges Nell under the table and when Nell looks at her pulls down the flesh under one eye. Nell sees something white and squirming but looks away.

Nell sits on the bed in her hotel room and Otto sits in the chair by the window and asks her if she likes Price and does she think she'd like living there. Price is too far away, she says. His brother's wife doesn't like her, she adds.

In Randolph, Eleeda and Clyde and Brother Snowball ask her if she got married to Otto while she was in Price. She says yes.

Otto comes to Randolph and sits in the front parlor of the hotel and asks her to marry him. She says no.

Guess you've thought about this, Otto says.

In the pale light from the fireplace she can see his eyes are wet.

Guess there's somebody else, he says.

Maybe not, she says.

Maybe you want him like I want you, Otto says. And maybe he don't want you.

I won't cry about it if he doesn't, she says.

On the Fourth of July the famous Walton Band from Woodruff plays in the Randolph town square. Nell watches Arthur, who plays the trombone and who she thinks is looking at her when she looks away. Arthur's father plays the banjo, rocking back and forth on his chair with his eyes closed. Arthur's sister plays the upright piano that some of the men wheeled out of the social hall and pulled to the square on a cart. An older brother plays the clarinet and two smaller children, a boy and a girl, play spoons. An Indian that lives with the family plays the fiddle and sometimes sings, and a man Nell doesn't know plays the bull fiddle. They play "Hindoostan" and "The Transatlantic Cable Rag," and some patriotic songs Nell isn't interested in. When the band quits Arthur makes his way over to Nell. She stands with her back against the flagpole, her hands behind her, one knee bent.

Dave's sister, isn't it? he asks.

Maybe, she says.

She follows him away from the people at the picnic tables to his motorcycle chained to a fencepost and enjoys the feel of his hand on her elbow as he helps her into the sidecar. On the road to Crawford

Mountain she feels her hair lash her neck, and sings "Hinnnn-do staaaan" at the top of her voice. The wind cuts her across the eyes and she pounds Arthur on the shoulder and peers at him through her fingers. He stops on the bridge, digs out a handkerchief and dabs her eyes. Here, he says, and takes off his goggles. He puts them on her face, pulling her hair out of the way. She wants his fingers to stay on her face.

She hears his motorcycle in the street and prepares to look composed. When he flings open the door she pays no attention. Her dog dances on its hind legs all around Arthur. She connects Lafe Pierce's line to Nelda Lamont's beauty shop and turns around to see Arthur kneeling on the floor ruffling her dog's ears. She cannot go to dances at Bear Lake with him in a motorcycle sidecar, she says. It makes her feel foolish. He sits back on his heels and makes kissing sounds at the dog, who tries to lick his mouth. He'll see what he can do, Arthur says.

Their favorite number is "It's Three O'Clock in the Morning."

While they dance Arthur holds her so tightly she gets a stomachache; he sings in her ear, and Nell feels the blood leave her head. On the drive back to Randolph she makes him stop the car and gets out because she needs to fart and doesn't want him to know. She wanders from the car, pretending to look for the moon.

Are they having a fight? Arthur calls.

She's in love, she calls back, she needs to be alone a minute.

In love? Arthur says.

Arthur's sister is having an illegitimate baby and the famous Walton band is breaking up. Arthur's brother has gone to California, taking his clarinet. He writes inviting Arthur to join him for the winter. He hasn't found work himself yet but he's sure that the two of them can make money together playing at the hotels. Nell cries, but Arthur tells her he'll write every day and come back in the spring loaded with dough. Wouldn't she like to be married to a rich musician and live in California?

Arthur can't come to Randolph to see her every day because he has to earn every penny he can at the Woodruff Mercantile where he works so he'll have enough to get to Los Angeles and live on until he and his brother start clicking. They surely are burning the telephone wires between the Mercantile and the phone company, though, aren't they, she says. They surely are, Arthur says, his voice flattened out and abstract in her headphones.

The day before he is to leave he tells her he can't come up to Randolph to see her and say goodbye; he has to be with his sister, who is in a bad way. He'll write every day from Los Angeles. That night Nell hears the Walton phone ring and plugs in her jack to listen. She knows the woman: she is principal of the Woodruff school.

You have to take me to Salt Lake tomorrow morning, the woman says. I have to go to the capitol. It's school business.

I'm not sure my car can make it, Arthur says. The choke isn't working right. It may break down.

I have to go to Salt Lake, Arthur, she says.

In a week Nell gets a letter from Arthur, postmarked Salt Lake. There is no return address. He asks her not to hate him. He's sorry all this happened.

Fletch Wilson takes her on a picnic in his car, which is swankier than Arthur's car was, with red leather upholstery and a chrome-plated horn. They sit huddled in blankets at the Monte Cristo summit and eat frogs' legs and biscuits. He takes her to a melodrama in Evanston and watches her during the performance so he will know what jokes she thinks are funny.

He takes her to a dance at Bear Lake, where he doesn't dance as well as Arthur did, and furthermore pinches her on the back. Don't do that. I don't like it, she says. His hand goes inert against her waist and he hums with the music. Soon, though, she feels his hand become restless, creep up her spine. In an instant he has pinched her on the shoulder blade and she has grabbed him by the hair and pulled so hard she feels it give in her hands. People stop dancing and watch.

Christ, you didn't have to do that, he says when she lets go. His eyes are streaming.

She hits his chest and face with her fists while he backs away. She is shaking with rage. She feels herself become lyrical. You wouldn't leave me alone when I told you a hundred times to stop it.

People look away and start dancing again.

11

They're all driving to Salt Lake City, where Nell has never been, to see Lillian Gish in "Orphans of the Storm." They will stay overnight at a rooming house near the theater and come back in time for church on Sunday. Nell has not mentioned this to her mother.

Nell hears the cars pull up and runs downstairs, carrying her bag. Her mother turns from soaping the front parlor window, the dripping cloth still in her hand.

We're going to see Lillian Gish, she says. In Salt Lake. I guess I forgot to tell you.

The parlor door opens and Eugene and Eleeda and Tom and Tom's brother and Edna and the other friends come in, hilariously. Tom kisses Nell's mother on the cheek. Edna grabs Nell's hands and dances her in a circle. Nell's boyfriend Eugene takes her bag to carry it for her.

Nell's not going, her mother says.

The friends stand and look at each other. Nell takes off her coat. Her mother soaks the wet cloth in the basin of soapy water and soaps the next pane in the window. The friends go out the door and Eugene pulls it shut behind him.

Nell's sister Ruth has a friend, also named Ruth, who goes to Salt Lake often, and knows about things. There is a sewing school, she tells Nell, run by a French lady, where you can learn to make clothes like they wear in New York and San Francisco. Nell tells her mother she wants to go to sewing school in Salt Lake City because when she is married and has children she will need to know how to make clothes for them. Her mother thinks it's a fine idea. They'll find a place and live together.

The sewing school is upstairs in a tall house near the Catholic cathedral. The teacher is a small wrinkled woman who cannot pronounce the sound "th," and wears bright clothes. Nell likes to listen to her speak and watch her quick, darting movements as she goes from girl to girl at the sewing machines or the dress dummies. Nell makes a skirt out of a green print fabric and the teacher praises her in front of the other girls.

They live in a rooming house, and Nell's mother makes pies at a private school for girls.

When her sister Ruth visits they rent bathing suits and swim in the hot springs plunge near the capitol. The suits come to their knees, and they pin the front of their long black stockings to the legs of the swim suit, so the backs of their knees are bare. Nell comes up from the bottom of the pool to find one leg bare; the safety pin has torn through. They hunt for the stocking at the bottom of the pool but never find it. Nell wants to get out and go home. Ruth says, Take the other one off and nobody will notice. If they do they won't give a damn. Nell takes the other stocking off and they swim the rest of the day. She feels naked and pretty.

12

Her best friend from the sewing school, Leone, comes to Randolph for the summer to visit Nell. They watch the street from the upstairs window of the telephone office and wave at Henry Crosby and Glen Mitchell who run the ice cream parlor. Henry and Glen give them dishes of ice cream free, with molasses poured over it and a raspberry from Bear Lake stuck on top like a nipple. Sometimes Nell's brother Joe goes with them and pays for Leone's ice cream.

Nell has not had a boyfriend for a long time. When Henry asks her out she goes with him but doesn't like the way he talks only about himself.

Joe and Leone drive to Logan to be married in the temple, and they all drive to Bear Lake for the honeymoon. They have dinner at the resort and at bedtime go to their cabins. Nell and Ruth and their mother take the cabin with curtains on the window; Henry shares a cabin with one of Nell's brothers from Evanston. In the night Nell has stomach cramps and runs outside to the privy. On her way back she passes Ruth in the dark. Ruth is holding her nightgown tightly around her and swearing softly as she runs. All night Nell hears cabin doors slam and the sounds of scrambling along the path to the privy. In the morning Leone comes to Nell, shyly.

Were you paying your dues last night too? she asks.

Nell says yes; so was her mother, so was Ruth. Sounded like Henry and Marion did too. Craziest thing, Nell says.

I thought it was just me, Leone says. I thought it was what happens when a man does that to you.

Late in the summer Henry kneels in her mother's house and asks Nell to marry him. She says she'll have to think about it. When winter comes on, Henry and Glen sell the Ice Cream Parlor and move back to Salt Lake. At Christmas Henry sends her a stupid work basket full of candy. She and Ruth eat the candy.

Lying in bed, Nell hears Mr. Johnson pass her door and go into the kitchen. She hears him rummaging in cupboards and drawers, whistling. She does not know if she is supposed to get up and fix his breakfast. She smells bacon and coffee, and in a while she hears the clatter of silverware on a plate. She holds her knees to her chest and keeps her eyes closed so that if Mr. Johnson opens her door he will think she's asleep and didn't hear him get up. When she hears the front door close behind him, she gets up and goes to the children's room. The girls cry when she comes in and fight her while she dresses them; the boy crawls under the crib and peers out at her with his thumb in his mouth. She makes them oatmeal in the kitchen and makes them eat it. Mrs. Johnson is still in bed when Nell leaves for the university, leaving the children to play in their room.

Nell's piano teacher at the university smokes cigars in the small practice room where he gives her her lesson. She learns about the circle of fifths, authentic and plagal cadences, secondary dominants; she learns to recognize every interval except a minor ninth down. She learns the minor scales and the modes.

Her mother makes pies at the girls' school again, and when Nell complains about the Johnsons, gets her a job at the school setting and waiting on tables, and clearing them after the girls have eaten, and washing pots and pans in the kitchen with sweating walls. This is satisfactory.

Nell's mother goes to Randolph to take care of Uncle Ike's wife. When Uncle Ike's wife dies Nell takes the train to Evanston, where her brother Marion picks her up and drives her through a blizzard to Randolph. He has to get out once to break the compacted snow off his wiper blades. Bad business, he says when he gets back in the car. At the funeral Nell and Ruth and Marion sit together. Nell's mother sits with Uncle Ike on the mourners' pew across the aisle.

14

Ruth comes to Salt Lake City for the sewing school and lives with Nell in the boarding house on North Main. She has a blind date with her friend Ruth's husband's nephew Frank but has appendicitis on the day of the date, so Nell goes. They meet at the pavilion on the Great Salt Lake. Nell is not impressed by Frank. He has red hair, and acne on the back of his neck which he tries to hide by keeping his shirt collar up. He is wearing pointy-toed shoes that squeak on the pavilion floor when they dance. When they go on the roller coaster Frank's wallet flips out of his pocket and sails into the lake. He has to borrow money from his uncle to entertain her the rest of the night. When she's ready to go home, the rest of Frank's family have already gone, so he takes her home on the Bamberger train. They eat popcorn and Nell talks about her boyfriend Clyde.

Frank trades his motorcycle in for a yellow Ford coupe, which he tells Nell he is so proud of that he parks it in front of his house every night and goes inside to stand at the window and look at it. His sister Gladys calls it Frank's hatbox.

Frank's sister Gladys likes Nell, but his other sister, Irene, does not, and his mother does not. When Frank brings Nell home for dinner Irene and her mother have put pictures of his dead wife on the shelves in the living room and on the mantle and hung them on the walls in the dining room.

Frank explains in the car that his mother doesn't want him to get married again; she wants him to stay home and care for her.

Are you going to do what she wants? Nell asks.

She's my mother, Frank says.

Frank works as a stillman at Utah Oil and Refining Company, where his best friend, Ted Holmes, whispers in his ear.

It's a chance that won't come again, Frank tells Nell. The California oil fields are booming. He'll write every day, and when he and Ted have built the refinery in Oxnard he'll come back and get her.

On the day Frank leaves, Nell sulks while he kisses her at the curb in front of the school. She watches him drive away from the school in his little yellow coupe loaded with suitcases and tries to imagine California. There are orange trees along the roads, she knows.

She calls them her taxi boys. One of them always drives by the corner in the pre-dawn where she waits to catch the streetcar and offers her a ride to the dispatch office where she works, and she always pretends she's not going to accept. When she gets in, Jack always gives her a squeeze and she always pushes him away and says Don't do that.

Hyrum always smells of cigarettes and dirty shirts when she gets into his cab; he never touches her but he says such funny things that Nell is shrieking with laughter when he drops her off at the dispatch office. Lavar would be handsome but his chin pulls back into his neck when he smiles, and all she can see are his front teeth that hang there with nothing to clamp down on. She knows Lavar is sweet on her, but she can't bring herself to like him. Still, it's Lavar who pleases her by asking one cold morning to see the ring Otto gave her before he moved to Price. She takes the ring off and hands it to him.

Guess I'll just take this home and look at it where the lights's better, Lavar says, and slips the ring into his pocket.

I guess you just won't, Nell says.

Maybe tomorrow you can have it back, he says.

If you really wanted me to like you you'd give it back now, she says.

Maybe I'll find me another girl who loves me and give it to her.

Nell grabs at his pocket. Give me that ring and I don't mean maybe, she says.

I'm driving, Lavar says, correcting a swerve across the streetcar tracks.

She reaches for his hair and he blocks her with an arm and stops the taxi in the middle of the street.

Give it to me this instant, she screams.

Here, he says. He gropes in his pocket and hands her the ring.

That's better, she says. She puts the ring back on her finger and sits back, waiting for him to drive her to work.

She gets a letter from Frank. Things haven't worked out with the refinery in Oxnard. Ted Holmes has gone to Los Angeles to work for a guy named Hisey. Frank guesses he'll come back to Salt Lake and try to get his old job back. She looks for another sheet of paper in the envelope but there isn't one.

Nell's mother goes back to Randolph to help take care of her stepdaughter Lucy's baby. Her sister Ruth goes back to Randolph and marries a good man. Her brother Dave has finished barber college and gone back to Randolph. Her brother Joe has a job with the railroad and has moved to Ogden. Nell is alone.

One of the taxi boys takes her to see "The Thief of Bagdad," and she lets him lick her ear when they sit in the parlor of her rooming house afterward.

She gets a letter from Frank. He has stopped to visit his dead wife's family in Bakersfield and they have insisted he stay and apply for a job on a lease in Fellows, so that's what he's done. The California fields are booming, he reminds her. It would make sense to stay and give it another try.

Nell sits in the parlor of her rooming house with a different taxi boy, and sees a yellow Ford coupe pull up to the curb. Frank gets out.

Who's that? the taxi boy asks.

Oh good hell, Nell says.

What might your name be? Frank asks, wiping his feet on the mat inside the door.

Frank's letter arrives the next day. They read it together. Boss sez he's sick of me deciding one day to go home to my best girl and the next day to stay and work for him. Told me to pack my bag and go to Utah and get married and come back and settle down like I was serious. Sounded like a good idea to me. I'll be there, as fast as my little hatbox can get me there. Hoping you're ready to get married and come to California with your best beau.

Suppose you might do that little thing? Frank asks.

Frank is the only one left.

Yes, she says.

Frank drives back to California and Nell goes to Randolph with her new last name to be with her mother for a month of showers and parties. They all go to Sister Snowball's funeral. At the gravesite, while the grave is being dedicated, Nell looks across at Brother Snowball, who used to call her Nellie Pope. It serves him right, she thinks.

Franklin Fisher's fiction has appeared or is forthcoming in *The Gettysburg Review, Massachusetts Review, Iowa Review,* etc.

BIG IDEA / *Pamela Greenberg*

Sometimes my bones hum like Bunyan's
must have; world turned vassal to my will,
whole cornfields swaying at my footsteps,
thistles fleshed into fruit. Then I think
I could live in a lighthouse, be happy
without an arm curled around me at night.
Or wander perhaps the forsaken farmland,
pilfering from silos, surviving
off the goodwill of the land. But when
is the truth ever like that? Once
I caught a catfish in the Adirondacks.
The thing wouldn't die even after I knifed it,
yanking out whatever I could find in its gut.
By the time it was finished frying
I could hardly swallow one forkful.
Self-sufficiency, I now say, is for giants.
Me, I need a mouth to greet mine after chores,
a stranger's words to bring me wonder,
a name to call my name urgent in the dark.

A CUP FOR ELIJAH/*Pamela Greenberg*

It is 1975, the year before my parents stop speaking.
Old, rabbinical, Uncle Leo takes his glasses off to gesture,
while on my shoulder my brother softly dozes.
At last, triumphantly, my aunt holds the plate
of offerings aloft. On it a broken eggshell
and the shankbone of a lamb. My father still
is happy; not manic, not depressed.
He stands with an electric carving knife
near the windowsill geraniums
in a pinstriped Brooks Brothers suit.
My mother, a stylish urban hippie, takes off
her sparkling turban to kiss him.
From the kitchen drifts the smell
of pot roast and string beans and sweet potato pie.
And it is beautiful and fragile, that instant,
but I can't keep it from what happens next:
my mother swings the door open to starlight;
my father pours an extra glass of wine.
Dazed, I gulp at my grape juice,
watching the pendulum of the grandfather clock
flicker in the candle's light. A dish falls
in the kitchen, cracking. Someone curses.
My now-dead uncle taps me on the back.

LAGUNITAS, 1978/*Pamela Greenberg*

Always, it seems, it has been like this:
the phone cradled on my mother's shoulder,
her too-loud boyfriend laugh. When she whispers
fork and spoon windchimes jangle on fish line
and from downslope comes the plaintive
mewl of the goats. (my mother's secrets,
her spicy burnt perfume) I cannot
get small enough, creaking out the screen door,
past blackberries fat with sweetness,
to the salt block even starker in moonlight,
the newborn fumbling on her knees to get up.
Everything strange and elusive,
even the goats—who, when I try to hold them—
stubbornly muzzle away. My mother
shouting my name then, with a tone that means,
In God's name what have you done.
When I get back she's standing barreled
across the doorway, hair wondrous and frizzled,
turquoise earrings perfectly still. As I gaze up,
her eyes grip me with their shrillest blue.
Behind her my two-thousand-piece zebra puzzle
unsolved near the woodburning stove.

FLOOD/*Pamela Greenberg*

All day we watched it—my mother, brother,
and I—the relentless wrath, the furious
downpour of God. Our zucchini plants
torn loose from the soil, lumber and stovepipe
roiling in the creek. Mid-afternoon
the bloated carcass of a muskrat sped by,
pummeled along in the swill. When the electric pole
threw blue sparks and died, we watched
by lantern light. We had entered that domain
where it is easier to look than not,
where the flood seemed lovely
because it had nothing to do with us.
And strangely enough—walled in
those years by turmoil—we *were* safe.
By morning the rain had slowed to a patter,
and our stove was working again.
A great, giddy weight had slid off us,
one we hadn't even known was there.
My mother sang as she flipped pancakes
and I rubbed knuckles into my brother's hair.
The first white sun thundered in.

THE EMPIRE STRIKES BACK/
Pamela Greenberg

On a bucket outside the Saint Nowhere feed barn,
cold, stolen apple juice dribbling down my chin,
I looked out toward the madrones along the coast.
Above my head hung a starfish and lucky
horseshoe and a stencil of a ram.
When the sun dulled orange and green,
I ducked into the theater down the street.
Han Solo, my idol, was frozen in a pit:
invulnerable, brazen, closed. I wanted
to kiss him; I wanted to be him; I couldn't tell.
Afterwards, pedaling my dirt bike home
I pulled daredevil wheelies in the road,
jumped over stones and gulches and farmland.
When I got back my pants were muddy,
my skin luminous with a newfound glow.
Now, the selfsame myth of the invincible
keeps me most nights alone. And I am rent
with a gnostic's nostalgia, glum elbows
under my chin. Back then I was so tough,
I could brave even the most inclement weather;
so young, I was not torn apart by awe.

PRAIRIE/*Pamela Greenberg*

High atop a playground's fuchsia frog
a girl spits pomegranate seeds
into the mammoth armful of meadow.
The field troubles her with longing
and culmination of longing:
the yellow spikeweed at her feet
and the unreachable furthermost prairie.
Spurring the ungiving flanks, she thinks
of bucking into the wildest West.
She could swallow fullthroat the horizon,
and never be seen again. Then again
she could strangle in this sweetness:
the smell of milk thistle and eucalyptus,
the firetower glinting, the wheeze
of hay fever caught up in her throat.

WHERE ONCE IT STOOD/*Pamela Greenberg*

I was looking for a horse, but there was
no horse, only the feed barn and above it
the purple meat of sky: the smell
of birch smoke and burlap and grain.
Yes, yes, now I remember. It was fall,
the same fall my mother bought a gun, the fall
we studied architectural perspectives in Art.
In the barn a bridle shimmered cold on its hook.
Light chinking in from the cracks,
mouse prints etched in sawdust on the floor.
And then—or was it another day?—
a horse did appear, a palomino in the pasture,
alone near a rock. Flanks prickly with hoarfrost,
mane the color of car fumes and snow.
Clearly he must have been there from the start.
Yes, the horse must have been an emissary
long unseen. When I reached to touch him,
he bolted away, leaving the child—who was me—
framed by the half-wide door of the barn.
Wait! I wanted to say, hold on!
But the horse—who was also me—
already had jumped the fence,
softening into the dark strand of trees.
Near the tractor a red candy wrapper
floated shipwrecked in the ditch.
Somewhere an ancient door hinge swung.
Hours passed, or days and years, and I grew hungry.
As for the horse, even my sharpest
finger whistle could not call him back.

Pamela Greenberg has had poems previously in *The Salt Hill Journal* and *Plainsongs Review*.

A NEW YOUTH/*Debora Freund*

THE SCENT of petrol hit my nose on my first day of school in Israel in 1959. I was a ten year old used to the processed smells of an American schoolroom: the artificial sweet scents of chewing gum, cheap nail polish and hair spray, blended with those of dusty chalk and vinyl floors. The stench came from the back of the room, where a girl with shorn hair sat fingering her pencils, eyes lowered.

"*Kinim*," a girl with long tresses announced loudly, pointing at her.

I stared in horror mixed with fascination. The word *kinim* was familiar to me from the Passover hagada. It was the plague of lice sent to the Egyptians. I wondered what was so unique about the girl, that God had bothered to send a plague just for her.

Her name, I soon learned, was Hanna Shaloush. A thin girl with shoes curling at the toes, she was chosen to sit next to me when the lice were gone. Our classmates envied her her proximity to my sixty-four, triple-decker Crayola set and the privilege of using my pencil sharpener with the attached can. She was the only one in class who had learned a few English sentences, mastered while serving behind the counter of her parents' fish stall.

"Fresh today," she would say when she wanted to convey to me the teacher's instruction to write on a new page in our notebooks. "Please come again," she would tell me at the end of each day. The coins she dropped into the green collection can—passed around for the planting of new trees in Israel—glistened with fish scales.

Although I didn't understand much of Hanna's jumbled English, the new palette of smells to which she introduced me was a language in itself. She reeked of camphor oil rubbed into her chest on cold days. Whereas my American friends had arrived at school on Fridays with curlers in their hair, hopeful to unravel thick Shirley Temple curls by sunset, Hanna's hair on Fridays glistened in the winter sun, rinsed with tangy-smelling vinegar in honor of the coming Sabbath. A more subtle odor emanated from her head on the days she fancied a special hairdo: Sugar mixed with lemon kept in check the loose strands of her uncoiled braids.

My American paraphernalia was a source of constant wonder to Hanna. She saved the silver paper in which my sandwiches were wrapped, and decorated her notebooks with little cutouts of the "mirror paper." She never tired of watching me blow bubbles with the gum constantly in my mouth, and I fed on her admiring gaze.

We became real friends primarily because of my inexhaustible supply of Scotch tape. Large horn-rimmed glasses slid down Hanna's snub nose; a thick Band-Aid held together the ridge of her broken frame. The Band-Aid curled into an ugly brown and swelled at the edges after a few hours of perspiration, and by noon, the rash between her long-lashed, squinting eyes had turned into an angry red. I changed that. After a week or so of watching this ugly transformation, I began to yank off a strip of transparent tape from its plastic holder in my pencil case and carefully mend Hanna's frame. She let me do this without a word. From then on we were friends.

In the first few weeks of school the favorite pastime of my classmates at recess was to play with the invisible nylon zipper on my sweater. Back and forth, back and forth.

"Like a train on tracks," a freckled girl from a higher class exclaimed to me in German, the language we spoke at home.

"Do snowflakes stay in your hand?" several of them wanted to know.

"Is it soap that bubbles in your mouth?"

"What is it like to watch TV?"

"Weren't you afraid to sit inside a metal box the shape of a hollow bird racing in the sky?"

No, I answered through my German translator. Snowflakes melted like ice cream, and an aeroplane was like a flying bus, without a bell to tug at stops.

The girls listened avidly, gathered around me under the blossoming orange tree that washed us with its fragrance. They wore cotton skirts with faded designs, the hems heavy from the spare fabric folded over until the skirts ballooned like limp tires around their scraped knees.

The bubbles in my mouth were from chewing gum, I explained. With my tongue I stretched the pink ball of Bazooka and blew a bubble that grew rounder and rounder until it burst on my face. The girls squealed. The gum proceeded from mouth to mouth, cheers erupting for the triumphant one who had managed an "American balloon."

"Is your mother an American movie star?" they asked, the first day she came to fetch me in her high heels and wide-brimmed straw hat.

I didn't tell them that my mother was dressed up because she was a newlywed. Nor that I had not been afraid on the flight because I had been too absorbed fantasizing about her new husband.

My imagination—well-oiled by hours of watching TV—conjured up a Clark Gable awaiting my beautiful mother with a bouquet of red roses. Instead, Nathan, met us with a bag of peanuts, a deep crease in his suit jacket around his middle, where the button strained to meet the buttonhole, a gold tooth glinting in the sun.

He settled my mother in the front seat of the metallic gray Chevrolet as if she were precious cargo. When Nathan drove with his hands off the wheel, my brother squealed like he did at a lurching merry-go-round. I wasn't that impressed. There were hardly any cars on the road. The traffic was nothing compared to the racetrack that was Kingston Avenue back home in New York.

Two months earlier, my mother had collected us from the aunt who had taken care of us during our mother's three-day trip abroad. Boxes were piled into a pyramid on the faded oilcloth of our kitchen table in the little flat above the garage on Kingston Avenue.

"These are gifts from your new father in Israel," my mother said.

The wrapping paper on the offerings had come from the corner store, I noted. But in my excitement at the news that our new father owned an ice cream factory, I forgot to comment on it. I saw a ring with layers of diamonds on my mother's finger, the shape of a miniature wedding cake.

My mother was only thirty years old when my father died. She was left with striking good looks, little money and a dowry of four children. Nathan was a childless widower—an old family friend from prewar Hungary—who, unlike my parents, had chosen to build a new life in Israel. Old friends they had in common had been the matchmakers. And now he had walked into my life to change it forever. Within the span of a few weeks, I had a new father, a new country, new classmates and a new name.

The name did not seem to fit at first. In class, I felt as if I were concealing a dark secret.

"Bronfeld," the teacher would repeat several times before I jumped up with a start, realizing from the silence around me that she had called my name. After a few occasions on which I failed to respond, I noticed that whenever the teacher addressed me, she moved her lips, exaggerating the syllables. When this also failed to elicit my immediate response, she solved her problem by transferring me—along with my "fishy" interpreter—to the front row, calling on me as little as possible.

In America, my peers had viewed my fatherless status with pity, mingled with admiration. The fact that I had no grandparents from either side made me even more pitiable. It took me some time to realize that in this country I could relax about my past. Death, here in Israel, seemed to be everyone's relative. Loss and confusion were a daily occurrence. Brothers and fathers were frequently summoned to the army, names of fresh victims—killed in ambush at the precarious borders— were broadcast daily. Death, over here, was a neighbor who made himself part of family life.

After the initial flurry of excitement over the whiff of Americanism I had brought across the sea, I became uninteresting to my new playmates. While they were tall, strong girls with already budding breasts, I was small, pale, prone to sickness in spite of the hateful spoonful of cod-liver oil I was obliged to swallow every day. I was never included in their giggles behind a girl's back, as they casually patted her between her shoulders to find out whether a hook was concealed beneath her cotton camisole. I felt my classmates were treating me the way I treated my little sister.

Neither was I adept at their games. Hours of fastening cutout clothes on cardboard dolls had not prepared me for the art of throwing dice in the air and catching them with one swift manipulation of the wrist. Nor did I thrill at the prospect of rolling down the ill-paved street, tucked inside an abandoned truck tire. I longed for the hours I had spent curled up on the sofa with a book. Reading material in English was scarce, my knowledge of Hebrew still very limited.

"I found something for you in English," Nathan came home beaming one day, and handed me an English translation of the Bible.

"Thank Aba," my mother whispered. She insisted we call him Father. "How thoughtful of you, Nathan," she said.

I spent most of my afternoons tagging behind our sixteen-year-old Yemenite au pair, Pnina, the oldest of fourteen children, who worked so that her father could afford to offer her future husband the dowry of two donkeys. She slipped around barefoot on the tiled floor as she threw bucketfuls of water that wetted the tips of her embroidered pantaloons. On Pnina, I practiced the new Hebrew words I learned in school.

She tolerated me. "You are lucky," she liked to remind me. I remember one time when she prepared a pile of shirts to iron. She sprinkled them with water and rolled them into thick sausage-like shapes, piling them into a plastic bag in the fridge. "So lucky, do you understand?" she kept saying. "No one ever ironed my underpants."

The other person in our household was Geveret Chaya, a cook who wore orthopedic shoes and the white coat of a nurse, her flat curls kept under a transparent net while she stirred with a wooden spoon the goulash simmering in our pots. My stepfather had hired her as soon as he discovered that my mother despised cooking. But the woman was no ordinary cook. As a sign of respect, my mother served tea to Geveret Chaya in her best teacups.

"Before the war in Hungary, I used to watch her ride past my house in a carriage pulled by four horses." My mother liked to tell this story repeatedly, as if it contained some special truth that we should grasp.

"Their house was so beautiful that it was the first Jewish house in Budapest confiscated to house the Nazi general. And now," she would shake her head with wonder, "now she is my cook." In her mind she still perceived portly Geveret Chaya as a young girl wearing satin shoes, descending the narrow steps of a carriage. The only sign of superiority I detected in Geveret Chaya was the way she sprinkled salt into the food: She shook it from far above the pot, as if, instead of the grey, lump salt, she aspersed the meal with a scented powder.

Only on days when my mother arrived at school did my classmates' interest in me revive. She was an impeccably groomed beauty who caused any room she entered to look suddenly shabby. The smell of her French perfume overpowered the odors of petrol and chlorine.

I noticed how the austere school principal's hand flew up to her dark chignon—held with many pins—patting it into place, while her other hand straightened the cameo attached at the throat of her starched, long-sleeved blouse. The mothers of my other schoolmates wore heavy nylon stockings held up with elastic bands, that sagged on their bandaged, varicose-veined legs. They wore loose shirts, which they were often unable to button completely over their swelling bellies. The country was busy procreating, and vanity in dress was considered unzionistic. Behind their backs, women like my mother, who sat idle in their living rooms the whole day, were called "salon ladies." The only other hourglass-shaped woman familiar to my classmates was Miss Ama, the curly-lashed, smiling woman on the label of the sole cleaning product manufactured locally. A frilly white apron was tied about Miss Ama's tiny waist, and cheerful slogans issued from balloons in her mouth. They were a pleasure to look at, Miss Ama and my mother.

I don't know if my mother was conscious of the impression she made on my young schoolmates, but she was aware of my loneliness and wanted to do something to help me adapt to my new circumstances.

"Your eleventh birthday is coming up," she said after one of her visits to inquire about my progress in school. "Let's invite your friends to our house."

Geveret Chaya offered to bake her famous apple strudel—a recipe received straight from the mouth of the owner of the largest café on the main street of Budapest. I said no.

The girls, I believed, liked only *garinim* (salted sunflower seeds) and falafel. I had no idea that for most of my peers, homemade cakes on a weekday, baked with eggs and sugar, were delicacies beyond their means.

Pnina brought in her mother to produce authentic Yemenite falafel. Geveret Chaya brought the popular roasted sunflower seeds that she denounced as "bird food spit out by humans like cows." My mother shopped for the coarse cotton skirt and the colorfully embroidered blouse that was as much a symbol of festivity in those days as was the white and blue national flag with which she decorated our living room.

The birthday party was a catastrophe. My friends swayed into our apartment in an exaggerated imitation of my mother's gait. They were dressed in layers of skirts for a petticoat effect. Crimson geranium petals were stuck to their nails, a substitute for nail polish.

"Hi," they uttered in American, chewing hard on toffee, pretending it was gum.

"Shalom," my mother greeted each of them courteously, trying to keep a straight face. In a nearby bedroom, Nathan was guffawing loudly at the charade.

"Whoever thought that one day we should worry again about the color on the tips of our fingernails," I heard Geveret Chaya muttering to herself. "Who would believe it. WHO?"

They sat on the edge of our sofa; the straight pencil-lines drawn on their pre-adolescent legs—an imitation of my mother's nylon stockings—smudged when they crossed and recrossed their legs.

"They have no American Coca-Cola, nor popcorn," I heard someone whisper in a disappointed tone when they were shown to the table laden with refreshment. "Only *garinim* and falafel."

They turned their attention to the tinkling chandelier above the table, taking turns rotating the delicate crystal pieces. "Like those in Franz Joseph's palace," they marveled, forgetting their put-on sophistication. "Sissy," the story of the Austrian-Hungarian Empress, starring Romy Schneider, was then being serialized on the movie screens, giving my little friends their first glimpse into opulence.

When they tired of looking at the chandelier, they discovered the two air conditioners my mother had brought with her from America; an air conditioner was a wonder they had never seen before. They held their hands against the cold stream of air, squealing when it blew the geranium petals off their nails.

"Winter in the summer," a girl marveled. "How can that be?"

"Her father manufactures ice cream and ice air," Miri, the number one student in our class explained to the others. The girls nodded in assent. This made sense to them.

After the party I fell back into anonymity. My Hebrew vocabulary gradually improved, and my mother stopped her frequent visits to school. When I eventually made one more attempt to be part of the gang, I failed dismally again.

The whole class was looking forward to the coming Pourim party at school. Weeks before the Jewish Carnival, the girls in my class plotted, exchanging secrets about their "tachposet." Disguise. Masquerade, the dictionary explained, when I looked up the word "tachposet."

My mother offered her wide lace skirt, her ivory fan and red blouse. "With your jet black hair you could be a perfect Spanish dancer," she said.

I turned down the offer. A better idea for an unrecognizable disguise was brewing in my mind.

I went to the backyard of the local chicken store for my "tachposet." There, surrounded by noisy chicken crates, four women sat on low wooden stools, plucking feathers from freshly slaughtered birds with nimble fingers. They hummed a throaty oriental tune that clashed with the cacophony of the nervous fowl. Willingly, they parted with the feathers I needed.

Back home, I spread copious layers of glue, then stuck feathers all over the white sheet with which I had covered myself. I cackled all the way to the schoolyard, proud about my ingenious disguise. My self-satisfaction lasted, however, only until I reached the classroom: "Tachposet," I soon realized, meant costume, not disguise. The celebration was an occasion to carry out one's fantasy, not conceal one's identity. My friends all strutted, resplendent in stiff, shiny attire, gold cardboard headgear crowning their proud heads.

"The American Hen," the queens, brides and dancers called after me, holding their noses whenever I passed. The feathers stank, and the name clung to me long after the feathers blew off the sheet.

The principal of the school must have heard of my new nickname because she asked me one day to step into the small cubicle that was her office. She took a leather-bound book off the shelf, folded a deep pleat in one of its heavy pages, bent the page backwards, in the opposite direction, and put it upright again. The page stood erect, restored to its previous condition.

"The author of this book is the Rambam," she said. "An illustrious sage and scientist. He believed that the middle path of behavior in life is the Golden Path. Sometimes, he says in this book, you have to bend your behavior to the extreme, so that when you change back to your current behavior, you are onto the Golden Path. Do you understand?"

I didn't understand exactly what she meant, but the restored page somehow left me reassured that with time things would straighten out.

"For example," she went on, "if a person suffers from stinginess and wants to repair this flaw in his character, the Rambam advises him to spend money excessively. After a period of time, he should stop. He will then spend his money in a normal way.

"You are trying hard to be like one of us," she said as she accompanied me to the door. "Don't worry. One day, sooner than you think, no one will remember that you ever were a newcomer."

While I was trying to adapt to the new country and the ways of my classmates, my mother had her own adjustments to make.

She came to Israel well-equipped: two air conditioners, soft toilet paper, various kinds of kindly smelling pesticides, heaps of nylon stockings, a large refrigerator and many other electrical appliances.

A week after turning on all these appliances at once, she ran into Israeli reality: the electrical system balked at this excess, and the main fuse of the building blew, causing Mrs. Albo, our corpulent neighbor, to run breathless down the stairs.

"A military attack," she warned us, trotting down to the cellar for cover.

Through the dressing gown loosely draped around her, I could see the hastily hooked metal eyes of her salmon-colored corset, one with a pocket for her jewelry sewn inside, in case of just such emergencies.

It turned out that no spare parts were available anywhere in the country for our electrical wonders. Soon we were like everyone else, rushing down the stairs at the sound of the ice man jingling his bell, trying to be first in line when the horse-drawn cart rattled into view. Daily, we purchased a block of ice to slide into our lifeless refrigerator, where it melted into a large plastic tray.

"An insult to our modern fridge," my mother complained each time we hauled the block of ice up the stairs. But there was nothing she could do.

The meagerness of material life in Israel affected us in all sorts of little ways. My father shaved with cream that smelled like tar. The little bottle of Chanel No. 5 on my mother's dresser transformed into a large one containing rose water. The shortage of my mother's beloved nylons meant that I was sent to a Bulgarian woman on the corner who made repairs, a well-endowed lady in a flowered dress who frowned while she counted, and charged each loose stitch by the length it had run. On a wooden chest stood faded photographs of three little girls with floppy satin bows in their hair and sailor suit dresses. A thick candle burned in a glass, throwing a flickering light on their faces, almost giving them live expressions. A scratched record sobbed Bloch's Kaddish (a prayer for the dead) on her gramophone. Each time the violin faltered on a scratch, Mrs. Milovitz would stop, her needle held in midair above the stocking extended on a wooden mushroom. Her husband with the brilliantined mustache would put down his cigarette—made of tobacco rolled in newspaper—and slowly rise to touch the needle. As soon as the music resumed, Mrs. Milovitz would begin working on my mother's stockings again.

After our washing machine followed the ways of the other American appliances, my mother considered employing additional staff.

"In our house we had servants, of course," Geveret Chaya sniffed. "But girls had to learn how to be good housewives."

My mother took this comment to heart, and soon my sisters and I were taking turns treading on the laundry that was soaking in the bathtub, dancing on it as if it were grapes that someday would become wine.

We took turns beating the Persian carpets too, while the latest model of upright Hoover leaned against the wall. After a few weeks of watching us drag the carpets to the balcony for their beating, my mother rolled up "those dust nests" and stacked them in a corner, remembering to unroll them only on the High Holidays.

"Shaloush?" The teacher called out Hanna's name from the roll a few weeks after Pourim. There was no answer. Almost a week had gone by since Hanna had been to school.

"Is she ill?" the teacher asked. "Has anyone been to visit her?"

No reply. Hanna was not one of the popular girls in class. She was the oldest child of a large family and never had time for after-school activities.

"A classmate is absent for a week and no one has bothered to find out why?" the teacher said. "Who is going to visit her? Today."

I raised my hand. By now, I felt confident enough to explore new surroundings on my own. Besides, Hanna was the only friend I had, and I had never been to the market before.

I found out that afternoon that Hanna was not sick. Her father was.

"Fresh today. Fresh today," I heard her calling. I found Hanna beckoning to a group of American tourists. She stood on a low stool that made her slight figure seem taller behind the fish stall. Hanna's father, of Moroccan origin, sat in a little room behind, peering under the fin of a fish with a magnifying glass, in search of stowaway, unkosher worms. His gray beard was soft and clean, his fingers long and bony. On the wall above the sink was taped a blood-splashed Talmud page that he frequently consulted. His skin had a transparency that I associated with the radiance of a saint. I was too young to connect it with heart disease, nor had I ever heard of diabetes. He had become very weak lately, Hanna said. She had to help until he got better.

Hanna's mother sat in front of the door, gutting fish, throwing the viscera and the fish into large metal pails on either side of her swollen knees. Unhealed cuts ran under her chipped nails. "Hanna's American friend," she said, fastening the flowered kerchief into a tighter knot around her head. Her face shed years when she smiled, revealing white, even teeth. An alarm clock with three feet performed a jig in a soup plate, ringing in a loud tone.

"Medicine time," Hanna's mother announced, looking at her husband. "You must eat something now."

He sat motionless in the chair, a bluish tinge around his mouth.

"Go call the doctor, Hanna," her mother instructed. "It is his sugar level again." The father lifted his hand in a feeble protest, but Hanna was already at the door.

"Come," she said to me. "We'll go to the phone." She hoisted a long wire from a hook on the wall; its end was bent into a loop.

I ran, attempting to match Hanna's quick steps, skipping over swarms of tiny flies feasting on rotten fruit. The thought of being reprimanded at home for ruining my good shoes nagged at the back of my mind.

At the phone booth, Hanna fished a hollowed token out of her pocket and attached it to the looped wire. She pushed it down the phone and dialed the doctor's number.

"Doctor Krautstein?" She dipped the wire at the sound of the click. "Doctor, this is Hanna Shaloush. My father needs an injection."

At a signal that came from the phone's belly, down went the wire again. "Can you please come?"

"People are watching," I whispered to Hanna, eyeing the queue that was forming behind us.

"My mother said I should tell you that he needs ins-u-lin." Hanna fed the phone's belly again. She covered the mouthpiece with her hand. "Stop worrying," she whispered to me. "They all do it."

The woman behind us, protecting herself from the warm winter sun with a faded parasol, listened openly to the conversation with the doctor, her lips mouthing Hanna's words. From her pocket peeped a similar looped iron wire.

I returned to visit Hanna every afternoon. The smells and the ever-changing scenes of the market fascinated me. Housewives swinging rigid plastic baskets marched between the stalls, drunk on the power they had over the wooing vendors. Stopping in front of fruit stalls, they palpated the fruit with the seriousness of those who had known hunger. Elderly ladies reeked of mothballs, frayed pieces of fur co-quettishly thrown over their shoulders. The children stomped along in their winter shoes, made to last longer with metal half-moons on the soles. When it rained, they stepped and leaped into water puddles and then were dragged off by scolding mothers into nearby shelters, where the adults fashioned dry linings into their shoes for them from the newspapers wrapped around their purchases.

From Hanna's brothers I mastered the climbing of guava trees. I learned to shake their branches, causing the cloying fruit to plummet on indignant passersby. The place was a mine of adventures, far more exciting than those in my beloved Bobbsey Twins books. Besides, it was far away from Nathan fawning over my mother.

When the weather changed and the hot sun came out, the tableau at the market was transformed, as if the curtain had dropped on a stage and a new scenery had been wheeled in. Fat caterpillars on glistening leaves raised their heads toward the glaring sun. Sweat ran like tears down the faces of women carrying overflowing baskets of fruit, live chickens and fish. They wore sunglasses with long pieces of paper tucked under them to shade their noses from the harsh sun.

Slow-moving men knotted the corners of large handkerchiefs to fit the shape of their heads. Some wore shapeless, light-colored straw hats, the brims stained with sweat. Most had cotton hats shaped like lampshades perched on their heads: Tembel hats—idiot hats—they were called because, as Hanna pointed out, you must be a tembel if you didn't shield your head from the blazing sun.

The heat magnified the odors. Scents of brilliantine came through the barber's open door. The smell of pickles in barrels of brine made my mouth water. Cheese reeked sourly behind the protection of thin cotton veils.

I soon became immune to the glassy stare of a dead fish. I learned to clean one without spattering the scales all over the wall and shouted at the top of my lungs "Fresh today!" whenever I saw someone with a camera. Each day, I proudly brought Hanna's parents bundles of yesterday's newspapers, thrown away by residents on our street unaware of their value. On this side of town, old newspapers were weighed on the vegetable scales, bought and sold as wrapping paper. Nowhere was I happier than in this live opera.

"You stink of fish," my mother hissed.

"She is growing wild," she complained to Nathan. "Children are given too much freedom in this country."

"Not wild," Nathan replied. "Strong and uninhibited, unlike the children of the ghetto we knew. Besides, it will do her no harm to see how other people live."

I was told to shower and change as soon as I came home, and to leave my clothes to air on the balcony. Soon, however, my head swarmed with a colony of lice.

My mother went out to a faraway pharmacy to buy a special product, but came home empty-handed.

"You go," she told Pnina. "I am too embarrassed."

Pnina returned with a densely toothed comb and soaked my head in petrol. Now in school, I was the one who sat in the back of the class.

After spending afternoons in the market, I returned to life on our street with the feeling that I was entering another country. Not far from us was Habima, an auditorium surrounded by sand. The inhabitants of the five buildings around it were very proud of living nearby, as if being *near* culture were equivalent to having it.

Once a month, on the day the Philharmonic played solely for subscribers, my mother dressed in one of her Parisian outfits, pulled on long gloves and shaded her face under a wide-brimmed millinery confection. Thus attired, she traversed the two unpaved streets separating us from Habima to bathe herself in culture.

To Hanna, my mother's life was a dim mystery. "Your mother has a cook, a cleaning lady, a woman to iron," Hanna once puzzled. "What does she do the whole day?"

I had to give the question some thought. What actually *did* she do the whole day?

"She shops," I answered thinking of the pretty frocks she brought home from Ivanir, the only shop in the country which claimed to offer the latest styles from Paris.

This explanation seemed to satisfy Hanna. She must have pictured my mother going to the market every day, taking her time to haggle over prices. I tried to conjure the image of my mother displaying the slippery fish on the counter as Hanna's mother did. But even in my imagination, it seemed foolish.

In reality my mother didn't do much, and Nathan was proud of the fact. "You struggled enough as a child and a widow," I heard him say to her. "I want you to enjoy life."

In Israel, my mother found many ex–Eastern Europeans like her, still recuperating from the idea that they were thrown into an Asiatic world. They all deeply loved the country, yet none of them spoke Hebrew or made an effort to study the language. They clung to the far past and sought to reproduce it. None had photographs to bring the past closer. They only had each other to prove that there ever was one. They went out every afternoon to the only fashionable coffee house on Dizengof Street. There, they exchanged Hungarian recipes and reminisced about their early youth, inevitably sliding, I later surmised, into the painful subject of lost relatives and the Holocaust. Their children knew nothing of the Holocaust. We were the future; they wanted that for us, and they expected us to let them live in the past. In exchange, they concealed from us the recent horrors they had experienced.

As for us children, we wanted to speak Hebrew only. Its guttural accents sounded bold. My German—which my mother insisted we speak, even though she vetoed the tiniest kitchen appliance that was German-made—was fading; my sentences were sprinkled heavily with Hebrew words.

I came home late one evening, elated after a busy afternoon in the market. "You were helpful. A good girl," Hanna's taciturn father had praised me. I felt useful and proud.

There were guests in our living room: a woman with peroxide curls, in linen clothes, and her tall husband with diamond cufflinks on his snowy sleeves. Next to them, my mother—tan in spite of the straw hats—and Nathan, the sleeves of his unstarched shirt rolled up to his elbows, seemed slightly provincial.

"The Mandelstams," Pnina whispered. "He is a judge. They just moved to Israel." Pnina wore shoes for the occasion, and a frilly white apron that was supposed to give her the look of a parlor maid.

The plastic covers had been removed from the satin settees in the living room, the carpets unrolled, and the light bulbs, shaped like dripping candles, were all turned on. The Mandelstams were important people, I assumed. I could hear it from the way my mother was careful with her German accent, allowing no trace of Hungarian.

"Hi," I barged in, holding up the newspaper with herring I had received from Hanna's mother as a gift for my mother.

"I learned to skin herring today," I announced proudly to my mother. "This is for you."

The Mandelstams' nostrils widened. My mother's face darkened, but she emitted a tinkling laugh that sounded like a spoon on a tin cup.

"Debora has a passion for the sea world," my mother said, her accent under control. "When she grows up she will do research in that field."

I felt let down. The picture of Hanna's mother refusing to close the stall before she had ferociously scrubbed the chipped wooden board floated in my mind. I felt as if her honor was at stake.

My eye caught a Lilly Romance peeping from under the sofa cushion—one of those thin magazines that my mother enjoyed reading when no one saw her. On its cover was a blonde maiden, the helpless expression on her face intended to convey femininity. My mother must have shoved it there at the last minute. On the nearby coffee table, a few issues of *Time* were casually scattered, as if they had just been put down before the guests arrived.

"Did you misplace your magazine, Mother?" I asked in a sweet voice, holding up the Lilly Romance for all to see.

Mrs. Mandelstam snickered. Her husband threw her a furious look, and she covered her mouth, uttering a cough.

From the expression on my mother's face, I felt I had hurt her far beyond my understanding.

Nathan followed me out of the room into the kitchen and slapped me hard on the face.

"At your age," he thundered, "your mother did not work, she labored. And not after school, but *instead of* school. And not because she enjoyed playing poor, but because her life and the life of her little sisters depended on that work. So live your youth all you want, but don't you dare spoil her new life now. Is that clear?"

It was the only slap I ever received from Nathan, and the longest explanation about my mother's childhood during the war. I had a red mark on my cheek for days after, and a vague new unease about the fact that I didn't know anything of my mother's past.

"Where was my mother during the war?" I asked Geveret Chaya a few days later.

"In a camp," she answered. Coming through her clenched teeth, the word "camp" had none of the associations of fun that I attached to the word.

"You mean some kind of orphanage?" I persisted.

"I said camp," she snapped, closing her lips over her teeth. That was all she would divulge. No point in asking more. Since the Mandelstam incident, I was not in her favor.

The bubble of secrecy burst when Eichmann was caught and put to trial, and the horrors of our parents' childhoods seeped into our lives. In the market, vendors held tiny transistors to their ears. None of the clients inspected the food they purchased, neither did they haggle over prices. They pointed at the items they needed and handed over the necessary coins. People's eyes had the fixed stare of fish; their attention was tuned inwardly, to an inner voice retelling them the story of their own pasts. The whole country seemed to be in a daze, silent.

At home, my mother's tears streamed down her unmade face while she leaned on the kitchen counter beside a dry-eyed Geveret Chaya. They listened in silence to endless witnesses put on the stand. Details of the past were torn out of some of them, like inflamed teeth extracted on a public square. Others started speaking haltingly at first, then continued in a gush of words, as if a painful boil had been squeezed open. I had never seen my mother cry before. Now it seemed that she couldn't stop.

"You are lucky you can cry," Geveret Chaya said to my mother in a dull tone. Never before had I heard a tinge of envy in her voice.

I wanted to shut my ears. The horrors were too great to absorb. I hated Eichmann for my own personal reasons. He was like a party crasher: the world of crowded smells and new impressions I had landed in was no more the bountiful little Eden I had thought it was. It was just a hole in a cheese. Outside loomed the world. I was grateful that my mother shut off the transistor whenever I was in the room.

But there was no way of avoiding the trial. The tormented voices followed me everywhere. I wished my mother back in her petticoats. I wished she would scold me for smelling of fish. One day I brought home a Lilly Romance and shyly put it beside her. She looked at it with the revulsion of a sick person offered rich food.

It seemed as if her supply of tears were endless. "Cry," Nathan said when he came home to find her still in her dressing gown. "Only now can we afford tears."

I slowly began to understand the gift Nathan was trying to give my mother: the youth she had been robbed of. I also understood that without our parents' silence, our own carefree youth would not have been possible.

Eichmann's clipped, monotonous voice no longer filled our household, yet my mother continued to spend most of her days leaning on the kitchen counter, blowing rings of smoke into the air.

"Come with me to the market," I begged her one day, convinced that if I could get her there, she would feel the magic of the place.

"Go," Nathan urged.

No response, just a dismissing shrug. But as I skipped around her, trying to make her go, she seemed to be studying me through the smoke rings.

"My little gypsy," she whispered at last.

Her face contorted again, and I steeled myself for a fresh batch of tears. But no, she simply ground her cigarette into the stone ashtray and said, "Okay. You can take me there."

It's only to stop my pestering, I told myself. Still, I couldn't help anticipating the pleasure of bringing together the two important people in my life.

"My mother," I said to one the next day.

"Mrs. Shaloush," I announced to the other.

I had imagined the opening of the scene perfectly: Mrs. Shaloush reacted to my mother's beauty with the same grunt she emitted at the sight of an exceptional silver-finned carp. She hastily wiped a hand on her apron and with something close to reverence, held it out.

For a second my mother recoiled. A filament of fish gut, a thin pink worm, was caught between two fingers of the outstretched hand.

"Debora speaks so much about you," she said, recovering. In her best "how do you do" manner, she held the crooked hand firmly, as if testing her endurance. The damage, however, had already been done. The blue vein on Mrs. Shaloush's forehead stood out and started throbbing. It was the one that appeared whenever she began to drive away a bargaining customer with a torrent of insults. My mother, I knew, was under attack.

"Where are you from?" Mrs. Shaloush asked courteously.

"Hungary."

"Hmmph," Hanna's mother sniffed, her eyes sparking with a fire that, I thought, could burn all of Hungary and everyone in it. "Ashkenaz. European Jews. God didn't send Hitler to the Sephardic Jews because they didn't try to become like the locals. We knew who we were."

"You *still* know who you are," my mother said affably as if discussing the weather while holding a cocktail glass. "That's why you will always remain behind this counter."

Baffled, I watched the two women I loved. My mother's face wore a mask of European civility, but I saw the deep contempt in her eyes. And although I had often watched Mrs. Shaloush lose her temper, I had never before seen such ferocity in her expression; her lips parted to reveal a flash of angry fangs.

I stood there, paralyzed. Then I felt my mother's hand on mine, pulling me away. Somewhere behind me, Hanna's voice was calling. She was asking if I would be back tomorrow.

My mother marched ahead, gripping my hand. Very soon, we would be out of Hanna's hearing range. I didn't try to fight my mother's steady pull, but I turned my head and at the top of my lungs, I shouted yes, yes.

Debora Freund recently earned an MFA from Bennington College and has published previously in *Tikkun Magazine*.

THE REST OF HER LIFE/ *Steve Yarbrough*

T HE DOG was a mixture of god-knows-how-many breeds, but the vet had told them he had at least some rottweiler blood. You could see it in his shoulders, and you could hear it when he barked, which he was doing that night when they pulled up beside the gate and Chuckie cut the engine.

"Butch is out," Dee Ann said. "That's kind of strange."

Chuckie didn't say anything. He'd looked across the yard and seen her momma's car standing in the carport, and he was disappointed. Dee Ann's momma had told her earlier that she was going to buy some garden supplies at Western Auto and then eat something at the Sonic, and she'd said if she got back home and unloaded her purchases in time, she might run over to Greenville with one of the other teachers and watch a movie. Dee Ann had relayed the news to Chuckie tonight when he picked her up from work. That had gotten his hopes up.

The last two Saturday nights her momma had gone to Greenville, and they'd made love on the couch. They'd done it before in the car, but Chuckie said it was a lot nicer when you did it in the house. As far as she was concerned, the major difference was that they stood a much greater chance of getting caught. If her momma had walked in on them, she would not have gone crazy and ordered Chuckie away, she would have stayed calm and sat down and warned them not to do something that could hurt them later on. "There're things y'all can do now," she would have said, "that can mess y'all's lives up bad."

Dee Ann leaned across the seat and kissed Chuckie. "You don't smell *too* much like a Budweiser brewery," she said. "Want to come in with me?"

"Sure."

Butch was waiting at the gate, whimpering, his front paws up on the railing. Dee Ann released the latch, and they went in and walked across the yard, the dog trotting along behind them.

The front door was locked—a fact that Chuckie corroborated the next day. She knocked, but even though both the living room and the kitchen were lit up, her momma didn't come. Dee Ann waited for a few seconds, then rummaged through her purse and found the key. It didn't occur to her that somebody might have come home with her momma, that they might be back in the bedroom together, doing what she and Chuckie had done. Her momma still believed that if she could tough it out a few more months, Dee Ann's daddy would recover his senses and come back. Most of his belongings were still here.

Dee Ann unlocked the door and pushed it open. Crossing the threshold, she looked back over her shoulder at Chuckie. His eyes were shut. They didn't stay shut for long, he was probably just blinking, but that instant in which she saw them closed was enough to frighten her. She quickly looked into the living room. Everything was as it should be: the black leather couch stood against the far wall, the glass coffee table in front of it, two armchairs pulled up to the table at forty-five degree angles. The paper lay on the mantelpiece, right where her momma always left it.

"Momma?" she called. "It's me and Chuckie."

As she waited for a reply, the dog rushed past her. He darted into the kitchen. Again they heard him whimper.

She made an effort to follow the dog, but Chuckie laid his hand on her shoulder. "Wait a minute," he said. Afterwards he could never explain to anyone's satisfaction, least of all his own, why he had restrained her.

Earlier that evening, as she stood behind the checkout counter at the grocery store where she was working that summer, she had seen her daddy. He was standing on the sidewalk, looking in through the thick plate glass window, grinning at her.

It was late, and as always on a Saturday evening, downtown Indianola was virtually deserted. If people wanted to shop or go someplace to eat, they'd be out on the highway, at the Sonic or the new Pizza Hut. If they had enough money, they'd just head for Greenville. It had been a long time since anything much went on downtown after dark, which made her daddy's presence here that much more unusual. He waved, then walked over to the door.

The manager was in back, totalling the day's receipts. Except for him and Dee Ann and one stock boy who was over in the dairy aisle sweeping up, the store was empty.

Her daddy wore a pair of khaki pants and a short-sleeved pullover with an alligator on the pocket. He had on his funny-looking leather cap that reminded her of the ones policemen wore. He liked to wear that cap when he was out driving the MG.

"Hey, sweets," he said.

Even with the counter between them, she could smell whiskey on his breath. He had that strange light in his eyes.

"Hi, Daddy."

"When'd you start working nights?"

"A couple of weeks back."

"Don't get in the way of you and Buckie, does it?"

She started to correct him, tell him her boyfriend's name was Chuckie, but then she thought *Why bother?* He'd always been the kind of father who couldn't remember how old she was or what grade she was in. Sometimes he had trouble remembering she existed: years ago he'd brought her to this same grocery store, and after buying some food for his hunting dog, he'd forgotten about her and left her sitting on the floor in front of the magazine rack. The store manager had carried her home.

"Working nights is okay," she said. "My boyfriend'll be picking me up in a few minutes."

"Got a big night planned?"

"We'll probably just ride around a little bit and then head on home."

Her daddy reached into his pocket and pulled out his wallet. He extracted a twenty and handed it to her. "Here," he said. "You kids do something fun. On me. See a movie or get yourselves a six-pack of Dr. Pepper."

He laughed, to show her he wasn't serious about the Dr. Pepper, and then he stepped around the end of the counter and kissed her cheek. "You're still the greatest little girl in the world," he said. "Even if you're not very little anymore."

He was holding her close. In addition to whiskey, she could smell after-shave and deodorant and something else—a faint trace of perfume. She hadn't seen the MG on the street, but it was probably parked in the lot outside, and she bet his girlfriend was in it. She was just three years older than Dee Ann, a junior up at Delta State, though people said she wasn't going to school anymore. She and Dee Ann's daddy were living together in the apartment above the pharmacy he used to own and run. He'd sold the pharmacy last fall, just before he left home.

He didn't work anymore, and Dee Ann's momma had said she didn't know how he aimed to live, once the money from his business was gone. The other thing she didn't know—because nobody had told her—was that folks said his girlfriend sold the kinds of drugs you couldn't get in a pharmacy. Folks said he might be involved in that too.

He pecked her on the cheek once more, told her to have a good time with her boyfriend and to tell her momma he said hello, and then he walked out the door. Just as he left, the manager hit the switch, and the aisle lights went off.

That last detail—the lights going off when he walked out of the store—must have been significant, because the next day, as Dee Ann sat on the couch at her grandmother's house, knee to knee with the Sunflower County sheriff, Nick Colter, it kept coming up.

"You're sure about that?" Colter said for the third or fourth time. "When your daddy left the Piggly Wiggly, Mr. Lindsey was just turning out the lights?"

Her grandmother was in bed down the hall. The doctor and two women from the Methodist church were in the room with her. She'd been having chest pains off and on all day.

The dining room table was covered with food people had brought: two hams, a roast, a fried chicken, dish upon dish of potato salad, cole slaw, baked beans, two or three pecan pies, a pound cake. By the time the sheriff came, Chuckie had been there twice already—once in the morning with his momma and again in the afternoon with his daddy—and both times he had eaten. While his mother sat on the couch with Dee Ann, sniffling and holding her hand, and his father admired the knicknacks on the mantelpiece, Chuckie had parked himself at the dining room table and begun devouring one slice of pie after another, occasionally glancing through the doorway at Dee Ann. The distance between where he was and where she was could not be measured by any known means. She knew it, and he did, but he apparently believed that if he kept his mouth full, they wouldn't have to acknowledge it yet.

"Yes sir," she told the sheriff. "He'd just left when Mr. Lindsey turned off the lights."

A pocket-sized notebook lay open on Colter's knee. He held a ballpoint pen with his stubby fingers. He didn't know it yet, but he was going to get a lot of criticism for what he did in the next few days. Some people would say it cost him re-election. "And what time does Mr. Lindsey generally turn off the lights on a Saturday night?"

"Right around eight o'clock."

"And was that when he did it last night?"

"Yes sir."

"You're sure about that?"

"Yes sir."

"Well, that's exactly what Mr. Lindsey says too," Colter said. He closed the notebook and put it in his shirt pocket. "Course, being as he was in the back of the store, he didn't actually see you talking with your daddy."

"No," she said, "you can't see the check-out stands from back there."

Colter stood, and she did, too. To her surprise, he pulled her close to him. He was a compact man, not much taller than she was. Before he ran for sheriff he'd been a high school football coach.

She felt his warm breath on her cheek. "I sure am sorry about all of this, honey," he said. "But don't you worry. I guarantee you I'll get to the bottom of it. Even if it kills me."

Even if it kills me.

She remembers that phrase in those rare instances when she sees Nick Colter on the street downtown. He's an old man now, in his early sixties, white-haired and potbellied. For years he's worked at the catfish processing plant, though nobody seems to know what he does. Most people can tell you what he doesn't do. He's not responsible for security—he doesn't carry a gun. He's not front-office. He's not a foreman or a shift supervisor, and he has nothing to do with the live-haul trucks.

Chuckie works for Delta Electric, and once a month he goes to the plant to service the generators. He says Colter is always outside, wandering around, his head down, his feet scarcely rising off the pavement. Sometimes he talks to himself.

"I was out there last week," Chuckie told her not long ago, "and I'd just gone through the front gates, and there he was. He was off to my right, walking along the fence, carrying this bucket."

"What kind of bucket?"

"Looked like maybe it had some kind of caulking mix in it—there was this thick white stuff sticking to the sides. Anyway, he was shuffling along there and he was talking to himself to beat the band."

"What was he saying?"

They were at the breakfast table when they had this conversation. Their daughter, Cynthia, was finishing a bowl of cereal and staring into an algebra textbook. Chuckie glanced toward Cynthia, rolled his eyes at Dee Ann, then looked down at the table. He lifted his coffee cup, drained it and left for work.

But that night, when he crawled into bed beside her and switched off the light, she brought it up again. "I want to know what Nick Colter was saying to himself," she said. "When you saw him last week."

They weren't touching—they always left plenty of space between them—but she could tell he'd gone rigid. He did his best to sound groggy. "Nothing much."

She was rigid now too, lying stiffly on her back, staring up into the dark. "Nothing much is not nothing. Nothing much is still something."

"Won't you ever let it go?"

"*You* brought his name up. You bring his name up, and then you get this reaction from me, and then you're mad."

He rolled onto his side. He was looking at her, but she knew he couldn't make out her features. He wouldn't lay his palm on her cheek, wouldn't trace her jawbone like he used to. "Yeah, I brought his name up," he said. "I bring his name up, if you've noticed, about once a year. I bring his name up, and I bring up Joe Tierce's name, and I'd bring up Larry Lancaster's name, too, if he hadn't had the good fortune to move on to bigger things than being DA in a ten-cent town. I keep hoping I'll bring one of their names up, and after I say it, it'll be like I just said John Doe or Cecil Poe or Theodore J. Bilbo. I keep hoping I'll say it and you'll just let it go."

The ceiling fan, which was turned off, had begun to take shape. It looked like a big dark bird, frozen in mid-swoop. Three or four times she had woken up near dawn and seen that shape there, and it was all she could do to keep from screaming. One time she stuck her fist in her mouth and bit her knuckle.

"What was he saying?"

"He was talking to a quarterback," Chuckie said.

"What?"

"He was talking to a quarterback. He was saying some kind of crap like 'If they're in a roll-up zone, hit Jimmy over the middle.' He probably walks around all day thinking about when he was a coach, playing games over in his mind."

He rolled away from her then, got as close to the edge of the bed as he could. "He's like you," he said. "He's stuck back there too."

She had seen her daddy several times in between that Saturday night—when Chuckie walked into the kitchen murmuring, "Mrs. Williams? Mrs. Williams?"—and the funeral, which was held at the Methodist church the following Wednesday morning. He had come to her grandmother's house Sunday evening, had gone into her grandmother's room and sat by the bed, holding her hand and sobbing. Dee Ann remained in the living room, and she heard their voices, heard her daddy saying, "Remember how she had those big rings under her eyes after Dee Ann was born? How we all said she looked like a pretty little raccoon?" Her grandmother, whose chest pains had finally stopped, said, "Oh, Allen, I raised her from the cradle, and I know her well. She never would've stopped loving you." Then her daddy started crying again, and her grandmother joined in.

When he came out and walked down the hall to the living room, he had stopped crying, but his eyes were red-rimmed and his face looked puffy. He sat down in the armchair, which was still standing right where the sheriff had left it that afternoon. For a long time he said nothing. Then he rested his elbows on his knees, propped his chin on his fists, and said, "Were you the one that found her?"

"Chuckie did."

"Did you go in there?"

She nodded.

"He's an asshole for letting you do that."

She didn't bother to tell him how she'd torn herself out of Chuckie's grasp and bolted into the kitchen, or what had happened when she got in there. She was already beginning to think what she would later know for certain: in the kitchen she had died. When she saw the pool of blood on the linoleum, saw the streaks that shot like flames up the wall, a thousand-volt jolt hit her heart. She lost her breath, and the room went dark, and when it relit itself she was somebody else.

Her momma's body lay in a lump on the floor, over by the door that led to the back porch. The shotgun that had killed her, her daddy's Remington Wingmaster, stood propped against the kitchen counter. Back in what had once been called the game room, the sheriff would find that somebody had pulled down all the guns—six rifles, the other shotgun, both of her daddy's .38's—and thrown them on the floor. He'd broken the lock on the metal cabinet that stood nearby and he'd removed the box of shells and loaded the Remington.

It was hard to say what he'd been after, this man who for her was still a dark, faceless form. Her momma's purse had been ransacked, her wallet was missing, but there couldn't have been much money in it. She had some jewelry in the bedroom, but he hadn't messed with that. The most valuable things in the house were probably the guns themselves, but he hadn't taken them.

He'd come in through the back door—the lock was broken—and he'd left through the back door. Why Butch hadn't taken his leg off was anybody's guess. When the sheriff and his deputies showed up, it was all Chuckie could do to keep the dog from attacking.

"She wouldn't of wanted you to see her like that," her daddy said. "Nor me either." He spread his hands and looked at them, turning them over and scrutinizing the palms, as if he intended to read his own fortune. "I reckon I was lucky," he said, letting his gaze meet hers. "Anything you want to tell me about it?"

She shook her head no. The thought of telling him how she felt seemed somehow unreal. It had been years since she'd told him how she felt about anything that mattered.

"Life's too damn short," he said. "Our family's become one of those statistics you read about in the papers. You read those stories and you think it won't ever be you. Truth is, there's no way to insure against it."

At the time, the thing that struck her as odd was his use of the word *family*. They hadn't been a family for a long time, not as far as she was concerned.

She forgot about what he'd said until a few days later. What she remembered about that visit with him on Sunday night was that for the second time in twenty-four hours, he pulled her close and hugged her and gave her twenty dollars.

She saw him again Monday at the funeral home, and the day after that, and then the next day, at the funeral, she sat between him and her grandmother, and he held her hand while the preacher prayed. She had wondered if he would bring his girlfriend, but even he must have realized that would be inappropriate.

He apparently did not think it inappropriate, though, or unwise either, to present himself at the offices of an insurance company in Jackson on Friday morning, bringing with him her mother's death certificate and a copy of the coroner's report.

When she thinks of the morning—a Saturday—on which Nick Colter came to see her for the second time, she always imagines her own daughter sitting there on the couch at her grandmother's place instead of her. She sees Cynthia looking at the silver badge on Colter's shirt pocket, sees her glancing at the small notebook that lies open in his lap, at the pen gripped so tightly between his fingers that his knuckles have turned white.

"Now the other night," she hears Colter say, "your boyfriend picked you up at what time?"

"Right around eight o'clock." Her voice is weak, close to breaking. She just talked to her boyfriend an hour ago, and he was scared. His parents were pissed—pissed at Colter, pissed at him, but above all pissed at her. If she hadn't been dating their son, none of them would have been subjected to the awful experience they've just gone through this morning. They're devout Baptists, they don't drink or smoke, they've never seen the inside of a nightclub, their names have never before been associated with unseemly acts. Now the sheriff has entered their home and questioned their son as if he were a common criminal. It will cost the sheriff their votes come November. She's already lost their votes. She lost them when her daddy left her momma and started running around with a young girl.

"The reason I'm kind of stuck on this eight o'clock business," Colter says, "is you say that along about that time's when your daddy was there to see you."

"Yes sir."

"Now your boyfriend claims he didn't see your daddy leaving the store. Says he didn't even notice the MG on the street."

"Daddy'd been gone a few minutes already. Plus, I think he parked around back."

"Parked around back," the sheriff says.

"Yes sir."

"In that lot over by the bayou."

Even more weakly: "Yes sir."

"Where the delivery trucks come in—ain't that where they usually park?"

"I believe so. Yes sir."

Colter's pen pauses. He lays it on his knee. He turns his hands over, studying them as her daddy did a few days before. He's looking at his hands when he asks the next question. "Any idea why your daddy'd park his car *behind* the Piggly Wiggly—where there generally don't nothing but delivery trucks park—when Front Street was almost deserted and there was a whole row of empty spaces right in front of the store?"

The sheriff knows the answer as well as she does. When you're with a woman you're not married to, you don't park your car on Front Street on a Saturday night. Particularly if it's a little MG with no top on it, and your daughter's just a few feet away, with nothing but a pane of plate glass between her and a girl who's not much older than she is. That's how she explains it to herself anyway. At least for today.

"I think maybe he had his girlfriend with him."

"Well, I don't aim to hurt your feelings, honey," Colter says, looking at her now, "but there's not too many people that don't know about his girlfriend."

"Yes sir."

"You reckon he might've parked out back for any other reason?"

She can't answer that question, so she doesn't even try.

"There's not any chance, is there," he says, "that your boyfriend could've been confused about when he picked you up?"

"No sir."

"You're sure about that?"

She knows that Colter has asked Chuckie where he was between seven-fifteen, when several people saw her mother eating a burger at the Sonic Drive-in, and eight-thirty, when the two of them found her body. Chuckie has told Colter he was at home watching TV between seven-fifteen and a few minutes till eight, when he got in the car and went to pick up Dee Ann. His parents were in Greenville eating supper at that time, so they can't confirm his story.

"Yes sir," she says, "I'm sure about it."

"And you're certain your daddy was there just a few minutes before eight?"

"Yes sir."

"Because your daddy," the sheriff says, "remembers things just a little bit different. The way your daddy remembers it, he came by the Piggly Wiggly about seven-thirty and hung around there talking with you for half an hour. Course, Mr. Lindsey was in the back, so he can't say yea or nay, and the stock boy don't seem to have the sense God give a betsy bug. Your daddy was over at the VFW drinking beer at eight o'clock—stayed there till almost ten, according to any number of people, and his girlfriend wasn't with him. Fact is, his girlfriend left the country last Thursday morning. Took a flight from New Orleans to Mexico City, and from there it looks like she went on to Argentina."

Dee Ann, imagining this scene in which her daughter reprises the role she once played, sees Cynthia's face go slack as the full force of the information strikes her. She's still sitting there like that—hands useless in her lap, face drained of blood—when Nick Colter tells her that six months ago, her daddy took out a life insurance policy on her momma that includes double indemnity in the event of accidental death.

"I hate to be the one telling you this, honey," he says, "because you're a girl who's had enough bad news to last the rest of her life. But your daddy stands to collect half a million dollars because of your momma's death, and there's a number of folks—and I reckon I might as well admit I happen to be among them—who are starting to think that ought not to occur."

Chuckie gets off work at Delta Electric at six o'clock. A year or so ago she became aware that he'd started coming home late. The first time it happened, he told her he'd gone out with his friend Tim to have a beer. She saw Tim the next day buying a case of motor oil at Wal-Mart, and she almost referred to his and Chuckie's night out just to see if he looked surprised. But if he'd looked surprised, it would have worried her, and if he hadn't, it would have worried her even more: she would have seen it as a sign that Chuckie had talked to him beforehand. So in the end she nodded at Tim and kept her mouth shut.

It began happening more and more often. Chuckie ran over to Greenville to buy some parts for his truck, he ran down to Yazoo City for a meeting with the regional supervisor. He ran up into the north part of the county because a fellow who lived near Blaine had placed an interesting ad in *National Rifleman*—he was selling a shotgun with fancy scrollwork on the stock.

On the evenings when Chuckie isn't home, she avoids latching onto Cynthia. She wants her daughter to have her own life, to be independent, even if independence, in a sixteen-year-old girl, manifests itself as distance from her mother. Cynthia is on the phone a lot, talking to girlfriends, to boyfriends too. Through the bedroom door Dee Ann hears her laughter.

On the evenings when Chuckie isn't home, she sits on the couch alone, watching TV, reading, or listening to music. If it's a Friday or Saturday night and Cynthia is out with her friends, Dee Ann goes out herself. She doesn't go to movies, where her presence might make Cynthia feel crowded if she happened to be in the theatre too, and she doesn't go out and eat at any of the handful of restaurants in town. Instead she takes long walks. Sometimes they last until ten or eleven o'clock.

Every now and then, when she's on one of her walks, passing one house after another where entire families sit parked before the TV set, she allows herself to wish she had a dog to keep her company. What she won't allow herself to do—has never allowed herself to do as an adult—is actually own one.

The arrest of her father is preserved in a newspaper photo.

He has just gotten out of Sheriff Colter's car. The car stands parked in the alleyway between the courthouse and the Methodist church. Sheriff Colter is in the picture too, standing just to the left of her father, and so is one of his deputies. The deputy has his hand on her father's right forearm, and he is staring straight into the camera, as is Sheriff Colter. Her daddy is the only one who appears not to notice that his picture is being taken. He is looking off to the left, in the direction of Second Street, which you can't see in the photo, though she knows it's there.

When she takes the photo out and examines it, something she does with increasing frequency these days, she wonders why her daddy is not looking at the camera. A reasonable conclusion, she knows, would be that since he's about to be arraigned on murder charges, he doesn't want his face in the paper. But she wonders if there isn't more to it. He doesn't look particularly worried. He's not exactly smiling, but there aren't a lot of lines around his mouth, like there would be if he felt especially tense. Were he not wearing handcuffs, were he not flanked on either side by officers of the law, you would have to say he looks relaxed.

Then there's the question of what he's looking at. Joe Tierce's office is on Second Street, and Second Street is what's off the page, out of the picture. Even if the photographer had wanted to capture it in this photo, he couldn't have, not as long as he was intent on capturing the images of these three men. By choosing to photograph them, he chose not to photograph something else, and sometimes what's just outside the frame may be more important than what's actually in it.

After all, Second Street is south of the alley. And so is Argentina.

"You think he'd do that?" Chuckie said. "You think he'd actually kill your momma?"

They were sitting in his pickup when he asked her that question. The pickup was parked on a turnrow in somebody's cotton patch on a Saturday afternoon in August. By then her daddy had been in jail for the better part of two weeks. The judge had denied him bail, apparently believing that he aimed to leave the country. The judge couldn't have known that her daddy had no intention of leaving the country without the insurance money, which had been placed in an escrow account and wouldn't be released until he'd been cleared of the murder charges.

The cotton patch they were parked in was way up close to Cleveland. Chuckie's parents had forbidden him to go out with Dee Ann again, so she'd hiked out to 448, and he'd picked her up on the side of the road. In later years she'll often wonder whether or not she and Chuckie would have stayed together and gotten married if his parents hadn't placed her off-limits.

"I don't know," she said. "He sure did lie about coming to see me. And then there's Butch. If somebody broke in, he'd tear them to pieces. But he wouldn't hurt Daddy."

"I don't believe it," Chuckie said. A can of Bud stood clamped between his thighs. He lifted it and took a swig. "Your daddy may have acted a little wacky, running off like he did and taking up with that girl, but to shoot your momma and then come in the grocery store and grin at you and hug you? You really think *anybody* could do a thing like that?"

What Dee Ann was beginning to think was that almost everybody could do a thing like that. She didn't know exactly why this was so, but she believed it had something to do with being an adult and having ties. Having ties meant you were bound to certain things—certain people, certain places, certain ways of living. Breaking a tie was a violent act—even if all you did was walk out door number one and enter through door number two—and one act of violence could lead to another. You didn't have to spill blood to take a life. But after taking a life, you still might spill blood, if spilling blood would get you something else you wanted.

"I don't know what he might have done," she said.

"Every time I was ever around him," Chuckie said, "he was in a nice mood. I remember going in the drug store with Momma when I was just a kid. Your daddy was always polite and friendly. Used to give me free lollipops."

"Yeah, well, he never gave me any lollipops. And besides, your momma used to be real pretty."

"What's that supposed to mean?"

"It's not supposed to mean anything. I'm just stating a fact."

"You saying she's not pretty now?"

His innocence startled her. If she handled him just right, Dee Ann realized, she could make him do almost anything she wanted. For an instant she was tempted to put her hand inside his shirt, stroke his chest a couple of times, and tell him to climb out of the truck and stand on his head. She wouldn't always have such leverage, but she had it now, and a voice in her head urged her to exploit it.

"I'm not saying she's not pretty anymore," Dee Ann said. "I'm just saying that of course Daddy was nice to her. He was always nice to nice-looking women."

"Your momma was a nice-looking lady too."

"Yeah, but my momma was his wife."

Chuckie turned away and gazed out at the cotton patch for several seconds. When he looked back at her, he said, "You know what, Dee Ann? You're not making much sense." He took another sip of beer, then pitched the can out the window. "But with all you've been through," he said, starting the engine, "I don't wonder at it."

He laid his hand on her knee. It stayed there until twenty minutes later, when he let her out on 448, right where he'd picked her up.

Sometimes in her mind she has trouble separating all the men. It's as if they're revolving around her, her daddy and Chuckie and Nick

Colter and Joe Tierce and Larry Lancaster, as if she's sitting motionless in a hard chair, in a small room, and they're orbiting her so fast that their faces blur into a single image that seems suspended just inches away. She smells them too: smells after-shave and cologne, male sweat and whiskey.

Joe Tierce was a man she'd been seeing around town for as long as she could remember. He always wore a striped long-sleeved shirt and a wide tie that was usually loud-colored, perhaps to distract attention from the beer gut it could only partially hide. You would see him crossing Second Street, a coffee cup in one hand, his briefcase in the other. His office was directly across the street from the courthouse, where he spent much of his life, either visiting his clients in the jail, which was on the top floor, or defending those same clients downstairs in the courtroom itself.

Many years after he represented her father, Joe Tierce would find himself up on the top floor again, on the other side of the bars this time, accused of exposing himself to a twelve-year-old girl. After the story made the paper, several other women, most in their twenties or early thirties, would contact the local police and allege that he had also shown himself to them.

He showed himself to Dee Ann too, though not the same part of himself he showed to the twelve-year-old girl. He came to see her at her grandmother's on a weekday evening sometime after the beginning of the fall semester—she knows school was in session because she remembers that the morning after Joe Tierce visited her, she had to sit beside his son Edgar in senior English.

Joe sat in the same armchair that Nick Colter had pulled up near the coffee table. He didn't have his briefcase with him, but he was wearing another of those wide ties. This one, if she remembers correctly, had a pink background, with white fleurs-de-lis.

"How you making it, honey?" he said. "You been holding up all right?"

She shrugged. "Yes sir. I guess so."

"Your daddy's awful worried about you." He picked up the cup of coffee her grandmother had brought him before leaving them alone. "I don't know if you knew that or not," he said, taking a sip of the coffee. He set the cup back down. "He mentioned you haven't been to see him."

He gazed directly at her, and his big droopy eyelids gave him a lost-doggy look.

"No sir," she said, "I haven't gotten by there."

"You know what that makes folks think, don't you?"

She dropped her head. "No sir."

"Makes 'em think you believe your daddy did it."

That was the last thing he said for two or three minutes. He sat there sipping his coffee, looking around the room, almost as if he were a real estate agent sizing up the house. Just as she decided that he'd said all he intended to, his voice came back at her.

"Daddies fail," he told her. "Lordy, how we fail. You could ask Edgar. I doubt he'd tell the truth, though, because sons tend to be protective of their daddies, just like a good daughter protects her momma. But the *truth*, if you wanted to dig into it, is that I've failed that boy nearly every day he's been alive. You notice he's in the band? Hell, he can't kick a football or hit a baseball, and that's nobody's fault but mine. I remember when he was about this tall—" He held his hand, palm down, three feet from the floor. "—he came to me dragging this little plastic bat and said, 'Daddy, teach me to hit a baseball.' And you know what I told him? I told him, 'Son, I'm defending a man that's facing life in prison, and I got to go before the judge tomorrow morning and plead his case. You can take that bat and you can hitch a kite to it and see if the contraption won't fly.'"

He reached across the table then and laid his hand on her knee. She tried to remember who else had done that recently, but for the moment she couldn't recall.

When he spoke again, he kept his voice low, as if he was afraid he'd be overheard. "Dee Ann, what I'm telling you," he said, "is I know there's a lot of things about your daddy that make you feel conflicted. There's a lot of things he's done that he shouldn't have, and there's things he should've done that he didn't. There's a bunch of *should*s and *shouldn't*ts bumping around in your head, so it's no surprise to me that you'd get confused on this question of time."

She had heard people say that if they were ever guilty of a crime, they would want Joe Tierce to defend them. Now she knew why.

But she was not guilty of a crime, and she said so: "I'm not confused about time. He came when I said he did."

As if she were a sworn witness, Joe Tierce began, gently, regretfully, to ask her a series of questions. Did she really think her daddy was stupid enough to take out a life insurance policy on her mother and then kill her? If he aimed to leave the country with his girlfriend, would he send the girl first and then kill Dee Ann's momma and try to claim the money? Did she know that her daddy intended to put the money in a savings account for her?

Did she know that her daddy and his girlfriend had broken up, that the girl had left the country chasing some young South American who, her daddy admitted, had probably sold her drugs?

When he saw that she wasn't going to answer any of the questions, Joe Tierce looked down at the floor. It was as if he already knew that one day he'd find himself in a predicament similar to her father's: sitting in a small dark cell, accused of something shameful. "Honey," he said softly, "did you ever ask yourself why your daddy left you and your momma?"

That's one question she was willing and able to answer. "He did it because he didn't love us."

When he looked at her again, his eyes were wet—and she hadn't learned yet that wet eyes tell the most effective lies. "He loved y'all," Joe Tierce said. "But your momma, who was a wonderful lady—angel, she wouldn't give your daddy a physical life. I guarantee you he wishes to God he hadn't needed one, but a man's not made that way . . . and even though it embarrasses me, I guess I ought to add that I'm speaking from personal experience."

Personal experience.

At the age of thirty-eight, Dee Ann has acquired a wealth of experience, but the phrase *personal experience* is one she almost never uses. She's noticed men are a lot quicker to employ it than women are. Maybe it's because men think their personal experiences are somehow more personal than everybody else's. Or maybe it's because they take everything personally.

"My own personal experience," Chuckie told Cynthia the other day at the dinner table, after she'd finished ninth in the voting for one of eight positions on the cheerleading squad, "has been that getting elected cheerleader's nothing more than a popularity contest, and I wouldn't let not getting elected worry me for two seconds."

Dee Ann couldn't help it. "When in the world," she said, "did you have a *personal* experience with a cheerleader election?"

He laid his fork down. They stared at one another across a bowl of spaghetti. Cynthia, who can detect a developing storm front as well as any meteorologist, wiped her mouth on her napkin, stood up and said, "Excuse me."

Chuckie kept his mouth shut until she'd left the room. "I *voted* in cheerleader elections."

"What was personal about that experience?"

"It was my own personal vote."

"Did you have any emotional investment in that vote?"

"You ran once. I voted for you. I was emotional about you then."

She didn't even question him about his use of the word *then*—she knew perfectly well why he used it. "And when I didn't win," she said, "you took it personally?"

"I felt bad for you."

"But not nearly as bad as you felt for yourself?"

"Why in the hell would I feel bad for myself?"

"Having a girlfriend who couldn't win a popularity contest—wasn't that hard on you? Didn't you take it personally?"

He didn't answer. He just sat there looking at her over the bowl of spaghetti, his eyes hard as sandstone and every bit as dry.

Cynthia walks home from school, and several times in the last couple of years, Dee Ann, driving through town on her way back from a shopping trip or a visit to the library, has come across her daughter. Cynthia hunches over as she walks, her canvas backpack slung over her right shoulder, her eyes studying the sidewalk as if she's trying to figure out the pavement's composition. She may be thinking about her boyfriend or some piece of idle gossip she heard that day at school, or she may be trying to remember if the fourth president was James Madison or James Monroe, but her posture and the concentrated way she gazes down suggest that she's a girl who believes she has a problem.

Whether or not this is so Dee Ann doesn't know, because if her daughter is worried about something she's never mentioned it. What Dee Ann does know is that whenever she's out driving and she sees Cynthia walking home, she always stops the car, rolls her window down and says "Want a ride?" Cynthia always looks up and smiles, not the least bit startled, and she always says yes. She's never once said no, like Dee Ann did to three different people that day twenty years ago, when, instead of going to her grandmother's after school, she walked all the way from Highway 82 to the Sunflower County Courthouse and climbed the front steps and stood staring at the heavy oak door for several seconds before she pushed it open.

Her daddy has gained weight. His cheeks have grown round, the backs of his hands are plump. He's not getting any exercise to speak of. On Tuesday and Thursday nights, he tells her, the prisoners who want to keep in shape are let out of their cells, one at a time, and allowed to jog up and down three flights of stairs for ten minutes each. He says an officer sits in a straight-backed chair down in the courthouse lobby with a rifle across his lap to make sure that the prisoners don't jog any farther.

Her daddy is sitting on the edge of his cot. He's wearing blue denim pants and a shirt to match, and a patch on the pocket of the shirt says *Sunflower County Jail*. The shoes he has on aren't really shoes. They look like bedroom slippers.

Downstairs, when she checked in with the jailer, Nick Colter heard her voice and came out of his office. While she waited for the jailer to get the right key, the sheriff asked her how she was doing.

"All right, I guess."

"You may think I'm lying, honey," he said, "but the day'll come when you'll look back on this time in your life and it won't seem like nothing but a real bad dream."

Sitting in a hard plastic chair, looking at her father, she already feels like she's in a bad dream. He's smiling at her, waiting for her to say something, but her tongue feels like it's fused to the roof of her mouth.

The jail is air conditioned, but it's hot in the cell, and the place smells bad. The toilet over in the corner has no lid on it. She wonders how in the name of God a person can eat in a place like this. And what kind of person could actually eat enough to gain weight?

As if he knows what she's thinking, her father says, "You're probably wondering how I can stand it."

She doesn't answer.

"I can stand it," he says, "because I know I deserved to be locked up."

He sits there a moment longer, then gets up off the cot and shuffles over to the window, which has three bars across it. He stands there looking out. "All my life," he finally says, "I've been going in and out of all those buildings down there and I never once asked myself what they looked like from above. Now I know. There's garbage on those roofs and bird shit. One day I saw a man sitting up there, drinking from a paper bag. Right on top of Paul's Jewelers."

He turns around then and walks over and lays his hand on her shoulder.

"When I was down there," he says, "scurrying around like a chicken with its head cut off, I never gave myself enough time to think. That's one thing I've had plenty of in here. And I can tell you, I've seen some things I was too blind to see then."

He keeps his hand on her shoulder the whole time he's talking. "In the last few weeks," he says, "I asked myself how you must have felt when I told you I was too busy to play with you, how you probably felt every time you had to go to the old Honey Theatre by yourself and you saw all those other little girls waiting in line with their daddies and holding their hands." He says he's seen all the ways in which he failed them both, her and her mother, and he knows they both saw them a long time ago. He just wishes to God *he* had.

He takes his hand off her shoulder, goes back over to the cot and sits down. She watches, captivated, as his eyes begin to glisten. She realizes that she's in the presence of a man capable of anything, and for the first time she knows the answer to a question that has always baffled her: why would her momma put up with so much for so long?

The answer is that her daddy is a natural performer, and her momma was his natural audience. Her momma lived for these routines, she watched till watching killed her.

With watery eyes, Dee Ann's daddy looks at her, here in a stinking room in the Sunflower County Courthouse, on a September afternoon. "Sweetheart," he whispers, "you don't think I killed her, do you?"

When she speaks, her voice is steady, it doesn't crack and break. She will display no more emotion than if she were responding to a question posed by her history teacher.

"No sir," she tells her daddy. "I don't think you killed her. I *know* you did."

In that instant the weight of his life begins to crush her.

Ten-thirty on a Saturday night in 1997. She's standing alone in the alleyway outside the courthouse. It's the same alley where her father and Nick Colter and the deputy had their pictures taken all those years ago. Indianola is the same town it was then, except now there are gangs, and gunfire is something you hear all week long, not just on Saturday night. Now people kill folks they don't know.

Chuckie is supposedly at a deer camp with some men she's never met. He told her he knows them from a sporting goods store in Greenville. They all started talking about deer hunting, and one of the men told Chuckie he owned a cabin over behind the levee and suggested Chuckie go hunting with them this year.

Cynthia is out with her friends—she may be at a movie or she may be in somebody's back seat. Wherever she is, Dee Ann prays she's having fun. She prays that Cynthia's completely caught up in whatever she's doing and that she won't come along and find her momma here, standing alone in the alley beside the Sunflower County Courthouse, gazing up through the darkness as though she hopes to read the stars.

The room reminds her of a Sunday school classroom.

It's on the second floor of the courthouse, overlooking the alley. There's a long wooden table in the middle of the room, and she's sitting at one end of it in a straight-backed chair. Along both sides, in similar chairs, sit fifteen men and women who make up the Sunflower County grand jury. She knows several faces, three or four names. It looks as if every one of them is drinking coffee. They've all got styrofoam cups.

Down at the far end of the table, with a big manila folder open in front of him, sits Larry Lancaster, the district attorney, a man whose name she's going to be seeing in newspaper articles a lot in the next twenty years. He's just turned thirty, and though it's still warm out, he's wearing a black suit, with a sparkling white shirt and a glossy black tie.

Larry Lancaster has the reputation of being tough on crime, and he's going to ride that reputation all the way to the state attorney general's office and then to a federal judgeship. When he came to see her a few days ago, it was his reputation that concerned him. After using a lot of phrases like "true bill" and "no bill" without bothering to explain precisely what they meant, he said, "My reputation's at stake here, Dee Ann. There's a whole lot riding on you."

She knows how much is riding on her, and it's a lot more than his reputation. She feels the great mass bearing down on her shoulders. Her neck is stiff and her legs are heavy. She didn't sleep last night. She never really sleeps anymore.

"Now Dee Ann," Larry Lancaster says, "we all know you've gone through a lot recently, but I need to ask you some questions today so that these ladies and gentlemen can hear your answers. Will that be okay?"

She wants to say that it's not okay, that it will never again be okay for anyone to ask her anything, but she just nods.

He asks her how old she is.

"Eighteen."

What grade she's in.

"I'm a senior."

Whether or not she has a boyfriend named Chuckie Nelms.

"Yes sir."

Whether or not, on Saturday evening, August 2nd, 1977, she saw her boyfriend.

"Yes sir."

Larry Lancaster looks up from the stack of papers and smiles at her. "If I was your boyfriend," he says, "I'd want to see you *every* Saturday night."

A few of the men on the grand jury grin, but the women keep straight faces. One of them, a small red-haired woman with lots of freckles, whose name she doesn't know and never will know, is going to wait on her in a convenience store up in Ruleville many years later. After giving her change, the woman will touch Dee Ann's hand and say, "I hope the rest of your life's been easier, honey. It must have been awful, what you went through."

Larry Lancaster takes her through that Saturday evening, from the time Chuckie picked her up until the moment when she walked into the kitchen. Then he asks her, in a solemn voice, what she found there.

She keeps her eyes trained on his tie pin, a small amethyst, as she describes the scene in as much detail as she can muster. In a round-about way, word will reach her that people on the grand jury were shocked, and even appalled, at her lack of emotion. Chuckie will try to downplay their reaction, telling her that they're probably just saying that because of what happened later on. "It's probably not you they're reacting to," he'll say. "It's probably just them having hindsight."

Hindsight is something she lacks, as she sits here in a hard chair in a small room, her hands lying before her on a badly scarred table. She can't make a bit of sense out of what's already happened. She knows what her daddy was and she knows what he wasn't, knows what he did and didn't do. What she doesn't know is the whys and wherefores.

On the other hand, she can see into the future, she knows what's going to happen, and she also knows why. She knows, for instance, what question is coming, and she knows how she's going to answer it and why. She knows that shortly after she's given that answer, Larry Lancaster will excuse her, and she knows, because Joe Tierce has told her, that after she's been excused, Larry Lancaster will address the members of the grand jury.

He will tell them what they have and haven't heard. "Now she's a young girl," he'll say, "and she's been through a lot, and in the end this case has to rest on what she can tell us. And the truth, ladies and gentlemen, much as I might want it to be otherwise, is the kid's gone shaky on us. She told the sheriff one version of what happened at the grocery store that Saturday night when her daddy came to see her, and she's sat here today and told y'all a different version. She's gotten all confused on this question of time. You can't blame her for that, she's young and her mind's troubled, but in all honesty a good defense attorney's apt to rip my case apart. Because when you lose this witness's testimony, all you've got left is that dog, and that dog, ladies and gentlemen, can't testify."

That dog can't testify.

Even as she sits here, waiting for Larry Lancaster to bring up that night in the grocery store—that night which, for her, will always be the present—she knows the statement about the dog will be used to sentence Nick Colter to November defeat. The voters of this county will drape that sentence around the sheriff's neck. If Nick Colter had done his job and found some real evidence, they will say, that man would be on his way to Parchman.

They will tell one another, the voters of this county, how someone saw her daddy at the Jackson airport, as he boarded a plane that would take him to Miami, where he would board yet another plane for a destination farther south. They will say that her daddy was actually carrying a bag filled with money, with lots of crisp green hundreds, one of which he extracted to pay for a beer.

They will say that her daddy must have paid her to lie, that she didn't give a damn about her mother. They will wonder if Chuckie has a brain in his head, to go and marry somebody like her, and they will ask themselves how she can ever bear the shame of what she's done. They will not believe, not even for a moment, that she's performed some careful calculations in her mind. All that shame, she's decided, will still weigh a lot less than her daddy's life. It will be a while before she and Chuckie and a girl who isn't born yet learn how much her faulty math has cost.

Larry Lancaster makes a show of rifling through his papers. He pulls a sheet out and studies it, lets his face wrinkle up as if he's seeing something on the page that he never saw before. Then he lays the sheet back down. He closes his manila folder, pushes his chair away from the table a few inches and leans forward. She's glad he's too far away to lay his hand on her knee.

"Now," he says, "let's go backwards in time."

Steve Yarbrough is the author of two collections, *Family Men* and *Mississippi History*.

Reviews

¡*Yo!*
by Julia Alvarez
Algonquin, 309 pp., 1997, $18.95

Julia Alvarez' first two novels, *How the García Girls Lost Their Accents* and *In the Time of the Butterflies,* explore with pathos and humor the political plight of two Dominican families, the Garcías and the Mirabals. ¡*Yo!* is a less politically charged continuation of the García saga, but the Garcías do find a spy of sorts in their midst: Yolanda García, more familiarly known as "Yo." Yo is a writer who uses her own family as fictional fodder. This, of course, causes the Garcías much distress and confusion; her sisters find themselves inadvertently quoting their characters, and her mother threatens to sue her.

But Yo's encounters with her family are only a small part of the story. The novel, which spans Yo's life from her childhood to the present, is a collection of observations about Yo from family, friends, lovers, and even a stalker. The portrait that emerges is of a woman who carelessly plunges into several marriages, yet gingerly and patiently forges a complicated relationship with her stepdaughter. The Yo that is described in the first half of the novel is infuriating and ingratiating,

honest in her writing but often dishonest in life.

Unfortunately, Alvarez does not sustain this multidimensional characterization of Yo. Yo's encounters with her domestically abused landlady and an illiterate Dominican farmer are resolved too neatly; her ability to help them turn their lives completely around seems out of character for a woman whose own life is constantly in chaos. Such easy resolutions are also a somewhat contrived means of presenting Yo as a sympathetic character. Yet what makes Yo so engaging for the majority of the novel is that she *isn't* saintly; her artistic gift doesn't grant her moral authority over others.

Also troubling is that Yo is the most static character in the novel. One of the strengths of Alvarez' previous works was her deft handling of many speakers whose points of view both reinforced and contradicted one another, resulting in stories which were at once personal and sweeping. In comparison, ¡*Yo!* is an entertaining read and an interesting examination of the personal toll writing takes on those who find their own lives fictionalized, but the novel ultimately lacks the lingering emotional impact of Alvarez' prior work. (KL)

A Crime in the Neighborhood
by Suzanne Berne
Algonquin, 1997, 285 pp., $17.95

This startling debut novel presents a wholesome neighborhood in Maryland as a microcosm of the Watergate Era. The protagonist, Marsha, is an eerily observant ten year old whose peculiar misinterpretations of the problems surrounding her are by-products of this time of calamitous social change. Though the book's title primarily refers to the murder of a twelve-year-old boy from Marsha's presumably safe community, it also describes a multitude of other events that take place in the course of the novel: Marsha's father's affair with her eccentric aunt; his neglect of the family at a time when everything around them seems to be failing apart; and the scandals occurring right around the corner in Washington, D.C., which provide a backdrop for the story.

A naïve child surrounded by symbols of domestic and political turmoil, Marsha is overwhelmed by the question, "Why do people hurt each other?" Fascinated and frustrated with the confusing mechanics of pain, she records clues concerning the murder and other neighborhood "crimes" in a painstakingly detailed notebook. Recalling the start of this project, she remarks, "I had never realized our house contained so many damaged things. Soon it seemed I couldn't look at anything without finding something wrong with it." This statement foreshadows the paranoia with which Marsha comes to view her entire neighborhood, as she dedicates herself to monitoring the trivial activities of particular neighbors.

The adults in this story, much like Marsha, are propelled by fierce determination and a lack of understanding. When news of the boy's murder breaks, several fathers establish a "Night Watch," in which they take turns patrolling the community in a futile search for evidence. Marsha's next door neighbor, a single man out of place in a family neighborhood, becomes the prime murder suspect, both in her notebook and in the minds of frightened parents.

But the story is about more than a child's death and its burgeoning effects. It is evident that the neighbors mourn not only the loss of an individual but also the loss of a "safe neighborhood"—essentially a society that allowed them to trust their neighbors, their spouses, and their politicians. The paranoia of Marsha's notebook and the gossip of the community result from an inability to deal with the chaos of change. Although Berne clearly views the efforts of the characters to discover the child's murderer as a type of witch hunt, she refrains from villainizing them for this mistake. "Because the truth is, mistakes are where life really happens," the narrator observes midway through the book. "Mistakes are when we get tricked into realizing something we never meant to realize, which is why stories are about mistakes. Mistakes are the moments when we don't know what will happen to us next."

Berne successfully intertwines the domestic and the political in this suspenseful novel. Although most of Marsha's questions raised in the course of the story remain unanswered, she is changed by her grappling with them and, by the end, she has at least begun to understand why people hurt each other. Disturbingly, she learns this by hurting someone else.

Economical but far-reaching, *A Crime in the Neighborhood* offers a frighteningly believable account of how a small community reacts to a changing society. (MM)

Edouard Manet: Rebel in a Frock Coat
by Beth Archer Brombert
Little, Brown, 1996, 505 pp., $29.95

Edouard Manet may be the only impressionist whose work has retained its capacity to shock. Monet, Renoir, Dègas, Cézanne, Gaugin, all radicals in their time, have been sentimentalized almost into meaninglessness. Monets hang on dormitory walls, Dègas dancers (who were just a step above prostitutes in their time) hang in little girls' pink bedrooms. Even Van Gogh's most psychotic self-portraits are the stuff of postcards and children's art history books. The impressionists, for the most part, just aren't scary anymore.

But Manet's masterworks—the aggressively sexual prostitute in *Olympia*, the satiric decadence of *Déjeuner Sur L'Herbe*, the pathos of *Bar at the Folies Bergère*—have not been tamed. It is the great irony of Manet's life that he, more than any of his contemporaries, craved popular acceptance. The contradictions in Manet's character, the public's response to his art and the obstinacy that made him continue to paint unsettling, unpopular pictures while craving public acclaim, should be the makings of a good biography. Unfortunately, while

Beth Archer Brombert gives us a wealth of information about Manet's life, she somehow manages to miss the man.

Part of the problem is that much of the book is taken up with trying to solve the two great mysteries of Manet's life, yet Brombert comes to no new conclusions about them. Yes, Manet was almost certainly the father of an illegitimate son who carried his wife's maiden name and yes, Manet probably had an affair with the artist Berthe Morisot. Brombert spends page after page attempting to document these "transgressions," but comes up with neither definitive proof, nor any new insights into their effects on the artist's life. We learn much about the politics of the Salon, the tastes of the times and the fact that Manet was widely ridiculed. But we never get to the heart of what made Manet steady in his vision in the face of rejection, mockery and a consuming desire for popularity.

Finally, the book reproduces Manet's works in black and white, so when Brombert is discussing the artist's palette, one is left either to imagine what his pictures really look like, or to consult another book with color plates. This failing provides an apt metaphor for the whole book. While Brombert's biography seems, superficially, to be an accurate account of Edouard Manet's history, it lacks color; Manet's essence never comes across. (WJ)

Love Warps the Mind a Little
by John Dufresne
W.W. Norton, 1997, 315 pp., $23

Laf Proulx is an oft-rejected writer who's working in a fish and chips stand. He's just been kicked out by his wife for having an affair, so he's staying with his lover, Judi Dubey—whom he's not sure he loves. Luckily, the lack of feeling is mutual. Judi sets Laf up on the couch and encourages him to enter marriage counseling and see if he can reconcile with his wife. Laf goes along with this plan enthusiastically, but he eventually admits to himself that things just aren't going to work out.

About this time, Judi is diagnosed with cancer. Laf is the kind of person who isn't sure he knows how to love, but he does know how to do the right thing. He cares for Judi, taking her to the hospital, nursing her through graphically described chemotherapy, talking with her about dying—and in so doing, Laf falls in love with Judi for real.

All of which may make the book sound like a bad episode of Oprah: midlife-crisis men whose lovers get cancer. But it is much more than that. Laf and Judi are surrounded by a hilarious, if sometimes confusing, cast of supporting characters, including Judi's schizo father, Laf's gallant dog Spot, and Judi's trailer-trash family. Laf is an irresistibly funny narrator, possessing at once a kind heart and a mordant wit. The book keeps you turning pages, but at the same time manages to be moving and profound. In fact, *Love Warps the Mind a Little* is surely the funniest book you'll ever read about a midlife crisis and a battle with cancer. (WJ)

Inventing Mark Twain: The Lives of Samuel Langhorne Clemens
by Andrew Hoffman
William Morrow, 1997, 568 pp., $30

What distinguishes this biography of Samuel L. Clemens from predecessors like Albert Bigelow Paine's epic work, *Mark Twain: A Biography,* and Justin Kaplan's *Mr. Clemens and Mark Twain,* is Hoffman's equal interest in Clemens, deeply flawed man and writer, and Mark Twain, nom de plume and creation. Hoffman skillfully demonstrates the dichotomy between the brilliant, eccentric public man of letters, Twain, and the cowardly, self-destructive narcissist, Clemens. This division is described in an engrossing psychobiography that attributes Clemens' literary "schizophrenia" to childhood insecurities.

Clemens was born November 30, 1835, in the frontier hamlet of Florida, Missouri, to John Marshall Clemens, a lawyer whose poor fiscal management kept his family in dire straits, and Jane Lampton Clemens, an anxious mother who doted on the sickly child. Never receiving approval from his father, Samuel sought center stage from his mother and his older siblings, becoming a wild, unmanageable boy, given to explosions of unprovoked rage.

Driven out of Florida by debts, John Clemens moved the family to Hannibal, Missouri, where Sam, although a voracious reader, hung out with his fellow hooky players, smoking, drinking, and cursing. When his father died, the teenager traveled from city to city, working for various newspapers, becoming a man of influence and fortune at the age of twenty-five when he received his riverboat pilot's license. All he wanted now was fame, which he believed he would get through his pen.

He received his first taste of literary celebrity at thirty with "Jim Smiley and his Jumping Frog," a story written by Mark Twain, the pseudonym Clemens had first used while writing letters as a journalist. Clemens then had the idea of giving humorous lectures based on his travel experiences, making Mark Twain a theatrical attraction in order to gain an audience. His idea was so successful that when he married Olivia Langdon in 1869, newspapers reported the marriage of Mark Twain, not Samuel Clemens.

Hoffman recounts Clemens' history of personal tragedies: loss of family members and friends, attempted suicide, disastrous investments, and the eventual humiliation of being forced by enormous debts to tour as Mark Twain, an alter ego he was by then weary of. By 1902, between royalties and investments made for him by a close friend, Henry Rogers, he had regained financial security, but after the death of his wife in 1904, another cloud was cast on his fame by rumors of his appetite for association with young girls.

In *Pudd'nhead Wilson's New Calendar* (1897), Mark Twain wrote, "Every man is a moon and has a dark side which he never shows to anybody." Throughout this biography, Hoffman repeats the premise that Sam Clemens considered himself a failure and a coward and that he had constructed Mark Twain as a brave and successful alter ego behind whose image he could camouflage his private nature. Hoffman's clear style and his mastery of some of the excellent recent scholarship on Twain help elucidate the dark side of one of the most widely known writers in the world. (JB)

Tropical Classical: Essays from Several Directions
by Pico Iyer
Knopf, 1997, 313 pp., $25

This collection of Pico Iyer's magazine features suffers from having too many different kinds of writing in it. It includes some twenty denatured pieces from *Time* magazine, *Condé Nast Traveler*, and *Islands*, alongside heftier articles from *The Smithsonian* and the *New York Review of Books*. The book includes everything from longish travel pieces about Ethiopia and Kathmandu to glib toss-offs about the wonders of the comma and "Confessions of a Frequent Flier." Its section headings are "Places," "People," "Books," "Themes," and "Squibs"—in other words, everything the sedulous journalist could find in his files that still looked good.

Iyer tailors his features to the magazine, and differences in styles, lengths, and viewpoints make for a hodgepodge. One can have fun guessing the magazine that each article appeared in, because the permissions page, coyly tucked at the back of the book, is evasive about the original venue of all except the selections from *Time*.

Iyer first became known as a travel writer with books like *Cuba and the Night* and *Falling off the Map*. The "places" selections here are solid—full of mood and detail and enjoyment—but without the final stamp of individuality that could put them in the highest rank of travel writing.

The best pieces in this miscellany are longish review essays written in the style of the *New York Review of*

Books. Over half of the reviews are of works by post-colonial authors of mixed Indian, Pakistani, and English background—Salman Rushdie, Ruth Prawer Jhabvala, R. K. Narayan, and others—while the remaining ones are of books by American authors. Iyer is an enthusiastic and generous reader, writing jargonless, vivid, open-minded review essays. He is good at the primary job of a reviewer, inspiring readers to try certain authors. Also, he is perceptive at locating weaknesses, as when he describes Ruth Jhabvala's fiction, despite its many virtues, as being so obsessed by charlatans and manipulators—particularly spiritual charlatans and seekers—that she paints almost all of her characters as either manipulators or deserving victims.

An essay on Salman Rushdie begins with the provocative statement: "The great problem with Salman Rushdie, I have often felt, is that he is simply too talented. And no writer has seemed more captive to his gifts: his powers of invention and imagination are so prodigal and so singular that he often gives the impression of not knowing when to stop . . . the puns and polycultural references and paralleling images multiply to the point of overload." While holding to this criticism, Iyer goes on to praise Rushdie as perhaps the best of the new East-West writers.

Iyer's own style suffers a little from a similar talent: it is aphoristic sometimes to a fault. His prose occasionally falls into rhetorical autopilot, with one clever bon mot following another, until one wonders if the author has been reading too much Oscar Wilde and gotten drowsy over his word processor. Whatever its faults, this miscellany is worth picking up for Iyer fans and for those who want an introduction to the contemporary East-West literary renaissance. (SM)

*The Perfect Storm: A True
Story of Men Against the Sea*
by Sebastian Junger
W. W. Norton, 1997, 227 pp., $23.95

Junger's book is about a storm off the coast of Nova Scotia in October, 1991, in which the swordfishing boat *Andrea Gail* disappeared with its six crewmen. Since the boat was out of radio contact well before she sank, the scarcity of known details about the central event might seem to be a serious flaw. However, Junger turns a weakness to an advantage by taking lack of information as an occasion to discuss the larger picture of sea storms, the meteorology of storms, the nature of high waves, swordfishing, boat construction, anecdotes of previous sinkings, and the effect of this particular storm on other boats within its vicinity, including the extraordinary trials of ships that did make it through. The book's climax describes the spectacular rescue of the crew of an undermanned wooden sailing boat.

Like a lot of fishing boats, the broad-beamed *Andrea Gail* had been refitted by eyeball and welding-torch engineering. Her crew, from Gloucester, Massachusetts, were used to the rigors of swordfishing. Called longlining because of the miles of hooks set out on single lines, swordfishing is grueling work that occasionally results in baiters getting hooked and jerked overboard. Swordfishing requires staying at sea for four or five weeks at a time, sometimes making no money, and at other times hitting the jackpot.

Swordfishermen are an especially hard-bitten, fatalistic lot, who often carouse in port for a week or so before going back out to sea. They may earn five thousand dollars from a haul, much of which they manage to blow while ashore, bouncing between the three fishermen bars of Gloucester. At times, so many ebullient fishermen are buying rounds for the house that the bartenders put out plastic token bottles so the beer doesn't get hot.

The "perfect storm" itself resulted from the uncommon coincidence of an arctic eddy, or anticyclone, that created a low-pressure trough along its front, being met by a mature Hurricane Grace coming up from the south. This created something like two giant meteorological gears, called nor'easters by New Englanders, spinning everything between them toward the shoreline of North America, generating one-hundred foot waves capable of blowing out inch-thick porthole glass, drowning engines, or picking up a loaded boat like the *Andrea Gail* and flipping her end over end. Even when she made it up and over such waves, at any time she could careen down the other side and simply punch into the sea and never resurface.

Junger is fascinated by the archetypal elements of his story—the experience inside a sinking ship, what it's like to drown—but he generally maintains enough distance from such subjects to avoid becoming morbid.

The author himself is a New Englander, not accustomed to being in the limelight, who does not enjoy staying in motels and hotels and taking expensive taxis. Junger apparently feels more at home sleeping in his tent and prefers hitchhiking over expensive cab rides. His harried publicist at W.W. Norton is said to have pleaded with him in a recent phone conversation, "Please take the taxi. You can afford it. You're number three on the best-seller list!" *The Perfect Storm* is in the tradition of John McPhee—sturdy English prose, a fine sense of rhetoric and drama employed to describe extraordinary forces in nature. I highly recommend it. (SM)

Celibates & Other Lovers
by Walter Keady
MacMurray & Beck, 1997, 225 pp., $20

In Walter Keady's first novel, *Celibates & Other Lovers,* the comedy comes from the characters' incongruities, as saintly types harbor sinful longings and former sinners try to become saints. Fearfully pious Phelim O'Brian receives the Divine Call of priesthood, yet he longs for the evil delights of the flesh, particularly for the soft, fair skin of red-headed Catherine McGrath. Sensual, good-natured Philpot Emmet, or "Pisspot," as he is called in school, inherits, from his father's family, a "powerful libidinous strain." Despite the verbal castigations of his schoolmaster father, he has countless love affairs before becoming a devout Catholic and family man—for awhile anyway.

Set in Creevagh, Ireland, in the years right after World War II, Keady's book depicts a village that fears the wrath of a vengeful God, the spread of the yellow peril, Communism, and the talk of its own gossips. A product of Irish farm life himself, Keady writes about small town agrarian existence with respect and humor. His insight, declared early in the novel, that "a man's plans are subject to change when warranted by events," is borne out by the lives of his characters. Like Phelim and Philpot, the other inhabitants of Creevagh seldom get what they want, even though they struggle laboriously. Shy, soft-spoken Seamus Laffey wants to marry dreamy-eyed Eileen Maille, who wants to date the freckled townie who owns a fancy motorcar. City councilor Jack Higgins aspires to a more lucrative position, but his bank roller and most powerful political connection, Martin Mulligan, dies, leaving his future uncertain. And Phelim's Catherine McGrath does not want to give over her strapping young fellow to God. Overcome with passion, she asks why priests, who are "heirs to the flesh" as much as anyone, are forbidden to do "what nature was forever screaming out for."

When Creevagh's most eligible bachelor, Timmy Mulligan, marries a widow, believing she is still a virgin, Maura Higgins, feminist, Communist sympathizer, and one of the novel's more self-aware characters, declares to giggling Eileen Maille, "We're laughing at stupidity and innocence and deceit and greed and hope and despair; all things that make life worthwhile." All things

that make this novel a worthwhile read as well. (KS)

Into Thin Air
by Jon Krakauer
Villard, 1997, 294 pp., $24.95

This is an amazing account of the disastrous 1996 commercial expedition to the top of Everest by a mountaineer who was there. The clients of such expeditions pay tens of thousands of dollars to be guided to the summit. The trip takes a month or two because of the necessity of acclimatizing oneself to various elevations. Finally, after a sleepless (because of the altitude) night at Camp Four, the client makes the two-mile run to the summit—weather permitting—on the ropes and ladders that Sherpas have laid out for him some hours before.

Krakauer was funded by *Outside* magazine to investigate the phenomenon of such commercial expeditions, and he got much more than he bargained for. He was alarmed by the competitiveness of the Western guides, and also of the Sherpas, for whom a successful ascent leads to lifetime employment. Krakauer himself had a small role in the disaster. He misidentified one of his fellows as being in a safe location and so fatally delayed a search—a mistake that haunted him for months afterward.

As climbers say, getting to the top is easy, it's getting down that's the hard part. Everest, in particular, is not an especially "interesting" ascent; what it requires is not finesse, but almost superhuman endurance. Above 225,000 feet, even with supplemental oxygen, climbers grow dizzy, headachy and confused. When Krakauer reached the summit he spent only a few minutes there and experienced no elation whatsoever; he could think only of the fresh oxygen tank cached for him a few hundred yards down.

The critical feature of the final climb is the turnaround time, the time at which it's necessary to go back, for reasons of safety, no matter how close one is to the summit. The guides on Krakauer's expedition were adamant about the turnaround time (1:30 p.m.) until the day of the final ascent, when they broke their own rule. Then a storm moved in, and several climbers died, both from Krakauer's group and from the dozen other groups who were on the mountain at the same time.

Krakauer's account contains many astounding examples of foolhardiness and courage: the New York socialite who had the latest issues of fashion magazines brought to her by Sherpa runner; the Taiwanese group who ignored the death of one of their comrades; the man who was left for dead and who later walked into camp under his own power. All these tales are told in the plain voice of a humble but expert climber with fine moral sensibilities—a voice that is intrinsically believable.

With the help of a few maps and pithy descriptions of nature, the author places us on the Khumbu Icefall, the South Col and the Hillary Step, while making us keenly appreciate the warmth and safety of our reading rooms. What he doesn't do is make explicit judgments about expeditions like the one he took part in. He leaves it to readers to decide whether or not anyone at all should be paying to climb Everest and whether or not reaching the summit isn't an essentially dumb idea.

Krakauer has written three previous nonfiction books, including *Into the Wild*, the story of a young man who attempted to live off the land in an abandoned bus during the Alaskan winter. *Into Thin Air*, notable for its careful refusal to go beyond the facts, is his best yet. (JS)

Lightning Song
by Lewis Nordan
Algonquin, 1997, 273 pp., $18.95

Early in Nordan's hilarious fourth novel, Leroy, the lonely twelve year old from whose innocent perspective the story is told, resuscitates his grandfather, whom he's found lifeless in the attic of his family's house on a Mississippi llama farm. Hours later, Old Pappy dies for good, and Leroy's lazy Uncle Harris moves in, bringing with him dirty magazines, alcohol, the daily news, and a sensual excitement that captivates Leroy's romantic mother, Elsie. As the oddly stormy events of the summer that follows illustrate, when fantasy becomes reality, it does so like a lightning bolt: the force is quick, but the effects linger.

An extraordinary burst of seasonal thunderstorms batters the Mississippi countryside, and lightning frequently hits Leroy's house. Eerie fireballs regularly come down the chimney and bounce around the small farmhouse. Leroy is discovering his hormones, however, and his attention remains firmly focused on the sexual tension that electrifies his family more effectively than the harmless lightning balls: Elsie sneaks kisses from Uncle Harris; Swami Don, Leroy's father, begins an affair at his part-time job; and Leroy is infatuated with and seduced by a high-school baton-twirling beauty.

The strength of the story rests in the muddled view Leroy takes toward the summer's swirling events. As they unfold, his perception widens and his self-awareness grows, though much of his newfound knowledge is based on misconception. Leroy comes to understand his mother's desire for Harris after "creepy-crawling" through his uncle's skin magazines. Yet when the baton-twirling Ruby Rae tricks him into his first sexual experience, Leroy realizes that sex is "entirely different from the pictures in Uncle Harris' magazines. Entirely different."

As the novel progresses, we find that Leroy's emerging perspective is not all that different from that of the adults around him. Elsie constructs a romantic vision of herself and Harris as a way to escape the monotony of the farm. Swami Don, whose left arm is useless due to a shooting accident, forges a relationship to bolster his self-esteem. But when faced with actual sex, both are embarrassed to discover, like Leroy, the vast differences between fantasy and reality. Even Uncle Harris, the icon of fresh sexuality to Leroy at the summer's start, is reduced to "creepy-crawling" in the attic on the phone with his estranged wife.

If *Lightning Song* lacks the impact of Nordan's last book, *The Sharp-shooter Blues*, it's nevertheless a memorable novel. Nordan's sense of the vernacular is keen, and as always, he delights in finding humor in the apparently tragic and pathetic events of life. (GH)

The Universal Donor
by Craig Nova
Houghton Mifflin, 1997, 250 pp., $23

Nova is fully in the driver's seat in this tale of love and crime and medicine set in southern California; novels this well made don't come along every day. It's the story of Terry McKechnie, single, thirty-something emergency room doctor, whose type O blood makes him the universal donor of the title. Terry is committed to his profession and not yet hardened by his daily caseload of gunshot and stabbing victims. He's sensitive and lonely, and plagued by a sense of emptiness that he quells in his few free hours by taking Xanax.

When a young, on-the-edge scientist named Virginia Lee shows up in the ER after being bitten by an exotic venomous snake, Terry finds himself in over his head, both professionally and emotionally. The case is complicated by the fact that Virginia is allergic to the antivenom—a reaction is potentially as fatal as the snakebite itself—and by the lack of available information about how to treat such a bite. To make matters worse, Virginia's blood is a rare type that breaks down any donated blood unless it matches hers. Ironically, when she begins to hemorrhage, Terry, the universal donor, can't give blood to save her.

The story of Terry's past connection with Virginia, gradually revealed in the course of the novel, and that of his efforts to find a blood donor for her, are fraught with intrigue and daring coincidence. There's plenty of sex and passion and danger, all of which Nova, something of a romantic, seems to applaud as essential to human fulfillment. There's betrayal and adultery, and all the violence and tragedy that one would expect a Los Angeles ER physician to be witness to. There's also an ex-con/car thief/rapist with whom Terry develops a curious co-dependent relationship and has several serious heart-to-hearts.

If the plot sometimes seems a bit too contrived, and the whole a touch too stylized, these are forgivable flaws in a book that manages to entertain so eloquently. Nova's mastery of his craft is impressive and the moral question he poses is an important one: how much do we owe to ourselves and how much to others; and at what price does self-fulfillment become too costly? (ES)

Dickens' Fur Coat and Charlotte's Unanswered Letters: The Rows and Romances of England's Great Victorian Novelists
by Daniel Pool
HarperCollins, 1997, 282 pp., $25

As in his previous book about nineteenth-century British fiction, *What Jane Austen Ate and Charles Dickens Knew* (1993), Pool effectively transports his readers to another era, one that the reader will discover was only a little less media-driven than our own.

While his last book engagingly explicated the cultural allusions in popular Victorian novels, Pool's new work offers gossipy tidbits about Victorian publishing, and about the lives of the authors themselves. Pool begins with the advent of the "new" Victorian novel, citing Charles Dickens as the founding father whose fiction marked the beginning of a new generation of novelists energized by changes in the publishing industry. Much of Pool's "gossip" about the personal lives of nineteenth-century writers is already well-known: Dickens' disastrous marriage that ended after his affair with the young actress, Ellen Ternan; George Eliot's cohabitation with a married man; and Charlotte Brontë's unrequited love for her publisher, George Smith.

More interesting is Pool's account of a publishing industry characterized by an increasingly "Hollywoodesque" attitude that advocated celebrity gossip, the creation of public frenzy, and the manipulation of the literary market as acceptable techniques for inflating profits. Pool cites Henry Colburn, one of early nineteenth-century England's most prominent publishers, as the harbinger of hype, a man notorious for hiring people to dine in public and discuss his books, and even for creating news by having himself arrested for the purposes of publicity.

Unfortunately, the book's poor organization and Pool's tendency to repeat anecdotes are annoying and ultimately interfere with overall continuity. However, aside from those flaws, and the outworn nature of some of the material, *Dickens' Fur Coat and Charlotte's Unanswered Letters* is an entertaining read for anyone interested in the book world of Victorian England. (AW)

American Pastoral
by Philip Roth
Houghton Mifflin, 1997, 423 pp., $26

The prolific Roth shows that there is no such thing as a charmed life in this spectacular novel. "Swede" Levov, a blue-eyed, golden haired Jew and the greatest athlete in the history of Newark's Weequahic High, seems at first to have it all. Like a movie idol, he is adored by men and women, young and old. On the court or field, his magical name inspires a personalized cheer: "Swede Levov! It rhymes with The Love." But when former childhood admirer Nathan Zuckerman (Roth's alter ego in several of his novels), is contacted by the Swede fifty years later for professional advice on writing a tribute for his deceased father, Zuckerman discovers that Levov's life is falling apart. The Swede's specialty women's glove company, Newark Maid, is in trouble; his marriage to "an up-and-coming Irish looker," Miss New Jersey 1949, Mary Dawn Dwyer, has ended in divorce; and he battles prostate cancer, an illness Zuckerman himself is fighting.

Sometime later, when he sees Jerry, the Swede's less adulated heart-surgeon brother, at their forty-fifth high school reunion, Zuckerman learns that the legendary Swede has died, and that his adulthood was "plagued with shame and uncertainty and pain" thanks to his revolutionary daughter, Merry, the "Rimrock Bomber" who blew up a post office, killing the local doctor, during the Vietnam War.

Beautiful, stuttering Merry's transformation from a bright, inquisitive, though slightly high-strung, child into a terrorist is horrifying and at the same time enthralling. One of Roth's greatest accomplishments is his depiction of parental anguish. At the novel's most heartbreaking moment, after years of searching, the Swede finds Merry, a broken woman living in a squalid rented room. As a converted Jain—a member of a small Indian religious sect that preaches nonviolence—she is unable now, after killing four people, to wash or eat for fear of destroying microorganisms. Blinded until now by his own perfection and hampered by his inability to probe beneath mere surfaces, the Swede finally learns through Merry's catastrophe to "penetrate to the interiors of people" and discovers that they are never who one imagines.

Like all masterpieces, *American Pastoral* goes beyond the characters' personal histories: The Swede's story parallels America's postwar rise and then sudden fall during the turbulent 1960s. The Levovs' troubled father-daughter relationship mirrors the struggle between the peace and tranquillity of "the longed-for American pastoral" and "the fury, the violence and the desperation of the counterpastoral." In this novel, Roth presents an intelligent, realistic critique of late twentieth-century America. (KS)

The Bounty
by Derek Walcott
Farrar, Straus and Giroux, 1997,
78 pp., $18

Walcott's first collection of poems since *Omeros* (1990) has the lithe grace and lapidary richness of imagery that his readers will find familiar.

Walcott maps out an uneasy and surprising relationship between himself as mourner and the poem as elegy. He also considers the relationship of his birthplace, the Caribbean island of St. Lucia, to Europe, and the importance of his native *patois* with respect to the literary English he has come to love. The scope of his subject matter is impressive: he celebrates and glorifies the path of a line of ants and the vastness of the ocean; he alludes to John Clare's primitivist "Mouse's Nest," to Guy de Maupassant's folktales, and to Dante's *Paradiso*. The resulting poems, contemplative, often haunting, are as satisfyingly lush and complicated as one would expect from the Nobel laureate.

The Bounty is divided into two unequal sections. The first consists entirely of the title poem; the second, longer section features a sequence of elegies and meditations on art. In "The Bounty," an elegy for his mother and for the poet John Clare, Walcott reconciles the position of the poet as mourner with that of the poet as maker. Keeping the material in its place, he seems to say, is the only way for a poet to grieve fully and to offer consolation to himself and the reader. He concludes: "No, there is grief, there will always be, but it must not madden,/like Clare . . . "

The second section of the book begins with a short lyric that tells the reader: "Now, so many deaths, nothing short of a massacre/from the wild scythe blindly flailing friends, flowers, and grass . . ." This reflection introduces a series of poems on mortality, on the history of Europe and the Caribbean, and ultimately, on art. Walcott's goal seems to be one of reconciliation: to find consolation for death in art; to find, in tracing the differences between the Old and the New World, a love for both. In "Signs," Walcott begins: "Europe fulfilled its silhouette in the nineteenth century/with steaming train-stations, gas-lamps, encyclopedias,/the expanding waists of empires . . ." There follows a sweeping, yet deliberate consideration of Balzac's realism, opera, the Holocaust and the invasion of Poland, followed by a direct address to Adam Zagajewski, to whom the poem is dedicated.

Perhaps only Walcott could manage such a scope of subject matter without trumpeting his virtuosity or calling undue attention to his formidable technical mastery. *The Bounty* offers itself to the reader as a meditation on the struggle for reconciliation and consolation, and it is a moving record of this process and its relationship to making art. (NK)

Gut Symmetries
by Jeanette Winterson
Knopf, 1997, 223 pp., $22

Winterson's newest novel traverses the familiar territory of her previous books, where fairy tale meets sexual politics. The novel explores a trio of bizarre, but unflaggingly articulate, characters whose relationships are as complicated as Winterson's writing is elaborate. Alice, a physicist, meets Jove, another physicist, on an odd cruise where both lecture on scientific theory for the pleasure of the passengers. After starting an affair with Jove, Alice meets his wife, Stella, and begins an affair with her also. The narrative, which alternates between all three characters' points of view, progresses through the many intricacies of this arrangement while divulging the eccentric histories of this triangle: Alice was born on a tugboat in England to an upper-middle class family whose crone of a grandmother keeps a preserved rabbit as a talisman and introduces Alice to the music of the Beatles; Stella was born on a peddler's sled during a legendary blizzard in New York, with a diamond permanently embedded in her hip due to her mother's craving for the gems during her pregnancy; and Jove is raised in the shadow of his mother's famous Italian restaurant where he meets Stella and begins their romance with the gift of a Bowie knife.

The author sustains this dizzying array of lurid tales while entwining the separate points of view of Alice, Jove, and Stella so skillfully that the culmination of their narratives, though reliant upon an outrageous convergence of ghosts, disappearing ships, and cannibalism, seems like the only possible ending.

Fans of Winterson's other works, particularly *The Passion* and *Sexing the Cherry*, will relish the convoluted storytelling that she takes to new heights in this narrative, composed of fables, news clippings, poetry, passages of dialogue, scientific theories, and even transcripts of conversations between the characters. Her writing is perhaps more self-indulgent than ever before as her characters exhort the reader to "walk with me"—then meander through long passages about love and its connection to space and physics. The book's first chapters are almost painful in their deliberate and, in some cases, facile explanations of scientific and mathematical theories. Winterson also stumbles in the first chapters through some platitudinous revelations about love and time and history, like "We are what we know. We know what we are. We reflect our reality. Our reality reflects us." But once she relaxes into the world of her characters, the novel is entertaining, and often stunning in its imagery.

One of the pleasures of reading Winterson is her ability to blur the distinctions between the everyday and the fantastic, and in this respect, *Gut Symmetries* does not disappoint. At one point Alice as narrator remarks, "As I invent what I want to say, you will invent what you want to hear. Some story we must have." (TH)

Reviews by:
Kathy Lee, Willoughby Johnson, Mandy Michel, John Byrne, Speer Morgan, Kris Somerville, Jim Steck, Greg Hazleton, , Evelyn Somers, Annie Walsh, Noël Kopriva, Tina Hall

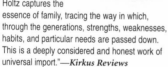

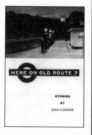

River City

presents

The Eighth Annual River City Writing Awards in Fiction

First Prize	$2000.00
Second Prize	$500.00
Third Prize	$300.00

CONTEST RULES

1. Any previously unpublished short story of up to 7,500 words is eligible. No novel chapters, please. Writers may enter only one manuscript in contest. **NO** simultaneous submissions.

2. All manuscripts should be typed, double-spaced, and accompanied by a cover letter. The author's name should **NOT** appear anywhere on the manuscript itself.

3. Please indicate Contest Entry on your outer envelope.

4. DEADLINE: All submissions should be **postmarked** by January 20, 1998.

5. All manuscripts should be accompanied by a **$9.50 entry fee**. The fee will automatically begin or extend a subscription to *River City*. Please make checks payable to The University of Memphis.

6. *River City* will publish the prize-winning story, and retains right of first refusal to publish any contest entry.

7. Entries will be screened by members of the Creative Writing faculty at The University of Memphis. Winners will be chosen from 15 finalists by a nationally prominent author.

8. **Winners** will be notified in April 1998.

9. All other entrants will receive the Winter 1999 issue of *River City*. **NO manuscripts will be returned.**

Send contest entries and subscriptions to: Contest Editor, *River City*, Department of English, The University of Memphis, Memphis, Tennessee 38152-6176, USA.

The 1998 Whiskey Island Magazine
Poetry and Fiction Contest

First Prize: $300.00 for poetry, $300.00 for fiction
Second Prize: $200.00 for poetry, $200.00 for fiction
Third Prize: $100.00 for poetry, $100.00 for fiction

All entrants will receive a copy of the
prize issue containing the winning submissions.

Submissions:
Poetry: As many poems as can fit on ten pages, single or double-spaced.
Fiction: Each entry should be one story. 600-6,000 words, double-spaced.

Entry Fee:
$ 10.00 money order or check (American bank only). Multiple entries (each story or collection of poems) will be accepted with an additional $10.00 fee per entry.

Deadline:
Entries must be postmarked or received between October 1, 1997, and January 31, 1998. Winners will be notified by May 30, 1998.

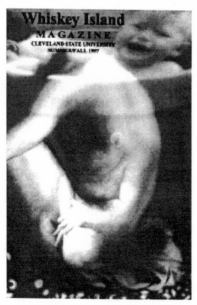

Fall 97 sample issue: $ 5.00

Manuscripts must be original and unpublished. No simultaneously submissions, please. Manuscripts must be clearly typed or printed. The author's name, address, phone number, and fax or E-mail number should appear only on a cover sheet. Please include a brief biography. No manuscripts will be returned. Send inquiries or entries to:

Whiskey Island Contest - MOR
Department of English
Cleveland State University
Cleveland, Ohio 44115

Phone: 216/687-2056
Fax: 216/687-6943
E-mail and Website:
whiskeyisland@popmail.csuohio.edu
http://www.csuohio.edu/whiskey_island